Routledge Revivals

American Literature in Context

First published between 1982 and 1983, this series examines the peculiarly American cultural context out of which the nation's literature has developed.

Covering the years from 1900 to 1930, this fourth volume of *American Literature in Context* focuses on how American literature dealt with the challenges of the period including the First World War and the stock market crash. It examines key writers of the time such as Henry James, Gertrude Stein, Ezra Pound, F Scott Fitzgerald and Eugene O'Neill who, unlike many Americans who sought escape, confronted reality, providing a rich and varied literature that reflects these turbulent years.

This book will be of interest to those studying American literature and American studies.

American Literature in Context

1900-1930

Ann Massa

Routledge
Taylor & Francis Group
Routledge Revivals

First published in 1982
by Methuen & Co Ltd

This edition first published in 2016 by Routledge
2 Park Square, Milton Park, Abingdon, Oxon, OX14 4RN
and by Routledge
711 Third Avenue, New York, NY 10017

Routledge is an imprint of the Taylor & Francis Group, an informa business

Publisher's Note
The publisher has gone to great lengths to ensure the quality of this reprint but points out that some imperfections in the original copies may be apparent.

Disclaimer
The publisher has made every effort to trace copyright holders and welcomes correspondence from those they have been unable to contact.

A Library of Congress record exists under LC control number: 81022302

ISBN 13: 978-1-138-69123-0 (hbk)
ISBN 13: 978-1-315-53553-1 (ebk)
ISBN 13: 978-1-138-69125-4 (pbk)
ISBN 13: 978-1-138-69132-2 (set hbk)
ISBN 13: 978-1-315-53545-6 (set ebk)

General Editor
ARNOLD GOLDMAN

AMERICAN LITERATURE IN CONTEXT, IV

1900–1930

AMERICAN LITERATURE IN CONTEXT, IV

1900–1930

ANN MASSA

METHUEN
LONDON AND NEW YORK

First published in 1982 by
Methuen & Co. Ltd
11 New Fetter Lane, London EC4P 4EE
Published in the USA by
Methuen & Co.
in association with Methuen, Inc.
733 Third Avenue, New York, NY 10017

Typeset by Scarborough Typesetting Services
Printed in Great Britain by
Richard Clay (The Chaucer Press) Ltd
Bungay, Suffolk

British Library Cataloguing in Publication Data

Massa, Ann
American literature in context.
4: 1900–1930
1. American literature—History and criticism
I. Title
810.9 PS88

ISBN 0 416 73920 2
ISBN 0 416 73930 X Pbk

Library of Congress Cataloging in Publication Data

Main entry under title:

American literature in context.
Bibliography: v. 4, p.
Includes index.
Contents: —4. 1900–1930/Ann Massa.
1. American literature—History and criticism—Addresses, essays, lectures. I. Massa, Ann.
PS92.A425 810′.9 81–22302
ISBN 0 416 73920 2 (v. 4) AACR2
ISBN 0 416 73930 X (pbk: v. 4)

Contents

General Editor's Preface

The object of the *American Literature in Context* series is to offer students of the literature and culture of the United States a coherent, consecutive and comprehensive sequence of interpretations of major American texts – fiction and non-fiction, poetry and drama.

Each chapter is prefaced by an extract from the chosen text which serves as a springboard for wider discussion and analysis. The intention of each analysis is to demonstrate how students can move into and then from the pages of literature in front of them to a consideration of the whole text from which the extract is taken, and thence to an understanding of the author's *oeuvre* and of the cultural moment in which he or she lived and wrote. The extract and its interpretation *ground* the wider interpretation: students need not just take the critic's overall view on trust, but can test it against the extract from the primary text.

The selection of texts is intended to represent the critic's choice from the variety, quality and interest of important American writing in the period. In these essays students can see how a literary and cultural critic responds to the page of writing before him or her, and how sustained critical response to particular passages can be linked to broader analyses of texts, authors, culture and society. With this integrated format, students can better see how background material relates to the text and *vice versa*. While the chapters are not precisely intended as models for students to imitate, those who are learning to write about literature are encouraged to treat extracts of their own choosing in a comparable manner, relating the particular response to wider matters.

Arnold Goldman

Acknowledgements

The author and publishers wish to record their thanks for permission to use the following copyright material:

Edith Wharton, *The House of Mirth*: Constable Publishers; Introduction (by Irving Howe) copyright © 1962 by Holt, Rinehart and Winston, Inc. Henry Adams, *The Education of Henry Adams*: copyright 1946 by Charles F. Adams, reprinted by permission of Houghton Mifflin Company. Gertrude Stein, *The Making of Americans*: by permission of the Gertrude Stein Estate; published (in the UK) by Peter Owen Ltd, London. Wallace Stevens, 'Sunday Morning': copyright 1923 and renewed 1951 by Wallace Stevens, reprinted from *The Collected Poems of Wallace Stevens*, by permission of Alfred A. Knopf, Inc.; also reprinted by permission of Faber and Faber Ltd. Ezra Pound, 'In a Station of the Metro' and 'Hugh Selwyn Mauberley': Ezra Pound, *Personae*, copyright 1926 by Ezra Pound, reprinted by permission of New Directions; also reprinted by permission of Faber and Faber Ltd from *Collected Shorter Poems*. Sherwood Anderson, 'Paper Pills' from *Winesburg, Ohio*: copyright 1919 by B. W. Huebsch, Inc., copyright renewed 1947 by Eleanor Copenhaver Anderson, reprinted by permission of Viking Penguin, Inc.; also by permission of Jonathan Cape Ltd and the Estate of Sherwood Anderson. Sinclair Lewis, *Main Street*: copyright 1920 by Harcourt Brace Jovanovich, Inc., copyright 1948 by Sinclair Lewis, reprinted by permission of the publisher; also by permission of Jonathan Cape Ltd and the Estate of Sinclair Lewis. Jean Toomer, selection from 'Box-Seat': reprinted from *Cane* by permission of Liveright Publishing Corporation, copyright 1923 by Boni & Liveright, copyright renewed 1951 by Jean Toomer. H. L. Mencken, 'In Memoriam: W.J.B.': copyright 1926 by Alfred A. Knopf and renewed 1954 by H. L. Mencken, reprinted from *A Mencken Chrestomathy* by permission of

Alfred A. Knopf, Inc. F. Scott Fitzgerald, *The Great Gatsby*: from *The Bodley Head Scott Fitzgerald*, Volume I, published by The Bodley Head; also reprinted with the permission of Charles Scribner's Sons. Ernest Hemingway, *The Sun Also Rises*: copyright 1926 by Charles Scribner's Sons, copyright renewed, reprinted with the permission of Charles Scribner's Sons; also by permission of Jonathan Cape Ltd and the Executors of the Ernest Hemingway Estate. Eugene O'Neill, *The Great God Brown*: copyright 1926 and renewed 1954 by Carlotta Monterey O'Neill, reprinted from *The Plays of Eugene O'Neill* by permission of Random House, Inc.; also by permission of Jonathan Cape Ltd and the Executors of the Eugene O'Neill Estate. William Faulkner, *The Sound and the Fury*: copyright 1929 and renewed 1957 by William Faulkner, reprinted by permission of Random House, Inc.; also reprinted by kind permission of Curtis Brown Ltd.

Introduction

In American history the period 1900–1930 is bounded by the emergence of the United States as a world power and the trauma of the stock market crash and the Depression; it is divided by the First World War. Broadly speaking, the literature of the period keeps pace with the history and the range of the literature is comparably great. Writers look outside America more readily and inside America more critically than before; internationalism and expatriatism (Stein, Pound, Hemingway) become major movements and major sources of creative insight. The certainties and uncertainties, the changes and reaffirmations of the period are all reflected in a literature which pushes enquiry and experiment to its limits, from the ironic novel of manners (Wharton) to the grotesque (Anderson), from the autobiography (Adams) to the newspaper article (Mencken). Gentility and caution, provincialism and middle-class values are replaced by styles and themes which parallel questioning, reforming, progressive American social philosophy. A radical literature which shrinks from nothing (Lewis, Toomer) becomes increasingly a literature of alienation, dissociation and defiance which finds wisdom, comfort and meaning in strange places. Through techniques of realism and naturalism, symbolism and expressionism, the writers of the period mirror America – its regions, its villages, its cities, its ethnicity. Yet this is also, and *par excellence*, an era of psychological literature, of the individual consciousness – an era which strikingly affirms the value of the imagination (Stevens, Fitzgerald, Faulkner).

A passage from *The Education of Henry Adams* could stand as a motif for the literature of the period.

> Satisfied that the sequence of men led to nothing and that the sequence of their society could lead no further, while the mere sequence of time was artificial, and the sequence of thought was

> chaos, he turned at last to the sequence of force; and thus it happened that, after ten years' pursuit, he found himself lying in the Gallery of Machines at the Great Exposition of 1900, his historical neck broken by the sudden irruption of forces totally new.[1]

Adams's perception of profound change was echoed throughout the next three decades. So was the profound concern with which he wrote about that sense of change. In novel and poem, in travelogue and polemical essay, the writers of the decades from 1900 to 1930 wondered what was the nature of so-called progress. Like Adams they felt their necks had been broken and that they had been forced towards new perspectives. In content and in form their writings reflected their sense of living in an age of challenge and redefinition, an age which differed more strongly from the nineteenth century than the post-Civil War period differed from the time before that war. Everything called for re-examination in an age of bewildering change, when the fact of change seemed the only certainty. Determinedly and defiantly, the writers engaged the issues and offered their conclusions. Science makes no more sense than Christianity, concluded Henry Adams; rural Minnesota and Washington, D.C. are as stultifying as one another, proclaimed Sinclair Lewis; the majority must always be wrong and therefore American democracy is doomed, lamented H. L. Mencken.

Nineteenth-century literature had been cosmic in its concerns and had assumed some principle of order in the universe. The end of that century saw the rise of a school of realism and naturalism which emphasized the difficulty of free will in an apparently determined universe in which environment, heredity and tradition governed regardless. Early twentieth-century literature fused the two in philosophical speculation of a high order married to an increasingly sophisticated discussion of fate and free will, nowhere more sophisticated than in Wallace Stevens's suggestion that we can make our own fictions, our own realities. Other writers responded less optimistically to events and philosophies which did violence to ideas, to places, to people. They had to come to terms with a violent shift in population from country to city, for instance, and with a violent change in the nature of immigration which came less from northern and western Europe and increasingly from eastern and southern Europe. Urban architecture underwent a radical change – the age of the skyscraper had dawned – so did transportation, consumer appliances and thus the home. In foreign policy America began to act as an effective world power and then proved a failure at the Versailles negotiating table; there was a subsequent shift from internationalism to isolationism. In domestic policy reform politics gave way to complacency, tolerance to nativism, restraint to hedonism. Psychology and psychiatry posed new questions and gave new answers. The range of Presidents was amazing, from big-game-hunter Theodore Roosevelt, aggressive and imperialistic, to Woodrow Wilson, the withdrawn scholar committed to the League of Nations, to Herbert Hoover, the engineer and thoroughly practical man.

Such a wildly and chaotically changing world was, argued Eugene O'Neill, effectively meaningless. Life was at worst a lie, at best a strategy, and called for violence of form and thought. Thus, in part, is explained the incidence of violence and death in the literature of the period: the suicides of Edith Wharton's Lily Bart and Faulkner's Quentin Compson, Pound's epitaph for Hugh Selwyn Mauberley and Mencken's for William Jennings Bryan, the murder of Jay Gatsby, the curious deaths of O'Neill's 'Great God Brown' and his antagonist Dion Anthony, deaths which mix murder, suicide and supernatural causes. If protagonists survive, there is a kind of violence in their living, in the pagan affirmation of the woman in 'Sunday Morning', in the religious abandon of Jean Toomer's Dan, in the hard-living, hard-drinking creed of Ernest Hemingway's expatriates. Adams and James note an increasing frenzy. Sherwood Anderson describes a village full of grotesques, twisted by one kind of violence or another, be it the violence of passion or inhibition. And those writers who offer an image of order make that order as appalling as the violence. James writes of the terrible conformity of America. Sinclair Lewis's *Main Street* – the typical American small town street – shows a smug community with little spiritual or emotional life. Pound's modern capital city is sterile and so is what passes for the best in culture. Gertrude Stein's emphasis on patterning and repetition communicates a terrifying limitation in humanity and art alike.

Henry James offers an answer of sorts to chaos. As he wrote to a despondent Henry Adams:

> I still find my consciousness interesting – under *cultivation* of interest. Cultivate it *with* me, dear Henry – that's what I hoped to make you do – to cultivate yours for all it has in common with mine. *Why* mine yields an interest I don't know that I can tell you, but I don't challenge or quarrel with it – I encourage it with a ghastly grin. . . . It's, I suppose, because I am that queer monster, the

> artist, an obstinate finality, an inexhaustible sensibility. Hence the reactions – appearances, memories, many things go on playing upon it with consequences that I note and 'enjoy' (grim word!) noting. It all takes doing – and I *do*. I believe I shall do yet again – it is still an act of life.[2]

O'Neill suggests a discriminating abandon to ecstasy; Fitzgerald advises attempting the impossible. Faulkner wrestles with the age's challenge to tradition, to belief and not least to the southern way of life, but he cannot escape the phenomenon of alienation, exemplified in Quentin Compson, who wants desperately to belong – but to what? Quentin finds himself defying his father, southern tradition and a nascent instinct to live and to affirm a new South. Adams defies history; Stevens, God; Hemingway, hopelessness. Stein affirms a new syntax, Fitzgerald the old dream. Toomer denies what is bourgeois and affirms what is black; Mencken affirms intellect and denies instinct. Each writer is himself, but there is common ground too. Faulkner's fiction, which ends the period, is idiosyncratic in conception and execution, yet it recalls Stein's prose style, Adams's perspective and the elegiac quality of Scott Fitzgerald's work.

Notes

1 Henry Adams, *The Education of Henry Adams*, Boston and New York, 1918, 382.

2 Quoted in John Carlos Rowe, *Henry Adams and Henry James: The Emergence of a Modern Consciousness*, Ithaca and London, 1976, 131.

I

Edith Wharton (1862–1937)

Bridge at Bellomont usually lasted till the small hours; and when Lily went to bed that night she had played too long for her own good.

Feeling no desire for the self-communion which awaited her in her room, she lingered on the broad stairway, looking down into the hall below, where the last card-players were grouped about the tray of tall glasses and silver-collared decanters which the butler had just placed on a low table near the fire.

The hall was arcaded, with a gallery supported on columns of pale yellow marble. Tall clumps of flowering plants were grouped against a background of dark foliage in the angles of the walls. On the crimson carpet a deerhound and two or three spaniels dozed luxuriously before the fire, and the light from the great central lantern overhead shed a brightness on the women's hair and struck sparks from their jewels as they moved.

There were moments when such scenes delighted Lily, when they gratified her sense of beauty and her craving for the external finish of life; there were others when they gave a sharper edge to the meagreness of her own opportunities. This was one of the moments when the sense of contrast was uppermost, and she turned away impatiently as Mrs. George Dorset, glittering in serpentine spangles, drew Percy Gryce in her wake to a confidential nook beneath the gallery.

It was not that Miss Bart was afraid of losing her newly-acquired hold over Mr. Gryce. . . .* But the mere thought of that other woman, who could take a man up and toss him aside as she willed, without having to regard him as a possible factor in her plans, filled Lily Bart with envy. She had been bored all the afternoon by Percy Gryce – the mere thought seemed to waken an echo of his droning voice – but she could not ignore him on the morrow, she must follow up her success, must

* Unless otherwise stated, ellipses indicate omissions from the original text.

submit to more boredom, must be ready with fresh compliances and adaptabilities, and all on the bare chance that he might ultimately decide to do her the honour of boring her for life.

It was a hateful fate – but how escape from it? What choice had she? To be herself, or a Gerty Farish. As she entered her bedroom, with its softly-shaded lights, her lace dressing-gown lying across the silken bed-spread, her little embroidered slippers before the fire, a vase of carnations filling the air with perfume, and the last novels and magazines lying uncut on a table beside the reading-lamp, she had a vision of Miss Farish's cramped flat, with its cheap conveniences and hideous wall-papers. No; she was not made for mean and shabby surroundings, for the squalid compromises of poverty. Her whole being dilated in an atmosphere of luxury; it was the background she required, the only climate she could breathe in. But the luxury of others was not what she wanted. A few years ago it had sufficed her: she had taken her daily meed of pleasure without caring who provided it. Now she was beginning to chafe at the obligations it imposed, to feel herself a mere pensioner on the splendour which had once seemed to belong to her. There were even moments when she was conscious of having to pay her way. . . .

For in the last year she had found that her hostesses expected her to take a place at the card-table. It was one of the taxes she had to pay for their prolonged hospitality, and for the dresses and trinkets which occasionally replenished her insufficient wardrobe. And since she had played regularly the passion had grown on her. . . .

. . . But of course she had lost – she who needed every penny, while Bertha Dorset, whose husband showered money on her, must have pocketed at least five hundred, and Judy Trenor, who could have afforded to lose a thousand a night, had left the table clutching such a heap of bills that she had been unable to shake hands with her guests when they bade her good night.

A world in which such things could be seemed a miserable place to Lily Bart; but then she had never been able to understand the laws of a universe which was so ready to leave her out of its calculations.

She began to undress without ringing for her maid, whom she had sent to bed. She had been long enough in bondage to other people's pleasure to be considerate of those who depended on hers, and in her bitter moods it sometimes struck her that she and her maid were in the same position, except that the latter received her wages more regularly.

As she sat before the mirror brushing her hair, her face looked hollow and pale, and she was frightened by two little lines near her mouth, faint flaws in the smooth curve of the cheek.

'Oh, I must stop worrying!' she exclaimed. 'Unless it's the electric light—' she reflected, springing up from her seat and lighting the candles on the dressing-table.

She turned out the wall-lights, and peered at herself between the candle-flames. The white oval of her face swam out waveringly from a background of shadows, the uncertain light blurring it like a haze; but the two lines about the mouth remained.

Lily rose and undressed in haste.

'It is only because I am tired and have such odious things to think about,' she kept repeating; and it seemed an added injustice that petty cares should leave a trace on the beauty which was her only defence against them.

But the odious things were there, and remained with her. She returned wearily to the thought of Percy Gryce, as a wayfarer picks up a heavy load and toils on after a brief rest. She was almost sure she had 'landed' him: a few days' work and she would win her reward. But the reward itself seemed unpalatable just then: she could get no zest from the thought of victory. It would be a rest from worry, no more – and how little that would have seemed to her a few years earlier! Her ambitions had shrunk gradually in the desiccating air of failure. But why had she failed? Was it her own fault or that of destiny?

The House of Mirth (1905)[1]

* * *

Much of Edith Wharton's fiction affirmed the right of women (and men) to choose a role, assert an identity, discover an individuality; but she recognized that the early twentieth century, suffering as it did from a hangover of nineteenth-century attitudes, was an especially difficult time for the successful affirmation of the self. Edith Wharton was brought up in a New York which for her was 'Fifth Avenue . . . with its double line of low brownstone houses, of a desperate uniformity of style',[2] and that image, taken from her autobiography, *A Backward Glance* (1934), could well stand for the exclusive social system of manners, mores and money which so appalled her and which seemed to her to linger on far too long. She was also the product of a society which cast every woman in the role of wife, mother and hostess, and which, above all, required women to be desirable. She remembered, as a little girl, her father's insistence that she look pretty when they went for walks; and 'the [precocious] birth of the conscious and feminine me in the little girl's soul'[3] was to Mrs Wharton a vicious feature of the society she was to damn in fiction.

Lily Bart knows that she is valued only for her surfaces, and she herself subscribes to this system of values, with disastrous consequences. She places too much emphasis on the importance of her appearance, she undervalues and underplays her generosity, her humour, her irony, her quick mind, her instinct to follow her own impulses, not society's dictates. And when age takes its toll of her looks, as she notices for the first time at the Bellomont house party, it is the beginning of the assumption of failure: 'She was frightened by two little lines near her mouth, faint flaws in the smooth curve of the cheek.' The scene prefigures a number of others in which Lily realizes she begins to look old: 'and when a girl looks old to herself, how does she look to other people' (p. 208).

She is the prisoner of her face and her body, and the emphasis in the Bellomont passage is on the premium of youth and beauty. No facial blemish, no maturation, no character is allowed Lily. She is valuable only so long as she is an unflawed surface. This she knows and this she in part resents. But she also delights in admiration, and admits to a pleasure-loving streak. She cannot resist the flattery of people and possessions; places look so much better when she comes down the staircase, steps into the room, sits at the table. Pictures compose themselves about her. She has been trained to excel at this, and has difficulty in retraining, however hard she tries. She has no talent for the social work which Gerty Farish undertakes, and the only alternative offered her is by her lawyer friend Lawrence Selden, in what he vaguely calls 'the republic of the spirit' (p. 79). As she points out to him, this, whatever it is, is easier for a man than for a woman.

> Your coat's a little shabby – but who cares? It doesn't keep people from asking you to dine. If I were shabby no one would have me: a woman is asked out as much for her clothes as for herself. The clothes are the background, the frame, if you like; they don't make success, but they are a part of it. Who wants a dingy woman? We are expected to be pretty and well-dressed till we drop – and if we can't keep it up alone, we have to go into partnership. (p. 14)

But she has not gone into partnership, and to be so decorative and not to have married while the less attractive Judy Trenors and Bertha Dorsets are secure wives and mothers make her conceive of some flaw in herself. For Mrs Wharton, the fact that Lily Bart has not married is no sin; it merely means that she has not fallen in love and that, while in theory she longs for the status and security of marriage, marriage has yet to appeal to her as a desirable way of life. But instead of being able to articulate and accept her state, Lily feels guilty and anxious. She does not understand why she has not married:

> Had she shown an undue eagerness for victory? Had she lacked patience, pliancy or dissimulation? Whether she charged herself with these faults or absolved herself from them made no difference in the sum-total of her failure. Younger and plainer girls had been married off by dozens, and she was nine-and-twenty and still Miss Bart. (p. 45)

What Lily does not realize is that it is her success to have held out against the inducements of comfort and ease – that the instinct for independence and the refusal to settle for anything less than a loving relationship have been working well within her in spite of the overlay of convention, and in spite of her belief that she wants to conform. As a woman friend says of her:

> She works like a slave preparing the ground and sowing her seed; but the day she ought to be reaping the harvest she oversleeps herself or goes off on a picnic. . . . Sometimes . . . I think it's just flightiness and sometimes I think it's because, at heart, she despises the things she's trying for. And it's the difficulty of deciding that makes her such an interesting study. (p. 218–19)

On Sunday morning at Bellomont she goes off for a long walk with Lawrence Selden, a man whose mind interests her, sending a message to Percy Gryce, whom she has worked so hard to impress – even boning up on his enthusiasm, Americana – that she is too unwell to go to church with him. Percy still plans to propose to her, but on his way back from church his carriage takes him past Lily and Selden, who are in animated and intimate conversation. Lily, seemingly both liar and flirt, has lost Percy Gryce. She does not think she has lost him deliberately; a psychiatrist might.

If Lily's inconsistency makes for her social failure, it also gives her an individuality beyond that of her predictable contemporaries. In her own way she is struggling to use her gifts of beauty and independence properly. Almost certainly she should be a dress designer or an interior decorator. She is frustrated both by 'society', which would not then countenance such roles, and by an only partially awakened self, which can barely contemplate them. In spite of knowing she must not be imprudent or unconventional, that she must always be ready with fresh compliances, she cannot, at crucial moments, conform. She is incapable of playing her cards carefully if something other than the object or the man in question engages her mind or her attention. She has what Mrs Wharton calls 'a warm fluidity', a capacity to respond, to give; and often the circumstances of this 'giving' are admirable if curious, for she has that compelling degree of self-knowledge which means that she wants to get away from herself. She is the only person in the novel who gives and who expects nothing in return; even Lawrence Selden expects to see an 'improvement' in her 'flirtatious' conduct after they have talked. But this responsiveness is, of course, weakness as well as virtue. 'Poor Lily, for all the hard glaze of her exterior, was inwardly as malleable as wax' (p. 62). Her very being is in transition, her very type in the process of formation, and she suffers from the adaptability which this uncertainty, this inner formlessness, gives her. Her faculty for adapting herself, for entering into other people's feelings, helps her survive socially and financially. It makes her an acceptable friend and secretary for Judy Trenor – she writes Judy's letters, helps organize her parties (and can go to them) and is obliged to listen to her – but it hampers her judgement. So does her excessive response to environment.

> Her faculty for renewing herself in new scenes, and casting off problems of conduct as easily as the surroundings in which they had arisen, made the mere change from one place to another seem, not merely a postponement, but a solution of her troubles. Moral complications existed for her only in the environment that had produced them; she did not mean to slight or ignore them, but they lost their reality when they changed their background. (p. 226)

She behaves with such pliancy after scandalous rumours link her name to Gus Trenor, Judy's husband. Judy drops her; another 'friend', who is going to Europe, takes her on as a companion (it is Bertha Dorset, and true to the character which Wharton depicts so well at Bellomont – 'glittering in serpentine spangles' – Bertha eventually accuses Lily of being her husband's mistress, so distracting attention from her own affair). Under the spell of the Mediterranean, Lily effectively forgets the complications of life in America. Such is her overdeveloped commitment to setting, to appearance and to place. Her swift change of mood demonstrates her capacity for obliterating her moral sense. The dangerous seeds of this responsiveness are evident at Bellomont where the lovely but superficial scene in the arcaded hall, brilliantly evoked by Mrs Wharton, 'gratified her sense of beauty and her craving for the external finish of life', where her luxurious bedroom seduces her into an unworthy affirmation of luxury for luxury's sake. She wants very much to be a full member of Bellomont society, yet she is already somewhat disenchanted with it; she 'could get no zest' from the thought of joining it as Mrs Percy Gryce, nor does she know any man with whom she wishes to enter that society. It begins to occur to her that for the real Lily Bart society is no catch; indeed, it is 'boring'. And yet she cannot turn her back. Her upbringing has so conditioned her that her intrinsic independence is frequently neutralized, and her sensitivity to art and beauty is becoming perverted to a response to the heavy luxury of Bellomont and an obsession with her own looks. Her longing for luxury also leads her to an unworthy condemnation of her friend and Selden's cousin, Gerty Farish. Gerty *is* unattractive, and so is the tasteless poverty of her apartment. But appearances, as Lily Bart knows when she is not under their sway, are deceptive, none more so than her own, the perfect surface which conceals rebellion. Gerty, who is to prove her most faithful friend and admirer, is seen to have a fineness which Bellomont cannot match. So deceptive are appearances that Gerty Farish, in her exceptional loyalty, comes to cast a reflected glory on Lily Bart.

If Mrs Wharton is critical of the restrictive ideals which nineteenth-century America tried desperately to carry on to the twentieth century, she sounds a cautionary note about the society immediately likely to replace or 'refresh' it: not Gerty Farish but the *nouveaux riches*. If the old ways of Percy Gryce and Grace Van Osburgh (the girl he marries) are narrow and hypocritical, the new rich – Sim Rosedale and Norma Hatch – who have earned, not inherited, their money, are, as their names suggest, vulgar. And when the outcast, exceptional Lily Bart, with her independent and artistic temperament, looks to these new men and women to help her survive in her emancipation, they are unable to understand her needs, unable to respect her sensitivity, her inherent sense of art, her complex beauty, at once refined and sensuous. They drag her down. Lily knew 'she was growing less sensitive. . . . a hard glaze of indifference was fast forming over her delicacies and susceptibilities, and each concession to expediency hardened the surface a little more' (p. 272). They imitate the old school's brutality. When circumstantial evidence suggests Lily is having an affair with Gus Trenor, she provides a perfect scapegoat for old New York, which excludes her with ritualistic precision. The new urban rich follow old New York's lead in dropping the tainted Lily, for she is not valued by them except as a means to their goal of moving in the highest social circles. There is little to choose between the crude pragmatism of the new and the refined hypocrisy of the old, though Lily, so nearly a member of the latter group, feels its attitude more keenly. Its members are those who inherited wealth, who doubtless made money in the scandalous Gilded Age stock market, and who turn an admiring and blind eye to political and economic corruption while publicly professing shock. A similar kind of hypocrisy informs their attitude to Lily Bart. They pretend to believe in probity and to be shocked by her conduct when they are in fact indifferent to such standards of conduct for themselves. It is their way of excluding her and of defining their exclusiveness. And they are not only mean people but greedy too; they allow the crude, the vulgar, the superficial – people who in no way compare with Lily Bart but who have the money she lacks – to buy what Lily's style and beauty cannot: the entrée to the 'best' society.

The poignant character of Lily Bart pinpoints the difficult transition in American culture from the frequent restriction and hypocrisy of late nineteenth-century America to the relative freedom and honesty of a less certain and more tolerant society. Mrs Wharton herself was one of those rare women able to make this transition with success. Money, status, talent and application enabled her to lead a distinguished, independent and unconventional life in America and in Europe. Lily Bart, however, is forced to desperate measures to retain her independence. When the aristocratic world of Bellomont decides to reject her as morally tainted, when her beauty begins to desert her and when she is disinherited, she gamely takes a job as a millinery assembler. But if she retains some self-respect, she nevertheless fails. Temperament, education and society have unfitted her for such independence; life becomes intolerable and, whether by accident or design, she takes an overdose of sleeping pills. She has lived and worked and died with dignity; she has all the hallmarks of an independent woman, but, sadly, she has been conditioned to believe that she cannot succeed or be fulfilled by striking out on her own. She assumes that she is the ill-fitting cog which cannot fit in the smoothly running social machine. But Mrs Wharton makes it clear that she thinks and hopes that Lily Bart is a pioneer in the battle for a self-realization unencumbered by the prejudices and pretensions of other people. The victim has in her the seeds of victory.

Edith Wharton formed her fiction in substantial part from her observation and analysis. She was haunted by the images of a society which in spite of change continued to limit and to be limited, to damage and to be deprived. She saw herself as 'a recording instrument' who gave expression to 'these people who haunt my brain . . . [who] speak within me in their own voices'.[4] It was her intention to be a recording angel, to give compassionate and diagnostic expression to her protagonists' dilemmas and to their tensions. 'Fate had planted me in New York, with its fashionable stiff upper class, its money and status oriented world,' she wrote,[5] and this, she rightly contended, was as fit for the pen of the writer and as realistic as 'the man with the dinner pail'. But no mere realist she. Fiction did not merely reflect life; it must have its own shape and integrity. To demonstrate in terms of encyclopaedic accuracy that New York was flat and futile was not enough:

> The problem was how to extract from such a subject the typical human significance which is the storyteller's reason for telling one story rather than another. In what aspect could a society of irresponsible pleasure-seekers be said to have, on the 'old woe of the world', any deeper bearing than the people composing such a society could guess? The answer was that a frivolous society can acquire dramatic significance only through what its frivolity destroys. Its tragic implication lies in its power of debasing people and ideals. The answer, in short, was my heroine, Lily Bart.[6]

Mrs Wharton conceived Lily Bart, then, as a tragic figure, and this at once gives the measure of her sense of the complex possibilities of realistic fiction. Ever since William Dean Howells had urged people to give due weight to common things expressed in ordinary speech, ever since the popularity of the theory of American fiction as a mirror of the age, it had been the limitations rather than the possibilities of that fiction which had been most apparent. Ordinary people – paint manufacturers like Howells's Silas Lapham – or lowly ones – wagon drivers and prostitutes like Stephen Crane's Jim and Maggie – were at best picturesque or pathetic, not heroic or tragic. Their capacity for dignity and self-knowledge, that 'average' capacity, was insufficient for scaling those kinds of heights. The theory of the average and of the commonplace also led to a kind of levelling down – to characters who were not so much individuals as types, characters with little philosophical depth, little response to culture, few 'ideals'. The author's role too had been diminished by the theory of realism: he was nearer the photographer or the historian than the painter or the creative writer. He would certainly need to select scenes and characters, to plot some, but all in the interests of life as it was, not of life as he saw it. Bias and point of view were inappropriate. The book must seem to tell all.

Howells's theory of realism was most opposed by Henry James, who preached that the 'house of fiction' had many windows, and who thought the artist could attempt what he chose and should be judged merely on the basis of how successfully he achieved his desired effects. Wharton, his friend and protégée, also agreed that 'there could be no greater critical ineptitude than to judge a novel according to *what it might have been about*,'[7] and in 1905, a year when the best-selling work of fiction was *The Jungle*, Upton Sinclair's exposé of the abuses of men, power and animals in the Chicago meat-packing industry, she had no compunction about setting her novel in upper-class New York. Her intention was to demonstrate that the novel of manners could be simultaneously a realistic novel (in its picture of society), a naturalistic novel (in its evocation of a helplessly conditioned Lily Bart), a muckraking novel (in its exposure of social hypocrisy, cruelty and false values) and a psychological novel (in its moving description of Lily's almost subconscious struggle not to knuckle under to society). By taking issue with the need to subscribe overtly to the harsh logic and the circumscribing characteristics of realistic literature, she gave an added dimension to realism in fiction. She saw herself as a more complex truth-teller than the average realist as she laid bare the brutality behind the veneer of civilization, the hypocrisy behind good manners, the money-lust behind well-bred restraint. With the passion of the muckraking journalist, Mrs Wharton analysed the difficulties of being single, the role of the Jew in New York society, the kind of life working girls were forced to lead. As naturalist Mrs Wharton suggested that Lily Bart was the victim of heredity and environment: formed by societal and parental conditioning, governed by animal impulses and fated by forces beyond her control.

Through such diverse means Mrs Wharton focuses our attention on Lily's struggle for success and happiness against the odds. The inevitability of Lily's defeat does not detract from the novel; it is the development of Lily's consciousness which is absorbing. She emerges as an individual trying to work through and within and upwards in society, never fully realizing how much at odds with it she is. *The House of Mirth* is an early treatment of socially oriented yet inner-directed woman, a new kind of woman trying hard to fit into an old, other-directed society.

Mrs Wharton makes Lily a woman striving for control over her destiny but not strong enough to buck the system successfully. The system, of course, is only in force for outsiders; insiders, those who already belong, can lie, cheat and fornicate. But Lily cannot.

It is a measure of Lily Bart's self-reliance and integrity that she says 'I won't blame anybody for my faults' when, as Mrs Wharton makes clear, it was from an extraordinarily materialistic mother that Lily imbibed the idea that if people were poor it was from choice (p. 261). Like her mother she has developed a 'naturally lively taste for splendour'; like her she says, 'I hate to see faded flowers at luncheon.' Lily has been brought up in the belief that, whatever it cost, one must have a good cook and one must be what Mrs Bart called 'decently dressed' (pp. 35–7) – that is, in the height of fashion. (Mrs Wharton recalled that her impeccably dressed father would murmur 'Fate cannot harm me' when he sipped a glass of Chartreuse after his gourmet dinner.)[8] Mrs Wharton leaves us in no doubt of the connection between possessions, environment and personality: 'She [Lily] was so evidently the victim of the civilisation which had produced her, that the links of her bracelet seemed like manacles chaining her to her fate' (p. 8). When Mr Bart becomes bankrupt, Lily is indeed unable to break the links with society and is forced to become a cross between a parasite and servant, the barely compatible roles in which we see her at Bellomont. She is part beautiful insider, part distraught outsider.

The scene at Bellomont shows how cleverly New Yorkers kept her half in and half out of their world; they could elevate her to equal or dismiss her as servant at any convenient moment. Indeed, 'it sometimes struck her that she and her maid were in the same position, except that the latter received her wages more regularly'. When she tries to shake off convention – by taking tea alone in a friendly and platonic atmosphere in Selden's apartment – she is seen coming out, and this is the beginning of the series of 'taints' that turn the world of Bellomont against her. Foolishly she listens to the confidences, again platonic, of George Dorset; foolishly she 'works' for Judy Trenor by entertaining a husband Judy declares she finds dull. Independence, kindness and an attempt to earn the hospitality she receives contribute to her undoing.

But most of all it is her lack of money which undoes her. Gus Trenor offers to invest what little money she has for her; he consults with her, reports to her, brings her substantial profits and then presumes on the 'relationship'. He has bought her, or has tried to; the profits, she discovers, are in excess of anything the stock exchange can offer – they come from his own pocket. Seen coming out of Gus's house late at night when Judy is out of town, Lily's taint is final. She has, in fact, been confronting him with her knowledge of the source of the money he has been giving her, and has ended their acquaintance. She spends the rest of her life trying to earn the money to repay him, as the aunt who was to leave her a fortune disinherits her on hearing rumours of the Bart–Trenor liaison.

'Why must a girl pay so dearly for her least escape from routine?' Lily asks (p. 18), in the terrible knowledge that 'the truth about any girl is that once she's talked about she's done for; and the more she explains her case the worse it looks' (p. 262). Convention, the hypocrisy and the brutality of society, Lily's lack of money, her upbringing, her received and too rarely questioned beliefs, all create a situation in which, inevitably, she will pay. Cruelly, her highest value for society, the looks that are so admired, make anything that she does in a man's company suspect.

In poverty, in her honest sense of self and in her honesty with the men who no longer want to marry her – she confronts them with the fact that they are worried that she is thought to be tainted, even though they know that she is not – Lily Bart is at once the effective indictment and the pitiful victim of the society which pretends she is fast. As the old New Yorkers' acceptance of the *nouveaux riches* shows, all she really needed was money, and then everything else could have been passed over. The limited self-reliance she achieves – she supports herself but finds the strain, the change, the physical hard work too much – indicates her own limitations, but her great strengths too. She underestimates her spiritual strength, her struggle for independence, her burgeoning adaptability. 'What can one do when one finds that one only fits into one hole? One must get back to it or be thrown out into the rubbish heap' (p. 358). Lily is admirably right to drop out, pathetically wrong in her wish to get back. May there be many more such dropouts, cries Edith Wharton, and so does the scene at Bellomont, which so clearly deforms Lily; but may the dropouts be fitted to shape better holes for themselves.

Notes

1 Edith Wharton, *The House of Mirth*, New York, 1962 (originally published 1905). All quotations from *The House of Mirth* are taken from this edition and, unless noted otherwise in textual parentheses, from pages 28–33.

2 Edith Wharton, *A Backward Glance,* New York and London, 1934, 2.
3 ibid.
4 ibid., 203.
5 ibid., 206.
6 ibid., 207.
7 ibid., 206–7.
8 ibid., 59.

*Further reading**

Auchincloss, Louis, *Edith Wharton: A Woman in Her Time*, New York, 1971. Evocative photographs.

Howe, Irving (ed.), *Edith Wharton: A Collection of Critical Essays*, Englewood Cliffs, NJ, 1962. Contains two fine essays: Diana Trilling, '*The House of Mirth* revisited', and Irving Howe, 'A reading of *The House of Mirth*'.

Kraditor, Aileen (ed.), *Up From the Pedestal: Selected Writings in the History of American Feminism*, Chicago, 1970. Useful turn-of-the-century selections.

Lewis, R. W. B., *Edith Wharton*, New York, 1975. Especially Part I, Old New York, 1862–1890, and Part II, The Writing of Fiction, 1891–1905.

Wharton, Edith, *A Backward Glance*, New York and London, 1934.

* Works cited in the further reading lists are first editions.

2

Henry Adams (1838–1918)

He left St. Louis May 22, 1904, and on Sunday, June 5, found himself again in the town of Coutances, where the people of Normandy had built, towards the year 1250, an Exposition which architects still admired and tourists visited, for it was thought singularly expressive of force as well as of grace in the Virgin. On this Sunday, the Norman world was celebrating a pretty church-feast – the Fête Dieu – and the streets were filled with altars to the Virgin, covered with flowers and foliage; the pavements strewn with paths of leaves and the spring handiwork of nature; the cathedral densely thronged at mass. The scene was graceful. The Virgin did not shut her costly Exposition on Sunday, or any other day, even to American senators who had shut the St. Louis Exposition to her – or for her; and a historical tramp would gladly have offered a candle, or even a candle-stick in her honor, if she would have taught him her relation with the deity of the senators. The power of the Virgin had been plainly One, embracing all human activity; while the power of the Senate, or its deity, seemed – might one say – to be more or less ashamed of man and his work. The matter had no great interest as far as it concerned the somewhat obscure mental processes of Senators who could probably have given no clearer idea than priests of the deity they supposed themselves to honor – if that was indeed their purpose; but it interested a student of force, curious to measure its manifestations. Apparently the Virgin – or her Son – had no longer the force to build expositions that one cared to visit, but had the force to close them. The force was still real, serious, and, at St. Louis, had been anxiously measured in actual money-value.

That it was actual and serious in France as in the Senate Chamber at Washington, proved itself at once by forcing Adams to buy an automobile, which was a supreme demonstration because this was the form of force which Adams most abominated. He had set aside the summer for study of the Virgin, not as a sentiment but as a motive power, which had left monuments widely scattered and not easily reached. The automobile alone could unite them in any reasonable sequence, and although the force of the automobile, for the purposes of a commercial traveller, seemed to have no relation whatever to the force that inspired a Gothic cathedral, the Virgin in the twelfth century would have guided and controlled both bag-man and architect, as she controlled the seeker of history. In his mind the problem offered itself as to Newton; it was a matter of mutual attraction, and he knew it, in his own case, to be a formula as precise as $s = \frac{gt^2}{2}$, if he could but experimentally prove it. Of the attraction he needed no proof on his own account; the costs of his automobile were more than sufficient: but as teacher he needed to speak for others than himself. For him, the Virgin was an adorable mistress, who led the automobile and its owner where she would, to her wonderful palaces and châteaux, from Chartres to Rouen, and thence to Amiens and Laon, and a score of others, kindly receiving, amusing, charming and dazzling her lover, as though she were Aphrodite herself, worth all else that man ever dreamed. He never doubted her force, since he felt it to the last fibre of his being, and could no more dispute its mastery than he could dispute the force of gravitation of which he knew nothing but the formula. He was only too glad to yield himself entirely, not to her charm or to any sentimentality of religion, but to her mental and physical energy of creation which had built up these World's Fairs of thirteenth-century force that turned Chicago and St. Louis pale. . . .

One late afternoon, at midsummer, the Virgin's pilgrim was wandering through the streets of Troyes in close and intimate conversation with Thibaut of Champagne and his highly intelligent seneschal, the Sieur de Joinville, when he noticed one or two men looking at a bit of paper stuck in a window. Approaching, he read that M. de Plehve had been assassinated at St. Petersburg. The mad mixture of Russia and the Crusades, of the Hippodrome and the Renaissance, drove him for refuge into the fascinating Church of St. Pantaleon near by. Martyrs, murderers, Caesars, saints and assassins – half in glass and half in telegram; chaos of time, place, morals, forces and motive – gave him vertigo. Had one sat all one's life on the steps of Ara Coeli for this? Was assassination forever to be the last word of Progress? No one in the street had shown a sign of protest; he himself felt none; the charming Church with its delightful windows, in its exquisite absence of other tourists, took a keener expression of celestial peace than could have been given it by any contrast short of explosive murder; the conservative

Christian anarchist had come to his own, but which was he – the murderer or the murdered?

The Virgin herself never looked so winning – so One – as in this scandalous failure of her Grace. To what purpose had she existed, if, after nineteen hundred years, the world was bloodier than when she was born? The stupendous failure of Christianity tortured history. The effort for Unity could not be a partial success; even alternating Unity resolved itself into meaningless motion at last. To the tired student, the idea that he must give it up seemed sheer senility. As long as he could whisper, he would go on as he had begun, bluntly refusing to meet his creator with the admission that the creation had taught him nothing except that the square of the hypothenuse of a right-angled triangle might for convenience be taken as equal to something else. Every man with self-respect enough to become effective, if only as a machine, has had to account to himself for himself somehow, and to invent a formula of his own for his universe, if the standard formulas failed. There, whether finished or not, education stopped. The formula, once made, could be but verified.

The effort must begin at once, for time pressed. The old formulas had failed, and a new one had to be made, but, after all, the object was not extravagant or eccentric. One sought no absolute truth. One sought only a spool on which to wind the thread of history without breaking it. Among indefinite possible orbits, one sought the orbit which would best satisfy the observed movement of the runaway star Groombridge, 1838, commonly called Henry Adams. As term of a nineteenth-century education, one sought a common factor for certain definite historical fractions. Any schoolboy could work out the problem if he were given the right to state it in his own terms.

Therefore, when the fogs and frosts stopped this slaughter of the centuries, and shut him up again in his garret, he sat down as though he were again a boy at school to shape after his own needs the values of a Dynamic Theory of History.

The Education of Henry Adams (1907)[1]

* * *

Edith Wharton gave us the difficult birth of the new woman; Henry Adams gave us the difficult education of modern mankind. 'My country in 1900 is something totally different from my own country of 1860,' he wrote to a friend. 'I am wholly a stranger in it. . . . The turning of a nebula into a star somewhat resembles the change. All I can see is that it is one of . . . terrific energy, represented not by souls, but by coal and iron and steam.'[2] In 1904 his sense of displacement became acute. He found himself at a crossroads. For this aristocratic product of western civilization, the highly cultivated descendant of one of America's first families, 'The old formulas had failed, and a new one had to be made.' He had to become a schoolboy again. First, to learn about the nature of the forces which play so dominating a role in the universe. Second, to understand that these forces, though in some senses made or harnessed by man, are ultimately autonomous and uncontrollable. Third, to accept the failure of man as master. Conventional education, he decided, was useless; through the perception of chaos we need to be educated out of the assumption of order into an informed silence. We must learn an ignorance which verges on helplessness. The 'Dynamic Theory of History' taught the powerlessness of human beings.

Adams saw himself as the aptly failed and paradoxical teacher of this sophisticated tale of failure and paradox. He was one professor of history at Harvard who sought to learn rather than to teach – who found he could not, morally, teach history because he did not understand it. He was interested in the methodology, the controlling principle behind the facts, but he could not discover the methodology. And history must explain; it was not enough for it to be 'the severe process of stating, with the least possible comment, such facts as seemed sure, in such order as seemed rigorously consequent' (p. 382).

Schoolmasters in Boston and Europe had taught Adams that the mind was the cause of form and sequence in the universe, and that therefore the form was comprehensible and the sequence predictable. Observation taught him that unexplained energy of all kinds was being generated, that unexplained phenomena abounded – too many for the mind to cope with. Experience taught him that 'millions of chance images [were] stored away without order in the memory' (p. 353). Nevertheless, ambitiously and with much of the skill and confidence of a Renaissance man, Adams set out to discover if the world which historians had traditionally seen as the logical product of God-given and man-made progress was rather the product of accidental force. He wanted to know whether chaos was an idea or a reality. Could he detect causes? Could he predict effects? If, as he suspected, life was a construct of irreconcilable opposites, anarchy and order would never be reconciled, and he would have to assert chaos as the controlling principle.

Appropriately for an age in which science seemed to offer the key to knowledge, Adams adopted a scientific approach to history, attempting to verify facts objectively and to approximate science by producing generalizations from the social sciences (political science, economics, sociology, anthropology and psychology). He decided against romantic, dramatic, heroic history in favour of a narrative seeking historical laws to match those of the sciences. But Adams's impulse towards a theory of history was also an aesthetic quest. Connoisseur of art and architecture that he was, he drew his evidence as much from art as from science; he hoped to arrive at a theory which would not only make scientific sense but also give artistic coherence to a world in which art was a marvellously accurate expression of man. His description of how he came to shape this theory interweaves the language and images, the concepts and the facts of both science and art. He looks for 'formulae' to explain Christianity; he attributes a 'force' to Catholicism symbolized by the Virgin Mary which he compares to the force of gravity; he ponders the paradoxical connection between Christianity, science and commerce as he tells us that the St Louis Exposition, having excluded religion from its exhibitions, observed Sunday closing. It was, as he puts it, shut 'to her' and 'for her'. He describes his attempt to feel at home in the universe as seeking 'a common factor for certain definite historical fractions'. The very phrase 'Dynamic Theory of History' suggests the fusion, the unity that Adams sought. At best he wanted to believe that art was central to an understanding of man and the universe. At worst he hoped that any governing scientific principle would have *form*. It did not seem to him at all improbable that force and energy could be redeemed by artistic expression, or would give rise to something admirably artistic. He had hoped this at the first World's Fair he had attended in Chicago, in 1893, when it had seemed that the fine arts and industry were made compatible by the unity which the classically styled White City, which housed the Chicago World's Fair, seemed to impose on exhibits which ranged from the maps which had brought Columbus to America to the Bell telephone. He was excited by the conjunction of such unlikely things: 'Educational game started like rabbits from every building' (p. 339). He had also been enthusiastic about the Paris Exposition of 1900, where he 'began to feel the forty-foot dynamo as a moral force. . . . One began to pray to it; inherited instinct taught the natural expression of man before silent and infinite force' (p. 380). But enthusiasm quickly gave way to foreboding and the forceful dynamo came to disturb Adams, nowhere more so than at the St Louis Exposition – a World's Fair which, unlike Chicago in 1893, seemed an indiscriminately boastful and ephemeral show of technological achievement in 'a third-rate town of half a million people without history, education, unity or art' (p. 466). Machine power was elevating such places, such people. The Exposition was a monument to existing industrial power and potential economic gain. It threatened. In temples lit by electric candles, mindless worship was taking place. The Exposition suggested a principle of change for change's sake, of power for power's sake, of force unleashed.

If, ultimately, Adams had to deny the beauty of the machine and instead affirm its terrifying power, his own writing, elegant, ironic, original, persuasively authoritative, charmingly serious, conferred a kind of art on such unlikely phenomena as the scientific equation and the car. Imaginatively he set the automobile in the context of culture and history. It enabled him to make his summer study of the Virgin, uniting as it did 'monuments widely scattered and not easily reached'; as one motive power it illumined the study of another, the powerful Virgin. It seemed an instrument that fate and the Virgin, rather than man or chauffeur or bag-man, had put at his disposal.

A sense of the alarming swiftness of change and a sense that any theory might quickly be outdated or disproved must account for Adams's reluctance to see the *Education* published. In 1906 he sent a hundred friends folio copies of the manuscript, printed with large margins and asking for comment. He insisted that his book was merely a collection of proof sheets. In fact, the book was, from the start, meticulously written and carefully modelled on the *Confessions* of St Augustine. It mirrors Augustine's search for a proper educative process and for a full understanding of life on earth. Augustine and Adams both pass through crisis and paradox – Adams most crucially in France in the summer of 1904 – until compelled to give some systematic explanation of their respective historical situations. But where Augustine perceives God's certain design, Adams can only detect the uncertainty of historical change, the certainty of uncontrollable and uncomprehended force. Adams is distressed by his own logic, for – quintessentially American in this – he cannot help being somewhat of a dreamer. He longs for law and synthesis, not for chaos and multiplicity. He longs to make optimistic connections between men and their actions, between past and present. He, the historical tramp, 'would gladly have offered a candle, or even a candle-stick in her honor, if she [the Virgin] would have taught him her relation with the deity of the senators'. But when he compares the twelfth-century Exposition, the fine Norman church in Coutances, with the twentieth-century St Louis Exposition, he can only deduce decline. Commercial function, not devotional purpose, had become the pivot of human activity. Disorder had replaced order.

In the *Education* Adams discussed the future of human activity in the universe, and the book is as wide-ranging in its application as in its command of a variety of disciplines. But Adams's book had its origins in his America, and derived much of its tone from his response to that country.

Henry Adams was the self-conscious descendant of a family whose history was closely connected with the birth of the American Republic and the preservation of its democratic institutions. His great-grandfather, John Adams, one of the Committee of Four who drafted the Declaration of Independence, was Vice President under George Washington and became the second President of the United States. Henry Adams's grandfather, John Quincy Adams, was the sixth President; his father, Charles Francis, was US Minister to the Court of St James, and his important duty was to prevent English recognition of the Confederacy. An upright man, Henry Adams felt out of place in the post-Civil War America in which he came of age. He held the chair of Medieval History at Harvard for seven years, and in 1877 moved to Washington, D.C., where he and his wife had a distinguished salon. Washington confirmed Adams's sense that government was no longer democratic but an extension of big business. After his wife's death in 1891, there was little Adams cared for left in America, and he spent most of his time abroad, wandering through Japan, Russia, China, Samoa and France, paying intermittent visits to America.

His was a life of much frustration. He had longed to play a leading role in American politics like his ancestors, and his inability to achieve significant influence and to lay hands on power perhaps intensified his preoccupation with power in all its forms. But if Adams sought significance for himself – and the third person narrative technique of the *Education* does not disguise his egotism – he was also and primarily seeking to understand the world as it had been, was and would be; and he undertook this search with as much humility as arrogance, describing himself as a 'manikin', a little man who sought to set his puny proportions of intellect and body against what he might discover to be the proportions and the moving impulses of the universe. If he was exceptional in his education, formal and informal – he had a layman's insight into science and art and a professional historian's training in history – he was also an average man, that 'every man with self-respect enough to become effective, if only as a machine, [who] has had to account for himself somehow'.

In the late nineteenth century Adams had not felt so strongly the need to account for himself. In *Mont St. Michel and Chartres*, conceived at that time though not published until 1904, he wrote with lyricism and erudition on the unity of art and science, religion and politics in medieval France, a unity of life which did not seem irrelevant or impossible in his lifetime. But by the early twentieth century the unity of things seemed to him to be specious. He found it difficult to make connections between original, primitive Christianity, symbolized in the Cross, and the urbanity of most cathedrals. He could not see a logical progression from steam to electricity. He sensed forces working towards disorder. Were they random? Malign? Why did things happen? Why did things change? Was there any discernible principle of power at work in the universe, he wondered. If so, was it divine, biological, chemical, historical or . . .? His overriding concern was ultimate energy: the force, physical and/or metaphysical, which moved the universe.

Idealistically, he wanted to believe that man was a force, either under God or over 'creation'; so he began his study with the contention 'that man as a force must be measured by motion from a fixed point' (p. 434). His fixed point was that time in history when man held the highest idea of himself as a unit in a unified universe, when everything hung together and made sense. He chose the century 1150–1250, expressed in Amiens Cathedral and the work of St Thomas Aquinas. But the unity he found there was gone by 1900, and he embarked on a study of twentieth-century multiplicity, a study of an aimless, fragmented, secular, pluralistic and confused society in which men did not unite in one faith or admire one art, and at a time when science changed the conditions and the possibilities and therefore the forms and the values of life itself. The recent immigrant to America and the old-established American citizen seemed to him to be alike

> the child of steam and the brother of the dynamo, and already, within less than thirty years, this mass of mixed humanities, brought together by steam, was [being] squeezed and welded into approach to shape; a product of so much mechanical power, and bearing no distinctive marks but that of its pressure. The new American, like the

> new European, was the sei.ant of the powerhouse, as the European of the twelfth century was the servant of the Church, and the features would follow the parentage. (p. 466)

Adams disliked such changes; he feared the pace of change and the chaotic implications of unassimilated change. He fled from St Louis to France, from fake temples to Christian ones, and to an object of worship which he preferred to the dynamo – the Virgin. For Adams as for Aquinas, the Virgin was the principle of love. 'Christ and the Mother are once Force – Love,' wrote Aquinas (p. 428). They were the modifiers of Old Testament Christianity, the embodiments and carriers of New Testament compassion and redemption.

He set aside the summer to study the cult of the Virgin in the vain hope that he would be able to affirm her superiority over the dynamo as a motive power in history. He wanted 'to yield himself entirely . . . to her mental and physical energy of creation'. But the very means by which he studied her – the automobile, which he disliked in theory as a dominant machine but yielded to in practice – presaged his defeat. Though he could affirm the dynamic role that the Mother of God had played in the formulation of Christian doctrine and hope – she was responsible for making Christ son of man as well as of God – Adams could not but acknowledge what he described as 'the scandalous failure of her Grace', the deceptive unity and benignity which she communicated. He could no longer attribute the harmonious and good things that happened to the Virgin and ignore her relationship to the persistent existence of evil. Either she was all powerful or she was a failure: 'The effort for Unity could not be a partial success; even alternating Unity resolved itself into meaningless motion at last.' He could not escape into the past any longer; he had to face the reality of the failure of Christianity and of his own knowledge and understanding. The appalling juxtaposition, on 5 June 1904, of the pretty church feast and the news of the assassination of the French ambassador in St Petersburg brought his head out of the sand. With characteristic prescience he saw the beginning of twentieth-century bloodshed. But the assassination also brought him sharply up against the fact that this was the continuation of the bloodshed of centuries before as well as during Christianity's primacy. He was assailed by the fact of bloodshed, whether communicated by the stained glass commemorating the martyr or by the telegraph machine. He could enter the church of St Pantaleon, but he could not take effective refuge there. For he now had to ask himself if the Christian martyr, who had encouraged people to live and die in the Christian faith, was murdered or murdering. He could not sit complacently on the steps of Ara Coeli in Rome, as he had often done in conscious imitation of Edward Gibbon, who had conceived there the idea for his historical masterwork, *The Decline and Fall of the Roman Empire*. He could no longer immerse himself in conventional history; he could no longer wander through Troyes imagining he had medieval French writers for company – he must look to the future. 'The standard formulas [had] failed' and he must 'invent a formula of his own'. He was thrown into what he had been fighting all his life, 'chaos of time, place, morals, forces and motive'. He must now, for the sake of self-respect, honestly admit that madness prevailed, that his state of being was vertigo. He must sit down again, not in homage to art, but 'as though he were . . . at school to shape after his own needs the values of a Dynamic Theory of History'.

Conventional education was little use to him here, Adams thought, though languages and mathematics were some help. In fact, he felt that he had been unfitted for life by his formal education and by Puritan assumptions of a God and intellect centred universe. Unfortunately life itself did not automatically re-educate; the miseducated needed to analyse as well as to observe. In Adams's process of self-education, Darwinism appealed because 'Natural Selection led back to Natural Evolution, and at last to Natural Uniformity' (p. 225) – he used the words Unity and Uniformity synonymously. But he found himself unable to deny that, in the evolutionary process, freaks of force, be they cosmic, chemical, solar or supersensual, seemed arbitrarily and unpredictably to upset the process and the theory. Humanism did not satisfy him either. Man pretended to create and command and to suggest order by making laws – but these were fictions. As for the dynamo, if it had become a symbol of infinity, a kind of cross – and he felt that it had such expressive force – that infinity was not the Christian world without end, that symbol did not point to anything as specific and delineated and understood as the Christian heaven, but towards an accelerating downward spiral. Energy would bring the planet to an end. The locomotive steam engine had given way to the electric train; the even swifter automobile was about to give way to the airship. Force could not always be productive. Eventually it would become a vis nova, a term scientists used to describe the sudden burst of a star which then sinks into relative obscurity. History would go the way of energy as defined in the second law of thermodynamics, which states that 'the potentiality of energy to do useful mechanical work in closed systems (societies) is constantly diminished by a universal tendency toward the dissipation of energy as heat'.[3] That law, predicted Adams, meant the breakdown or breakup of effective life or progress.

This then was the dynamic theory of history, and if the means by which Adams arrived at his theory – mixing as he did philosophy, theology, history, psychology, physiology and biology and the inner logic of his own argument – have been properly criticized as impressive but not, on examination, sound, the theory of social 'entropy' (irreversible social disorder and decreasing intellectual energy) has been affirmed by American literature from Nathanael West to Thomas Pynchon. It is now not uncommon to assert, with Adams, that of all the factors which account for historical development, the discovery and utilization of energy have been the most significant, and that the attracting energy, once called God and Nature, is simply force or forces, energy or energies. It was a theory which diminished the power of man over his destiny. 'No one denies that motives exist adequate to decide the will, even though it may not be conscious of them,' Adams wrote (p. 487). Man is and, for the most part, has always been ignorant of the forces at work in the universe. He has even been responsible for diminishing himself, because 'as the mind of man enlarged its range, it enlarged the field of complexity, and must continue to do so even into chaos' (p. 487). Ironically the discovery of the dynamic formula of history amounted to the discovery of what, to Adams, was a principle of meaninglessness in the universe.

Nevertheless, he could not help trying to verify it. Using his dynamic theory of history, Adams looked at his life and his country and found that the concept of force, the very word force, seemed to account for and describe most things. Education was at best a force from which one might hope for a reaction, at worst a force which crushed. Society created economic monopolies which were explicable in terms of force. The continent itself was a magnetically attractive force, as successive waves of immigrants demonstrated; the urge to develop new products to satisfy a consumer who should be content with already adequate models was a sign that the American people were already succumbing to pointless excess, spending energy and money alike simply for the sake of spending. Americans thought they controlled their finances, but in fact it was money which was the controlling, motive power. 'The American wasted money more recklessly than any one ever did before; he spent more to less purpose than any extravagant court aristocracy'

(p. 328). Excess would breed degradation in the scientific and moral senses. It was inevitable. Men were labouring under the illusion that 'this Eden [was] of their own invention, and could no more have . . . [quitted] it of their own accord than the pearl oyster could quit its shell' (p. 459). The dynamic theory of history posited that in the social and physical world alike, acceleration would lead to explosion or deceleration. This was similar to the entropical theory of creation, which argued that all matter was created in a moment of intense energy rushing out into space in an attempt to dissipate itself, and that matter would ultimately come to rest or explode. Adams summed it up: whichever way, it was 'meaningless motion'.

In his caring, curious, heightened response to the significance of the modern event and to the extraordinary advances of technology, Adams seems prophetic. He virtually predicted the atom bomb from his understanding of the properties of radium. But he was not simply a man who with insight and foresight and foreboding asked what it was and what it would be like to be a twentieth-century American, not simply a man who answered that man is rushing frenetically to self-destruction. He was a poignant human being, a man who above all was a lover of art and architecture and who, ruefully, had to cede to science. He could not even claim his baptismal name with certainty; he called himself, in scientific terms, a 'runaway star [born] Groombridge, 1838, commonly called Henry Adams'. He recognized that his researches and speculation, his analytical visits to cathedrals and industrial exhibits constituted 'this slaughter of the centuries'. When winter sent him to his rooms to write, he in effect slaughtered himself: he had to deny significance, to take away vitality from those things he most valued. His instinct was to be hostile to a scientific explanation of the universe – he did not want to admit 'that the creation had taught him nothing except that the square of the hypothenuse of a right-angled triangle might for convenience be taken as equal to something else'. He sought a larger answer – 'a spool on which to wind the thread of history without breaking it'. And though he mocked his search – 'one sought only a spool,' he said wryly, 'one sought no absolute truth' – his was a search for just such truth. He had hoped against hope that there were indefinite possible cometary orbits available to the runaway star, Henry Adams, that his journey would enable him to find and attain an orbit which suited him. He found only the terrifying path of the meteor.

Notes

1 Henry Adams, *The Education of Henry Adams*, Boston and New York, 1918 (privately published 1907). All quotations from the *Education* are taken from this edition and, unless noted otherwise in textual parentheses, from Chapter 32, 'Vis Nova (1903–1904)', pages 468–73.

2 *Letters of Henry Adams (1892–1918)*, ed. Worthington Chauncey Ford, Boston, 1938, 279–80.

3 William H. Jordy, *Henry Adams: Scientific Historian*, New Haven and London, 1963, 132.

Further reading

Jones, Howard Mumford, *The Age of Energy: Varieties of American Experience, 1865–1915*, New York, 1971.

Jordy, William H., *Henry Adams: Scientific Historian*, New Haven and London, 1952.

Levenson, J. C., *The Mind and Art of Henry Adams*, Boston, 1957.

Samuels, Ernest, *Henry Adams*, Cambridge, Mass., 1948, 1958, 1964. The classic, three volume biography.

Wagner, Vern, *The Suspension of Henry Adams: A Study of Manner and Matter*, Detroit, 1969.

3
Henry James (1843–1916)

Wherever I turned, I confess, wherever any aspect seemed to put forth a freshness, there I found myself saying that this aspect was one's strongest impression. It is impossible, as I now recollect, not to be amused at the great immediate differences of scene and occasion that could produce such a judgment, and this remark directly applies, no doubt, to the accident of a visit, one afternoon of the dire mid-winter, to a theatre in the Bowery at which a young actor in whom I was interested had found for the moment a fine melodramatic opportunity. This small adventure – if the adventures of rash observation be ever small – was to remain embalmed for me in all its odd, sharp notes, and perhaps in none more than in its element of contrast with an image antediluvian, the memory of the conditions of a Bowery theatre, *the* Bowery Theatre in fact, contemporary with my more or less gaping youth. Was that vast dingy edifice, with its illustrious past, still standing? – a point on which I was to remain vague while I electrically travelled through a strange, a sinister over-roofed clangorous darkness, a wide thoroughfare beset, for all its width, with sound and fury, and bristling, amid the traffic, with posts and piles that were as the supporting columns of a vast cold, yet also uncannily animated sepulchre. It was like moving the length of an interminable cage, beyond the remoter of whose bars lighted shops, struggling dimly under other pent-house effects, offered their Hebrew faces and Hebrew names to a human movement that affected one even then as a breaking of waves that had rolled, for their welter on this very strand, from the other side of the globe. I was on my way to enjoy, no doubt, some peculiarly 'American' form of the theatric mystery, but my way led me, apparently, through depths of the Orient, and I should clearly take my place with an Oriental public. . . .

. . . From the corner of the box of my so improved playhouse further down, the very name of which moreover had the cosmopolite lack of point, I made out, in the audience, the usual mere monotony of the richer exoticism. No single face, beginning with those close beside me (for my box was a shared luxury), but referred itself, by my interpretation, to some such strange outland form as we had not dreamed of in my day. There they all sat, the representatives of the races we have nothing 'in common' with, as naturally, as comfortably, as munchingly, as if the theatre were their constant practice – and, as regards the munching, I may add, I was struck with the appearance of quality and cost in the various confections pressed from moment to moment upon our notice by the little playhouse peddlers.

It comes over me under this branch of my reminiscence, that these almost 'high-class' luxuries, circulating in such a company, were a sort of supreme symbol of the *promoted* state of the aspirant to American conditions. He, or more particularly she, had been promoted, and, more or less at a bound, to the habitual use of chocolate-creams, and indeed of other dainties, refined and ingenious, compared with which these are quite *vieux jeu*. This last remark might in fact open up for us, had I space, a view, interesting to hold a moment, or to follow as far as it might take us, of the wondrous consumption by the 'people', over the land, of the most elaborate solid and liquid sweets, such products as form in other countries an expensive and select dietary. The whole phenomenon of this omnipresent and essentially 'popular' appeal of the confectioner and pastry-cook, I can take time but to note, is more significant of the economic, and even of the social situation of the masses than many a circumstance honoured with more attention. I found myself again and again – in presence, for example, of the great glittering temples, the bristling pagodas, erected to the worship in question wherever men and women, perhaps particularly women, most congregate, and above all under the high domes of the great modern railway stations – I found myself wondering, I say, what such facts represented, what light they might throw upon manners and wages. Wages, in the country at large, *are* largely manners – the only manners, I think it fair to say, one mostly encounters; the market and the home therefore look alike dazzling, at first, in this reflected, many-coloured lustre. It speaks somehow, beyond anything else, of the diffused sense of material ease – since the solicitation of sugar couldn't be so hugely and artfully organized if the response were not clearly proportionate. But how is the response itself organized, and what are the other items of that general budget of labour, what in especial are the attenuations of that general state of fatigue, in which so much purchasing-power can flow to the supposedly superfluous? The wage-earners, the toilers of old, notably in other climes, were known by the wealth of their songs; and has it, on these lines, been given to the American people to be known by the number of their 'candies'?

I must not let the question, however, carry me too far – quite away from the point I was about to make of my sense of the queer chasm over which, on the Saturday afternoon at the Windsor Theatre, I seemed to see the so domestic drama reach out to the so exotic audience and the so exotic audience reach out to the so domestic drama. The play (a masterpiece of its type, if I may so far strain a point, in such a case, and in the interest of my young friend's excellent performance, as to predicate 'type') was American, to intensity, in its blank conformity to convention, the particular implanted convention of the place. This convention, simply expressed, was that there should never be anything different in a play (the most conservative of human institutions) from what there had always been before; that *that place*, in a word, should always know the very same theatric thing, any deviation from which might be phrenology, or freemasonry, or ironmongery, or anything else in the world, but would never be drama, especially drama addressed to the heart of the people. The tricks and the traps, the *trucs*, the whole stage-carpentry, might freely renew themselves, to create for artless minds the illusion of a difference; but the sense of the business would still have to reside in our ineradicable Anglo-Saxon policy, or our seemingly deep-seated necessity, of keeping, where 'representation' is concerned, so far away from the truth and the facts of life as really to betray a fear in us of possibly doing something like them should we be caught nearer. 'Foreigners', in general, unmistakably, in any attempt to render life, obey the instinct of keeping closer, positively recognize the presence and the solicitation of the deep waters; yet here was my houseful of foreigners, physiognomically branded as such, confronted with our pale poetic – fairly caught for schooling in our art of making the best of it. Nothing (in the texture of the occasion) could have had a sharper interest than this demonstration that, since what we most pretend to do with them is thoroughly to school them, the schooling, by our system, cannot begin too soon nor pervade their experience too much. Were they going to rise to it, or rather to fall to it – to *our* instinct, as distinguished from their own, for picturing life? Were they to take our lesson, submissively, in order to get with it our smarter traps and tricks, our superior Yankee machinery (illustrated in the case before them, for instance, by a wonderful folding bed in which the villain of the piece, pursuing the virtuous heroine round and round the room and trying to leap over it after her, is, at the young lady's touch of a hidden spring, engulfed as in the jaws of a crocodile?) Or would it be their dim intellectual resistance, a vague stir in them of some unwitting heritage – of the finer irony, that I should make out, on the contrary, as withstanding the effort to corrupt them, and thus perhaps really promising to react, over the head of our offered mechanic bribes, on our ingrained intellectual platitude?

One had only to formulate that question to seem to see the issue hang there, for the excitement of the matter, quite as if the determination were to be taken on the spot. For the opposition over the chasm of the footlights, as I have called it, grew intense truly, as I took in on one side the hue of the Galician cheek, the light of the Moldavian eye, the whole pervasive facial mystery, swaying, at the best, for the moment, over the gulf, on the vertiginous bridge of American confectionery – and took in on the other the perfect 'Yankee' quality of the challenge which stared back at them as in the white light of its hereditary thinness. I needn't say that when I departed – perhaps from excess of suspense – it was without seeing the balance drop to either quarter, and I am afraid I think of the odd scene as still enacted in many places and many ways, the inevitable rough union in discord of the two groups of instincts, the fusion of the two camps by a queer, clumsy, wasteful social chemistry. Such at all events are the roundabout processes of peaceful history, the very history that succeeds, for our edification, in *not* consisting of battles and blood and tears.

The American Scene (1907)[1]

* * *

It is hard to think of anyone better qualified than Henry James to give a penetrating sense of the America which he revisited in 1904–5. He had not been in his native land for twenty years, having rejected its thin cultural soil and the thin literature which he felt went with it for the fertile lands and the rich cultural accretions of Europe, and in particular of England, where he settled and which he relished. But he remained an American citizen (until the outbreak of the First World War, when he felt impelled to commit himself to the adopted country from which he had derived so much), and he remained concerned about the character and the destiny of America. Indeed, the American, albeit in Europe, had provided the subject matter and had produced the distinction of much of his best fiction. His lifelong preoccupation was with the 'complex fate' of being an American, with that race of naive and impressionable individuals who needed to go to the Old World to mature but who could only do so at the expensive, inevitable and sad loss of New World virtues: innocence, idealism and independence. The experienced eye replaced the fresh one, only to become jaded.

Unlike the inexperienced and eminently corruptible fictional Americans James brought to Europe – Christopher Newman in *The American* (1877), Isabel Archer in *The Portrait of a Lady* (1881), Lambert Strether in *The Ambassadors* (1903), Maggie Verver in *The Golden Bowl* (1904) – James had wisdom and sophistication. He had also, he believed, retained 'much freshness of eye, outward and inward' (p. xxxv). He could straddle Old World and New. His responsive and perceptive piece on the Bowery demonstrates the lively sense of change and the strong sense of the past which coloured his serious attempt, from 24 August 1904 to 5 July 1905, to see, to feel and to express the America he now saw. He was scrupulous in his comparison of past and present, and careful to give way neither to novelty nor to nostalgia.

An inveterate traveller and a conscientious reporter, James did justice to America both on foot and in Pullman cars which, he wrote, 'so reverse the relation of the parties concerned, suggesting somehow that the country exists for the "cars" which overhang it like a conquering army, and not the cars for the country' (p. 27). In his case, as in Henry Adams's, convenience temporarily overcame principle, and James used the railroad to see New England, New York and New Jersey, St Louis, Los Angeles and Chicago, San Diego and Seattle, Philadelphia and Baltimore, Washington and Richmond, Charleston and Florida. He was determined to get a sense of the whole continent. He made painstaking attempts to revisit and reassess the various places in which he had lived or had known well: the houses in Washington Square and the Fourteenth Street district of New York, the streets of Boston and Cambridge. He spent time discussing the state of the nation with Edith Wharton, with Henry Adams and with his own brother William.

Henry James's brother William, the distinguished Harvard philosopher, felt that Henry, like the characters in his novels and stories, had become as much impoverished as enriched in Europe, and William figured dauntingly in Henry James's mind and imagination as he left for the States in 1904. William had not only made America his home (after spending much of his early life, like Henry, in Europe); he had made it his business to articulate a theory which defined one highly significant aspect of Americanness: its commitment to goals, its disregard for means. The Declaration of Independence had stated that all men were created equal and that they were endowed with certain inalienable rights – life, liberty and the pursuit of happiness – but it had been less specific as to how these were to be attained and safeguarded. William James's philosophy of 'pragmatism' argued that ends justified means and that flexibility was essential to the human condition, human success and human progress. In one sense this was very American: make it new, assume endless ingenuity, assume change as an index of progress. In another it went profoundly against the Christian concepts which had informed American thought in its earlier years. Pragmatism might undermine the egalitarian and democratic assumptions of common goals and a common good. It could be read as a justification of inequality and of dubious political and economic practices. It also struck at the heart of something Henry James cared specially about: forms, rituals and manners, which William saw as dispensable and fluctuating means but which Henry saw as the backbone of social relationships and as indispensable means to indispensable ends. Those ends were culture, civilization, maturity – elements in the picture for which social relationships provided the frame, the canvas and the paints. The two brothers had affectionately agreed to differ, but it was with a sense of trepidation as well as a sense of curiosity that Henry James arrived in America. Would the society to which William James had committed himself demonstrate William's justification? Or would it justify Henry's partial alienation?

In 1875 Henry James had left an America still preoccupied with the aftermath of the Civil War, inward looking and tending towards superficiality and vulgarity (Mark Twain christened this period the Gilded Age). But this America was still a country in which the idealist, if not the artist, could hope for a fine American difference, an acceptable American exceptionalism. By the time James returned in 1904, the possibility of such a difference seemed increasingly remote. Corruption prevailed in Washington. Industrial growth had become a national priority. Influential men were preaching a debased version of Emersonian self-reliance: a self-help which would lead to private material fulfilment. Economically and politically America had become a world power. She had become imperialistic, she had become pretentious – her 'World's Fairs' showed that. Theodore Roosevelt had become the international trouble shooter. In terms of reputation and ethos America seemed more Old World than New. Would Henry James find it a more palatable place than before?

No, for it seemed to him that America had taken upon itself the worst aspects of the Old World and had ignored its grace, style and culture. Change had been for the worst. He lamented the loss of the old Bowery Theatre he had visited as a young man, 'dim' and 'bleak' though it had been; he preferred the old 'bare ranting stupid stage, the grey void, smelling of dust and tobacco juice' to the 'improved' playhouse (p. 195). And while he was to find Americans addicted to change, there had been none where it was most needed: in literature, in art, in drama. The play he saw at the Windsor Theatre was derived from English melodrama of little merit, which kept as far away as possible 'where "representation" is concerned . . . from the truth and the facts of life'. As ever in America, there was no originality in the arts. Conventionality dictated that 'there should never be anything different in a play . . . from what there had always been before'. The only freedom from imitation within the play was not artistic; it consisted of a piece of 'Yankee machinery . . . a wonderful folding bed in which the villain of the piece, pursuing the virtuous heroine round and round the room and trying to leap over it after her, is, at the young lady's touch of a hidden spring, engulfed as in the jaws of a crocodile'.

And if imitative culture prevailed, so did many other things which James remembered distastefully. His heart sank when he saw the New York waterfront,

> only too confoundingly familiar and too serenely exempt from change, the waterside squalor of the great city put forth again its most inimitable notes, showed so true to the barbarisms it had not outlived that one could only fall to wondering what obscure inward virtue had preserved it. (pp. 1–2)

Things were, in fact, so much worse than when he had left for Europe in 1875 that the Puritanism, the joylessness which he had left America to escape now seemed attractive by comparison. Such universities as Harvard, such places as Cambridge, seemed to him to 'glow with all the vividness of the defined alternative, the possible antidote' (p. 57). For pleasure James was reduced to going to the Harvard Law Library to smell the dust.

Unerringly James singled out for comment those aspects of America which were to become her hallmarks in the twentieth century. The monotonous buildings and townscapes depressed him: the 'vast, featureless highway', the 'loud, assertive' houses (p. 8), the New York skyline, which looked like 'a hair comb turned upward and deprived of half its teeth' – or like a hideous pincushion (pp. 139–40). He detected a principle of appalling openness at work, a lack of evident demarcation between one house and another which conveyed 'an air of unmitigated publicity . . . from which there could be no appeal' (p. 9). He diagnosed a society in which judgement by one's peer was paramount. There was an obligation always to be open, as a demonstration of frankness, probity, democracy, Americanness. The lack of privacy appalled him. Not for him the open society or the open plan house, in which, he lamented, 'Thus we have the law fulfilled that every part of every house shall be, as nearly as may be, visible, visitable, penetrable, not only from every other part, but from as many parts of as many other houses as possible, it may be only near enough' (p. 167). And what was he to make of a society that had ruined Central Park by making it a park of 'ingratiation' (p. 176), split up and spoilt by having to be all parks in one, incorporating something for all tastes? Such physical and environmental openness was of a piece with 'the consummate monotonous commonness' (p. 83), the fact that every face he saw was a version of the 'unmitigated business man' (p. 64), with that face's terrifying – and misplaced – intensity, as misplaced as the intensity with which the 'American' theatre imitated English melodrama. What was he to make of a society which flew in the face of nature and attempted to deny the existence of intrinsic difference, a society which refused to discriminate, a society which made it impossible to know, when you rang a doorbell, whether the washerwoman or the lady of the house had answered, a society where people of all ages dressed alike?

Henry James commented that everyone was ground down into the same marginally civil and free relations by 'the endless electric coil, the monstrous chain that winds round the general neck and body' (p. 89). He was referring to the elevated railroad in New York, but what he says holds good for the car today. He noted, as foreigners still do, another example of American conformity: the importance they had come to place on regular teeth – supplemented, if necessary, by 'the far-shining dental gold' (p. 180). The vacuous and uniform smile was *de rigueur* – the American needed to demonstrate that he was pursuing happiness, he needed to show his success. There was no attempt to suggest that teeth were one of nature's gifts, and that the gift was, to a degree, individual and distinctive; the intention was simply to show ingenuity and money at work. They were at work in buildings, too. James anticipated the phrase 'built-in obsolescence' – 'eternal waste', he called it (p. 113).

What pointless energy, he lamented; if this meant a forever new, forever young society, it also meant 'unattempted, impossible maturity' (p. 111). It was not surprising that this society had, as its social and aesthetic ideal, the conspicuous consumption of the over-ornate Waldorf-Astoria Hotel. James was seeing for himself, and embodying in literature, the relevance of the sociologist Thorstein Veblen's analysis of American values as 'Pecuniary Emulation' and as the search to manufacture and purchase 'Vendible Imponderables': the gift for the man who has everything. This was show for its own sake, an imitation of the Old World at its profligate worst. There was no stylishness to the production or the consumption. If the goods and buildings were more lavish than those of Puritan New England, a 'hereditary thinness' still prevailed. He wondered if 'the cash register, the ice-cream freezer, the lightning-elevator, the "boys' paper" and other such overflows, do truly represent the sum of its [America's] passions' (p. 312). America seemed to equate art with ingenuity. Anything subtler would produce a grimace on the American face – an inconceivable image.

As much as Edith Wharton, and perhaps more savagely, James indicted money as a root American evil. If you are 'making no money, America is no place for you,' he declared. 'The preliminary American postulate or basis for any successful accommodation of life . . . is that of active pecuniary gain and of active pecuniary gain only' (pp. 236–7). The only principle or order which he could detect in America was 'the expensive as a power by itself, a power unguided and undirected, practically unapplied' (p. 9). In America property and money gave form to society, a lamentable contrast to Europe at her best, shaped by art, religion, social and political discrimination, and an affirmation of difference and variety.

Revulsion from an Anglo-Saxon American type even less congenial to him in 1904 than in 1875 led James to look at the recent immigrant as an alternative 'American'. His image of America, urban America especially, would indeed have been incomplete had it ignored the forceful immigrant presence and had it failed to contemplate the effect of immigration on American society and on the ultimate composition of the American character. 'The cauldron of the American character', as he called it, was 'about as vivid a thing' as he had encountered on the continent (p. 121). He was struck by the fact that when he had left America most of the immigrants had been from western and northern Europe. But between 1870 and 1930 more than 37 million immigrants came to America, most of them from Poland, Bohemia, Russia and

Italy. An 'odd scene', James commented: going to New York City's Bowery was as strange as going to the Orient! America was no longer the automatic preserve of the familiar middle classes; eastern and southern European artisans were increasingly present, diluting an already thin American character.

As the immigrant went, so the city; as the city, so the nation: immigration was therefore crucial to the fate of America. James christened immigration 'the great stew' – a messy and pedestrian mixture (p. 130). His hostile viewpoint was countered by the Jewish immigrant playwright Israel Zangwill, who, in his play, *The Melting Pot* (1909), wrote of a love he felt even for the humiliating procedures with which immigrants were vetted at Ellis Island before being admitted to America. Ellis Island appalled James for the thoughtlessness with which America altered itself and the idealistic misconceptions with which immigrants exchanged the honourable values of Europe for the dishonourable ones of America. Zangwill wrote:

> America is God's crucible, the great Melting Pot where all the races of Europe are melting, and reforming. Here you stand, good folk, think I, when I see them at Ellis Island, here you stand in your fifty groups and your fifty languages and histories and your fifty blood hatreds and rivalries. But you won't be long like that, brothers, for these are the fires of God you come to – these are the fires of God: A fig for your feuds and vendettas: Germans and Frenchmen, Irishmen and Englishmen, Jews and Russians – into the Crucible with you all! God is making the American.[2]

James: 'this visible act of ingurgitation on the part of our body politic and social . . . constitutes an appeal to amazement beyond that of any sword-swallowing or fire-swallowing of the circus' (p. 84).

James noticed the 'alien' wherever he went – in the upper reaches of Fifth and Madison Avenues, in the Maine woods, in Boston. His use of the word 'alien' was quite deliberate, for to him the alien still was an alien. Why had he not yet been dissolved in the melting pot, James wondered. He answered himself that he was, of course, noticing only those who had not yet been assimilated; but he continued to refer to this element of strangeness as the way into a discussion of precisely what constituted the Americanness into which the aliens would merge or which they might change. He considered some Italian workers – obviously Italian, but not relaxed, forthcoming and courteous as he had known them in Italy. 'It was as if contact were out of the question' – and this in the land of universal brotherhood. James found this 'rather a chill, straightway, for the heart, and rather a puzzlement, no less for the head' (p. 119). He did meet an Armenian in the New Hampshire woods who was almost aggressive in the assertion of his culture. But James felt, correctly, that this was a temporary over-reaction. One and all the aliens were being 'dressed and prepared' (p. 120) for brotherhood, and their children would be indistinguishably American, transformed by the common school and the newspaper. Why *were* the immigrants so anxious to relinquish such qualities as their natural friendliness (the Italians) and so prone to deny their ethnicity (the Armenians, even)? There was little in the established American character James could wish them to emulate. Could they not see, as he had seen when he took the New York elevated railroad to the Bowery, that America was something to fear – an 'animated sepulchre'?

James saw nothing in America that justified Europeans taking American citizenship when to become an American was to become first and foremost conscious of money and to throw off real identity in search of a non-existent one. He saw the immigrant as pitiable, as a 'dog who sniffs around the freshly acquired bone, giving it a push and a lick, betraying a sense of its possibilities' (p. 128). Only in the Jewish quarter of New York did it seem to him that the process might just be reversed. Yiddish culture might survive the ethnic dilution. It had forms, values and ageless traditions and an impetus to hang on to them: the age-old Jewish fear of persecution. Otherwise, call it melting pot, cauldron or stew, James disliked and feared the new wave of immigration. 'What meaning', he asked, 'can continue to attach to such a term as the "American" character? – what type, as the result of such a prodigious amalgam, such a hotch-potch of racial ingredients, can be so conceived as shaping itself?' (p. 121). He did wonder if the only hope for America's escape from the huge democratic broom, from the attempt to be all alike, from the zealous cultivation of the common mean was that the constituent alien groups in America – and all Americans were aliens once – 'may rise again to the surface, affirming their vitality and value and playing their part' (p. 129). He hoped that the qualities engrained in generations in Europe had not been finally extinguished. Could Americans not agree that what they had most in common was that they were *all* aliens, and that they should use their differences to make a rich diversity in America? Could they not learn from one another, as he had learned from French and Russian novelists? Must the American identity be composed of sacrifices of ethnic qualities and cultures; must it be negative and tasteless, could it not be positive and well flavoured?

Even while he speculated in this way, James found it difficult to be optimistic, for he was aware that above all the immigrants wanted to be baptized into America, to renounce what they had been before. They were

> consciously not being what they *had* been, and . . . this immediately glazed them over as with some mixture, of indescribable hue and consistency, the wholesale varnish of consecration, that might have been applied, out of a bottomless receptacle, by a huge white-washing brush. (p. 127)

But it seemed to him that it was not an act of piety, rather one of sacrilege, to be an 'aspirant to American conditions'.

James's essay on the Bowery brought together all the strands of his response to America. Here were the east Europeans whose cultural heritage was superior to the Yankee melodrama but who nevertheless obediently savoured American entertainment. Here was the silly, derivative Anglo-American literature; here was conspicuous consumption. The Bowery essay evoked in James his strongest impression of America: wherever he turned there was freshness, there was change. He experienced once again the 'queer chasm' between nineteenth- and twentieth-century America as he saw how the earlier Irish immigrants, with their familiar faces, had given way to 'the hue of the Galician cheek, the light of the Moldavian eye', to a 'pervasive facial mystery'. How altered America appeared, how different 'Americans' themselves looked; how sad that the immigrant should merely affirm America in all its blandness and grossness, and should in no way refresh and enrich that society. What improvement was there in the fact that the peanuts and oranges, natural American foods, had given way to fancy chocolates, that the shabby playhouse, appropriate to the Bowery, had been replaced by the inappropriately elaborate one? In one sense, however, James had to admit such buildings were appropriate: American theatres, candy stores, even American homes, 'great glittering temples' or 'bristling pagodas' that they were, reflected the 'many-coloured lustre' of money. In a savage and elaborate metaphor, he suggested that the expensive candy store, all cool marble inside, the luxury palace where America bought luxury items, was now the American church: the 'solid and liquid sweets' (hard and soft centred) were communion wafer and communion wine.

Remembering how the Bowery had been, James felt poignantly in this scene the reaction that coloured so much of his visit to America: 'all old signs . . . seemed visibly to fail and new questions, mockingly insoluble, to rise'. What was he to make of, on the one hand, the total lack of common culture between audience and artists and, on the other, the air of the audience, 'naturally, . . . comfortably, . . . munchingly' at home? What made them feel at home was the confectionery they so conspicuously consumed; this was the common cultural denominator, this was

> a sort of supreme symbol of the *promoted* state of the aspirant to American conditions. He, or more particularly she, had been promoted, and, more or less at a bound, to the habitual use of chocolate-creams. . . . The wage earners, the toilers of old, notably in other climes, were known by the wealth of their songs; and has it, on these lines, been given to the American people to be known by the number of their 'candies'?

A comic reflection, but a tragic one, too.

In the Bowery chapter James also set out his vain hope that 'their dim intellectual resistance, a vague stir in . . . [their] unwitting heritage' would lead the aliens to reject American culture. But he had to accept that though they still looked alien, they were already, in the only sense that mattered, typical twentieth-century Americans. They had acquired 'the diffused sense of material ease'. They had accepted that 'wages, in the country at large, *are* largely manners – the only manners . . . one mostly encounters'; they were already leading hollow lives. They had already effectively abdicated culture and individuality. He could only see this paradigmatic American scene of the period as an 'odd scene': 'the fusion of the two camps [western Europe's pioneer stock and the new wave of eastern European immigrants] by a queer, clumsy, wasteful social chemistry'. As a result the great stew of America was full of mediocrities. A country strongly committed to individualism, spirituality and the cutting edge was now the country of conformity, commerce and blandness.

Notes

1 Henry James, *The American Scene*, ed. Leon Edel, London, 1968 (originally published 1907). All quotations from *The American Scene* are taken from this edition and, unless noted otherwise in textual parentheses, from Chapter 5, 'The Bowery and Thereabouts', pages 195–9.

2 Israel Zangwill, *The Melting Pot*, London, 1914, 33.

Further reading

Auden, W. H., 'Henry James and the artist in America', *Harper's*, July 1948.

Edel, Leon, Introduction to *The American Scene*, London, 1968.

Edel, Leon, *The Master, 1901–16*, Philadelphia, 1972. Volume 5 of Edel's biography.

Jones, Maldwyn, *American Immigration*, Chicago, 1960. Especially Chapters 7 to 9.

Rowe, John Carlos, *Henry Adams and Henry James: The Emergence of a Modern Consciousness*, Ithaca and London, 1976.

4
Gertrude Stein (1874–1946)

I am writing for myself and strangers. This is the only way that I can do it. Everybody is a real one to me, everybody is like some one else too to me. No one of them that I know can want to know it and so I write for myself and strangers.

Every one is always busy with it, no one of them then ever want to know it that every one looks like some one else and they see it. Mostly every one dislikes to hear it. It is very important to me to always know it, to always see it which one looks like others and to tell it. I write for myself and strangers. I do this for my own sake and for the sake of those who know I know it that they look like other ones, that they are separate and yet always repeated. There are some who like it that I know they are like many others and repeat it, there are many who never can really like it.

There are many that I know and they know it. They are all of them repeating and I hear it. I love it and I tell it, I love it and now I will write it. This is now the history of the way some of them are it.

I write for myself and strangers. No one who knows me can like it. At least they mostly do not like it that every one is of a kind of men and women and I see it. I love it and I write it.

I want readers so strangers must do it. Mostly no one knowing me can like it that I love it that every one is a kind of men and women, that always I am looking and comparing and classifying of them, always I am seeing their repeating. Always more and more I love repeating, it may be irritating to hear from them but always more and more I love it of them. More and more I love it of them, the being in them, the mixing in them, the repeating in them, the deciding the kind of them every one is who has human being.

There is now a little of what I love and how I write it. Later there will be much more of it.

There are many ways of making kinds of men and women. Now there will be descriptions of every kind of way every one can be a kind of men and women.

This is now a history of Martha Hersland. This is now a history of Martha and of every one who came to be of her living.

There will then be soon much description of every way one can think of men and women, in their beginning, in their middle living, and their ending.

Every one then is an individual being. Every one then is like many others always living, there are many ways of thinking of every one, this is now a description of all of them. There must then be a whole history of each one of them. There must then now be a description of all repeating. Now I will tell all the meaning to me in repeating, the loving there is in me for repeating.

Every one is one inside them, every one reminds some one of some other one who is or was or will be living. Every one has it to say of each one he is like such a one I see it in him, every one has it to say of each one she is like some one else I can tell by remembering. So it goes on always in living, every one is always remembering some one who is resembling to the one at whom they are then looking. So they go on repeating, every one is themselves inside them and every one is resembling to others, and that is always interesting. There are many ways of making kinds of men and women. In each way of making kinds of them there is a different system of finding them resembling. Sometime there will be here every way there can be of seeing kinds of men and women. Sometime there will be then a complete history of each one. Every one always is repeating the whole of them and so sometime some one who sees them will have a complete history of every one. Sometime some one will know all the ways there are for people to be resembling, some one sometime then will have a completed history of every one.

Soon now there will be a history of the way repeating comes out of them comes out of men and women when they are young, when they are children, they have then their own system of being resembling; this will soon be a description of the men and women in beginning, the being young in them, the being children.

There is then now and here the loving repetition, this is then, now and here, a description of the loving of repetition and then there will be a description of all the kinds of ways there can be seen to be kinds of men and women. Then there will be realized the complete history of every one, the fundamental character of every one, the bottom nature in them, the mixtures in them, the strength and weakness of everything they have inside them, the flavor of them, the meaning in them, the being in them, and then you have a whole history then of each one. Everything then they do in living is clear to the completed understanding, their living, loving, eating, pleasing, smoking, thinking, scolding, drinking, working, dancing, walking, talking, laughing, sleeping, everything in them. There are whole beings then, they are themselves inside them, repeating coming out of them makes a history of each one of them.

Always from the beginning there was to me all living as repeating. This is now a description of my feeling. As I was saying listening to repeating is often irritating, always repeating is all of living, everything in a being is always repeating, more and more listening to repeating gives to me completed understanding. Each one slowly comes to be a whole one to me. Each one slowly comes to be a whole one in me. Soon then it commences to sound through my ears and eyes and feelings the repeating that is always coming out from each one, that is them, that makes then slowly of each one of them a whole one. Repeating then comes slowly then to be to one who has it to have loving repeating as natural being comes to be a full sound telling all the being in each one such a one is ever knowing. Sometimes it takes many years of knowing some one before the repeating that is that one gets to be a steady sounding to the hearing of one who has it as a natural being to love repeating that slowly comes out from every one. Sometimes it takes many years of knowing some one before the repeating in that one comes to be a clear history of such a one. Natures sometimes are so mixed up in some one that steady repeating in them is mixed up with changing. Soon then there will be a completed history of each one. Sometimes it is difficult to know it in some, for what these are saying is repeating in them is not the real repeating of them, is not the complete repeating for them. Sometimes many years of knowing some one pass before repeating of all being in them comes out clearly from them. As I was saying it is often irritating to listen to the repeating they are doing, always then that one that has it as being to love repeating that is the whole history of each one, such a one has it then that this irritation passes over into patient completed understanding. Loving repeating is one way of being. This is now a description of such feeling.

There are many that I know and they know it. They are all of them repeating and I hear it. I love it and I tell it. I love it and now I will write it. This is now a history of my love of it. I hear it and I love it and I write it. They repeat it. They live it and I see it and I hear it. They live it and I hear it and I see it and I love it and now and always I will write it. There are many kinds of men and women and I know it. They repeat it and I hear it and love it. This is now a history of the way they do it. This is now a history of the way I love it.

The Making of Americans (1906–8)[1]

* * *

Gertrude Stein is often seen as an eccentric expatriate, a celebrated personality whose main claim to distinction is as an early and perceptive patron of various young painters, most notably Picasso, Braque and Miro. Her famous salon at 27 Rue de Fleurus was hung with wonderful paintings. Without her image as the patron and perceiver of all that was important in European art, it is doubtful if expatriate and visiting American writers like Sherwood Anderson and Scott Fitzgerald would have sought her out so readily. However, it was her literary theories and her writing, formulated first as a response to the James brothers, William and Henry, which made her interesting and influential.

The Making of Americans, written in France and Switzerland over the years 1906–8, though not formally published until 1925, demonstrates a number of important things about the period and about its influential author. First, it shows how even a committed expatriate like Gertrude Stein was still conditioned and stimulated, in the themes and styles of her writing, by things American. Second, it marks the transition in Stein's own writing, in the early years of the twentieth century, from a relatively conventional prose to the idiosyncratic use of language and syntax that was to influence so many American writers – among them Sherwood Anderson, Ernest Hemingway and William Faulkner. Third, it constitutes a seminal attempt in American literature to respond to the turn of the century preoccupation with the nature of consciousness and how to give it effective expression. Fourth, it shows the period's growing interest in words – in the word *per se*, in words as patterns, in the autonomy of words, in endowing words with new life and that life their own, independent even of subject matter and of the object described. 'Successions of words are so agreeable,' theorized Stein,[2] and her practice proved her point: 'Living, loving, eating, pleasing, smoking, thinking, scolding, drinking'. The sequence of 'ing' sounds, modulated by their preceding syllables, conveys infinite clarity, infinite variety. The sounds suggest life and have life too.

Gertrude Stein represents the American dimension of what was happening elsewhere in the arts and sciences in the early twentieth century. She was part of the intellectual revolt against the art of previous eras, and she is properly associated with that time when Einstein, Bergson, Russell and Freud were making revolutionary advances in physics, metaphysics, philosophy and psychology, and when in music and in painting the Cubists, the Fauves and Schoenberg were making new 'harmonies', connecting sounds and shapes and colours in new and what seemed at first to be strange and dislocated ways, ways as strange as Gertrude Stein's prose. Indeed her writing resembled the cubist fragmentation of conventional perspective and its use of interlocking planes, and like the Fauves, she boldly dismantled traditional forms. She believed that if we abandon the 'structures' – be they visual or syntactical – which we have imposed on time and space, on our universe and on our language, we will achieve unimpeded access to our consciousness. Natural flow would replace artificial order. Literature would become like life: it would be always in motion. And as an American she felt she had a head start, as she explained in 1934.

> I am always trying to tell this thing that a space of time is a natural thing for an American to always have inside them as something in which they are continuously moving. Think of anything, of cowboys, of movies, of detective stories, of anybody who goes anywhere or stays at home and is an American and you will realize that it is something strictly American to conceive a space that is filled with moving, a space of time that is filled always filled with moving and my first real effort to express this thing which is an American thing began in writing The Making of Americans.[3]

She was as ambitious as her great contemporaries, and as convinced that she had achieved a breakthrough in understanding and communication.

> I began to be sure that if I could only go on long enough and talk and hear and look and see and feel enough and long enough I could finally describe really describe every kind of human being that ever was or is or would be living. . . . And I began writing The Making of Americans. . . . I was sure that in a kind of way the enigma of the universe could in this way be solved.[4]

It is no coincidence that Stein affirmed Henry James as one of the few significant modern novelists. She approved his reaction against a sparse culture. But something in American culture was part of James's genius and her own, she believed: the fact that it was a culture with a 'disembodied way of disconnecting something from anything and anything from something was the American one'. It was an independent culture, and a mobile one. Henry James made the paragraph float, said Stein; the Jamesian paragraph 'detached what it said from what it did, what it was from what it held'.[5] His paragraphs did not analyse and state, they *were*, they flowed. Each word was as clear and individual as a pebble seen through a stream's clear water. James's skill made the pebbles float above the sentence, the paragraph, the page, the book.

She particularly admired his technique in such difficult late novels as *The Awkward Age* (1899) and *The Wings of the Dove* (1902). Some criticized the un-lifelike dialogue in these novels; Stein saw that James was acutely conscious of words as words, and that by eliminating descriptive and explanatory passages he was giving dialogue, the uttered word, the word itself, an enigmatic power, a limitless possiblity for redefinition, expansion, permutation and combination. She was to imitate the effect James achieved when he had different characters repeat identical words and phrases in ways which pointed out not only the dissimilarity of the characters but the potential complexity and range of meaning which sound and repetition and patterning opened up. She also approved his realization that the novel and traditional syntax were devalued forms, and was as determined as he to refresh them. You can no longer say 'O moon, O sea, O love,' and expect to carry conviction, she said. And she claimed of her much criticized line 'a rose is a rose is a rose' that 'in that line the rose is red in English poetry for the first time in a hundred years'.[6]

Stein responded to William James as well as to his brother. As a student at Radcliffe College in 1897, she was able to hear the lectures James was giving at Harvard, and her interest in psychology led her to study the anatomy of the brain at Johns Hopkins. James had recommended that she go into philosophy, but she decided to become a doctor; and though she gave this up and went to live abroad in 1902, William James's influence on her was nevertheless profound. Not only did he articulate the theory of the stream of consciousness, the stream of thought, he held that knowledge does not consist of generally accepted information, it is what the individual 'knows', it is what is held for the individual within the experience of the present. To Stein, this meant an end to the usual understanding of history as chronologically ordered sequence, and it reinforced her understanding, through Henry James, of the limits of traditional narrative technique. And so, in Stein's application of the James brothers' theories, we find the breakdown of conventional plot structure and discursive writing, and discover instead a dependence upon other means of expressing a present which contained the past and anticipated the future. For instance, statements which are in part repetitive advance a theme step by step, giving a sense of uninterrupted sequence and of moment-to-moment reality, rather like a sequence of motion picture frames. Repeated sentence openings, followed by slight variations within the sentence as in the paragraph beginning 'Every one then is an individual being', show how successful her cinematic technique could be. And to Stein just as the so-called past called for immediate, cinematic treatment, the narrative past tense had to give way to the present tense and to the participial style. 'This is now a history of Martha Hersland. This is now a history of Martha and of every one who came to be of her living,' she wrote in *The Making of Americans*, and elsewhere: 'the business of Art . . . is to live in the present actual'.[7]

Gertrude Stein explored a range of American themes in her writing. She was almost as fascinated as Henry James when she revisited America (in the 1930s), and she found flying over the American landscape in a plane an experience which suspended time into a continuous present in the way her writing did. Immigrants and their place in America had concerned her in the Anna and Lena sections of *Three Lives* (1909), and the third of those lives, Melanctha's, was a marvellously acute analysis and affirmation of blackness which anticipated Jean Toomer's (see Chapter 9) in its treatment of the possibilities in black people for indolence and activity, and in its feeling for the beauty of black bodies and the vitality of black speech. (She had carefully observed the repetitive qualities of black speech and its less than orthodox grammar as a medical orderly in Baltimore in the 1890s.) Her lifelong commitment to America as place, inspiration and audience was evident in *The Geographical History of America* (1936), the work in which she set out definitively to explain and illustrate her literary theories, which continued to bewilder many people. One of her last works, *Brewsie and Willie* (1946), concerned the personal and social problems of American soldiers in France in the Second World War. But her most American work was *The Making of Americans*, an attempt to write a 'total history' of America by writing the fictional history of a typical family, the Herslands; the work ran to over 900 pages and half a million words. In form and length it was a deliberately ambitious book, a revolutionary book. Gertrude Stein consciously thought of herself as one of the great creative forces of her time; and as she said in an early passage from

The Making of Americans: 'There will then be soon much description of every way one can think of men and women, in their beginning, in their middle living, and their ending.' If, as she believed, Spain could be explained by Picasso, America could be explained by Americans. To write of one was to write of the other.

Some critics have seen *The Making of Americans* as autobiographical and have taken Martha Hersland to be Stein. But to attempt to make such analogies, to decide that Gossols is San Francisco and Bridgepoint Baltimore, is to run counter to Stein's intention, which was to universalize, to see things as typical, not as representative. It was important for her not to describe recognizable places, not to give well-known place names. That was a limiting act of naming, an act that put a halt to the extension of meaning. She did not want to name and thus define; she wanted to convey a sense of ceaselessness. As a result, she rarely used adjectives, for to do so was to judge, to label, to interfere with the flow of the style and the subject. The adjectives she used conveyed her sense of the processes of historical and individual growth: middle, every, complete, bottom, fundamental. She also avoided nouns, for nouns were names, and 'things once they are named the name does not go on doing anything to them and so why write in nouns'.[8] Commas too were a writer's way of forcing meaning on the reader 'by helping you along holding your coat for you and putting on your shoes keeps you from living your life as actively as you should lead it'.[9] She did not want anything to get in the way of the medium of the floating paragraph into which her readers could dive and retrieve meaning for themselves. Revising her text in the 1920s, she took out numbers of proper names and replaced them with 'the man', 'the woman'.

Linear time was also unimportant to her. Hundreds of pages might intervene between closely connected events in a character's life; a key character might not be mentioned for thousands of paragraphs. Julia Dehning and Alfred Hersland are married early in *The Making of Americans*, and then do not appear for another 500 pages. The curious order, or lack of it, can in part be attributed to Stein's attempt to show us in what arbitrary sequence and proportion the human consciousness remembers and recounts. If so, she was perhaps overdoing her determination to convey the sense of the liberated consciousness, and the difference between the nature of that consciousness and the artificial fiction and history to which we are accustomed. But the strange order had most to do with Stein's idiosyncratic intention in writing *The Making of Americans*. What she did was to arrange history to follow the pattern of her own stream of thought, which blurred the boundaries between fiction and history, between objectivity and subjectivity. She did not like such distinctions; she believed in oneness, in continuous flow. If a character was not mentioned by name he was present by type, for in *The Making of Americans*, Stein claimed,

> Then there will be realized the complete history of every one, the fundamental character of every one, the bottom nature in them, the mixtures in them, the strength and weakness of everything they have inside them, the flavor of them, the meaning in them, the being in them, and then you have a whole history then of each one.

She claimed to achieve this by encyclopaedic lists of activities and types and by writing about a typical handful of characters, from the Hersland and Dehning families, together with a few of their servants. They come from Europe to America, to Bridgepoint in the East and Gossols on the West Coast. But this is no orderly family saga; indeed it is only history if we take Croce's dictum that all history is contemporary to mean that history is the past as we see it in the present, and that since our thoughts, feelings and acts are themselves historical facts, our actions are historical actions and can thus constitute a model for writing and perceiving history.

Stein also argued that it was egalitarian American history that she was writing. Everyone had everything inside them, everyone had the same 'bottom nature.' In her theory American character contained everything, and that everything is released slowly, there is so much of it. Each character releases its contents at different times, at different intervals of time, in different amounts. So there is difference and sameness, diversity and unity: America.

One of the things Stein does in this keynote opening extract from *The Making of Americans* is to give the reader information about the scope and nature of her interests as a human being and as a writer, and she quickly makes it apparent that the two are synonymous. 'I write for myself,' she says, 'I write', suggesting she always does it, and 'I am writing', reminding us that this is what she is doing at this minute. This is what gives her fulfilment as a human being, for her writing is an expression of her love of her material. 'I love it and I tell it. I love it and now I will write it.' And what she loves and what she writes is what she calls 'repeating', which is writing, which is living, which is history. She loves especially to write that 'Everybody is a real one to me, everybody is like some one else too to me.' And 'They look like other ones . . . they are separate and yet always repeated'. This is a statement of her sense of the difference and likeness of people, an American affirmation of brotherhood coupled with an American affirmation of individuality.

But even here Stein sees herself as revolutionary, for in spite of Americans' professions of brotherhood and egalitarianism, she knows that they do not really like to think of themselves as anything but unique. 'Mostly every one dislikes to hear' what she's going to say: that the world consists of types, and that these types are evident to everyone. 'Every one reminds some one of some other one who is or was or will be living.' She is conscious of being set apart as the truth-teller, and this is how she sees herself, as a writer who is utilizing unconventional techniques and fictional characters to tell American truths.

Gertrude Stein does not regard her view of history and being as repeating as in any way diminishing human nature. On the contrary, she sees human nature as having 'mixtures', 'flavor', 'meaning', 'being', 'strength' and 'weakness'. This is an admirable wholeness. To deny any quality to any human being would be the diminishing thing. She intends to show the whole range of human activities – walking, dancing, working, talking, sleeping, for example – and she enumerates some of them in the paragraph beginning 'there is then now and here the loving repetition'. She intends to describe the whole range of human types, a type being a person in whom one characteristic is temporarily dominant. Everyone else, in fact, has that characteristic too, but not, concurrently, in dominant proportions.

The activities and types create a variety of patterns, and her work is a celebration of the patterning in theme and in style. She is not only writing about likeness, brotherhood, repeating, human continuity; she is writing with likeness, with love, with democracy – all words are equal – with repetition, with continuity. Her use of the word everyone, with the word split into two – every one – and not, as is usual, run together, fuses theme and style particularly well. The repeated splitting of this word gives a sense of individuality and universality, of the part and of the whole. Effective too is her syntactical confusion of singular and plural: 'Every one is a kind of men and women.' Nothing could be more idealistically American. Here we have not the individual versus society but the individual *and* society – self-reliance and democracy in harmonious existence. It has been suggested that Stein is un-American in that she sees the personality in terms of a fixed nature and not a *tabula rasa*. She does believe that certain elements in a character are always present and always operative; but given that any one element or any combination of elements can dominate a character at any time, the possibilities still seem endless.

All her technical devices serve two purposes: first, to focus on words and on structures (parts of speech, sentences, paragraphs) as having value and significance independent of overall content; second, to make everything expressive of content. Her dual use of the preposition offers a good example. In the paragraph beginning 'Always from the beginning' she uses, repetitively, a good number of prepositions to suggest incessant motion – from, as, of, to, in through, out from, or, over, with, into. These prepositions give increased impetus to the participles which also bear the content of the piece – loving, living, being and repeating. The prepositions are repeated so often and in such a variety of contexts that they become not only governing parts of speech but self-governing entities. We focus not only on motion but on the distinctive and almost metaphysical connotations of words in isolation: in – from – to. As she plays with words as if they were counters she can move around at will, we feel that Gertrude Stein can indeed stretch, extend, alter and redefine words and groups of words – or, if she chooses, use them conventionally. She can liberate a word and, in making us conscious of a new dimension of meaning, can make us feel the masters, even the makers, of reality. Take the word 'repeating', for instance, in the paragraph beginning 'Always from the beginning there was to me all living as repeating.' Repeating is initially defined – admittedly as 'all living'; nevertheless, 'repeating' is in some sense limited in its meaning and by its use in this first sentence. The conventional reading would be that life is repetitious, even boring. But by using 'repeating' in a variety of contexts, by associating it with listening, living, being and understanding, with the whole, with the complete, she convinces us that 'repeating' is, in the widest and most unlimited sense, all of living. It is what goes on inside each one of us; it is our quality, our difference, our character expressing itself, an essence which is there for the perceptive person to hear and to observe. Detect the pattern (the character and the characteristics expressing themselves) and you find the being. Stein describes how it is done; concentrate all senses and faculties in the act of responding to and studying people. Extend the act of 'listening' to each part of the body and mind.

> Soon then it [the repeating] commences to sound through my ears and eyes and feelings[,] the repeating that is always coming from each

> one, that is them, that makes then[,] slowly[,] of each one of them a whole one.

The soothing, hypnotic effect of her style, the feeling of infinity given by the accumulation of participles in the paragraph, reinforce the ever-widening meaning of 'repeating'. The Stein theory, then, can work in practice. She has conveyed 'a space of time that is filled, always filled with moving': a world of language in which the parts are active, a world of being in which nothing is passive. Certainly the skill with which Stein makes language serve her philosophical as well as her artistic purpose is itself suggestive of endless possibilities. For example, the word 'repeating' both describes and is history, which is a retelling and repeating of what has gone before; yet repeating is also what is happening now and what is going on in each individual. We may disagree with her philosophy; we cannot deny that her medium is, effectively, her message.

Everything in Stein's style is carefully calculated so that medium and message shall meld. She works with a limited vocabulary not because what she has to say is limited or narrow, but because this is an exemplary way of showing the versatility of words. She is, in effect, teaching us a new language, and so it is appropriate that to read Stein is to feel that we are reciting with her the parts of speech, declining verbs, mouthing lists of participles and conjunctions. Stein also sounds and looks biblical. The prose has an Old Testament flow and could be set out in verse. It gives the revolutionary a strange authority. But it is a new language, not the one we learned at school. She violates almost every rule of grammar and composition, using singular nouns with plural verbs and vice versa, inappropriate tenses and cases, unnecessary inversion, redundant phrases. Indeed, a conventional teacher of composition could well use *The Making of Americans* as a 'how not to do it' text.

In *The Making of Americans* Stein of course *wants* to shock. She intends us to be disoriented by the singular lack of imagery, metaphor and all the other usual figures of speech. Deprived of his usual guidelines, the reader has to work to follow her. This too is deliberate. First she makes a familiar language unfamiliar; then she makes the unfamiliar language exciting; then the reader realizes he is experiencing a new art form.

It has to be said, however, that the challenging prose she wrote was best suited to an essay or a short story; and that after, say, 5000 words

The Making of Americans becomes almost unreadable. It proves exhausting and monotonous. But could it be otherwise? The ultimately interminable tone was an inevitable result of Stein's intention. She was determined to tell all, to work with an extremely limited vocabulary and to use a demanding style.

At the end of a lecture she gave on *The Making of Americans* during a visit to America in 1934, Stein came to her theory of the unique American concept of time as space, and of the time–space medium as something physical, as something that can be moved about in and moved away from and experimented with.

> I felt this thing, I am an American and I felt this thing, and I made a continuous effort to create this thing in every paragraph that I made in *The Making of Americans*. And that is why after all this book is an American book an essentially American book, because this thing is an essentially American thing this sense of a space of time and what is to be done within this space of time.[10]

This essentially American thing was the American continent, densely settled in spots but still vast, often empty; it was the ever adventurous American spirit, which produced the confident Gertrude Stein, attempting to solve the enigma of being; it was a people with an endless, restless, mobile sense of possibility, of plasticity, of moving forward on all frontiers. Gertrude Stein's distinction was at once to convey this quintessential Americanness to the twentieth century – Melville had done so in the nineteenth in *Moby-Dick* – and to do so through an innovative use of language and a redefinition of the techniques of the writer and the role of the reader.

Notes

1 Gertrude Stein, *The Making of Americans*, in Carl Van Vechten (ed.), *Selected Writings of Gertrude Stein*, New York, 1962 (written 1906–8, originally published 1925). All quotations from *The Making of Americans* are taken from this edition and, unless noted otherwise in textual parentheses, from pages 261–7.

2 Gertrude Stein, *How to Write*, ed. Patricia Meyerowitz, New York, 1975, xxi.

3 Gertrude Stein, 'The Gradual Making of *The Making of Americans*', in Van Vechten, op. cit., 258.

4 ibid., 245–6.

5 Gertrude Stein, 'What is English Literature', in Patricia Meyerowitz (ed.), *Gertrude Stein: Look at Me Now and Here I Am, Writings and Lectures, 1911–45*, Harmondsworth, 1971, 57.
6 ibid., 7.
7 Stein, *How to Write*, op. cit., ix.
8 Gertrude Stein, 'Poetry and Grammar', in Meyerowitz, op. cit., 125.
9 ibid., 131.
10 Stein, 'The Gradual Making of *The Making of Americans*', in Van Vechten, op. cit., 258.

Further reading

Bridgman, Richard, *Gertrude Stein in Pieces*, New York, 1970.
Hoffman, Michael J., *The Development of Abstractionism in the Writings of Gertrude Stein*, Philadelphia, 1965.
James, William, *The Principles of Psychology*, New York, 1890.
Meyerowitz, Patricia (ed.), *Gertrude Stein: Look at Me Now and Here I Am, Writings and Lectures, 1911–45*, Harmondsworth, 1971.
Stein, Gertrude, *The Autobiography of Alice B. Toklas*, New York, 1933.
Stein Gertrude, *How to Write*, New York, 1975. A useful introduction by Patricia Meyerowitz.
Weinstein, Norman, *Gertrude Stein and the Literature of the Modern Consciousness*, New York, 1970.

5

Wallace Stevens (1879–1955)

Sunday Morning

I

Complacencies of the peignoir, and late
Coffee and oranges in a sunny chair,
And the green freedom of a cockatoo
Upon a rug mingle to dissipate
The holy hush of ancient sacrifice.
She dreams a little, and she feels the dark
Encroachment of that old catastrophe,
As a calm darkens among water-lights.
The pungent oranges and bright, green wings
Seem things in some procession of the dead,
Winding across wide water, without sound.
The day is like wide water, without sound,
Stilled for the passing of her dreaming feet
Over the seas, to silent Palestine,
Dominion of the blood and sepulchre.

II

Why should she give her bounty to the dead?
What is divinity if it can come
Only in silent shadows and in dreams?
Shall she not find in comforts of the sun,
In pungent fruit and bright, green wings, or else
In any balm or beauty of the earth,
Things to be cherished like the thought of heaven?
Divinity must live within herself:
Passions of rain, or moods in falling snow;

Grievings in loneliness, or unsubdued
Elations when the forest blooms; gusty
Emotions on wet roads on autumn nights;
All pleasures and all pains, remembering
The bough of summer and the winter branch.
These are the measures destined for her soul.

III

Jove in the clouds had his inhuman birth.
No mother suckled him, no sweet land gave
Large-mannered motions to his mythy mind.
He moved among us, as a muttering king,
Magnificent, would move among his hinds,
Until our blood, commingling, virginal,
With heaven, brought such requital to desire
The very hinds discerned it, in a star.
Shall our blood fail? Or shall it come to be
The blood of paradise? And shall the earth
Seem all of paradise that we shall know?
The sky will be much friendlier then than now,
A part of labour and a part of pain,
And next in glory to enduring love,
Not this dividing and indifferent blue.

IV

She says, 'I am content when wakened birds,
Before they fly, test the reality
Of misty fields, by their sweet questionings;
But when the birds are gone, and their warm fields
Return no more, where, then, is paradise?'
There is not any haunt of prophecy,
Nor any old chimera of the grave,
Neither the golden underground nor isle
Melodious, where spirits gat them home,
Nor visionary south, nor cloudy palm
Remote on heaven's hill, that has endured
As April's green endures; or will endure
Like her remembrance of awakened birds,
Or her desire for June and evening, tipped
By the consummation of the swallow's wings.

V

She says, 'But in contentment I still feel
The need of some imperishable bliss.'
Death is the mother of beauty; hence from her,
Alone, shall come fulfilment to our dreams
And our desires. Although she strews the leaves
Of sure obliteration on our paths,
The path sick sorrow took, the many paths
Where triumph rang its brassy phrase, or love
Whispered a little out of tenderness,
She makes the willow shiver in the sun
For maidens who were wont to sit and gaze
Upon the grass, relinquished to their feet.
She causes boys to pile new plums and pears
On disregarded plate. The maidens taste
And stay impassioned in the littering leaves.

VI

Is there no change of death in paradise?
Does ripe fruit never fall? Or do the boughs
Hang always heavy in that perfect sky,
Unchanging, yet so like our perishing earth,
With rivers like our own that seek for seas
They never find, the same receding shores
That never touch with inarticulate pang?
Why set the pear upon those river-banks
Or spice the shores with odours of the plum?
Alas, that they should wear our colours there,
The silken weavings of our afternoons,
And pick the strings of our insipid lutes!
Death is the mother of beauty, mystical,
Within whose burning bosom we devise
Our earthly mothers waiting, sleeplessly.

VII

Supple and turbulent, a ring of men
Shall chant in orgy on a summer morn
Their boisterous devotion to the sun,
Not as a god, but as a god might be,
Naked among them, like a savage source.

Their chant shall be a chant of paradise,
Out of their blood, returning to the sky;
And in their chant shall enter, voice by voice,
The windy lake wherein their lord delights,
The trees, like serafin, and echoing hills,
That choir among themselves long afterward.
They shall know well the heavenly fellowship
Of men that perish and of summer morn.
And whence they came and whither they shall go
The dew upon their feet shall manifest.

VIII

She hears, upon that water without sound,
A voice that cries, 'The tomb in Palestine
Is not the porch of spirits lingering.
It is the grave of Jesus, where he lay.'
We live in an old chaos of the sun,
Or old dependency of day and night,
Or island solitude, unsponsored, free,
Of that wide water, inescapable.
Deer walk upon our mountains, and the quail
Whistle about us their spontaneous cries;
Sweet berries ripen in the wilderness;
And, in the isolation of the sky,
At evening, casual flocks of pigeons make
Ambiguous undulations as they sink,
Downward to darkness, on extended wings.

Poetry, A Magazine of Verse (1916): stanzas I, VIII, IV, V, VII only
Complete poem published in *Harmonium* (1923)[1]

* * *

Wallace Stevens is unmistakably an American poet. His work is characterized by the economic evocation of American place, be it a stump in Oklahoma ('Life in Motion'), a hill in Tennessee ('Anecdote of the Jar'), 'Loneliness in Jersey City' or 'An Ordinary Evening in New Haven'. The protagonists of many of his poems have more than a little of the self-reliant American about them. But his writing is even more of the time than the place. Stevens made a unique response to contemporary assertions that God was dead, chaos loomed and man must desperately live for the moment. He did not chart decline, like Adams; he did not seek to defend tradition, like James; he did not define history in fresh ways, like Stein; he did not seek to refurbish old dreams, as Anderson and Fitzgerald were to do. He confronted the destruction of the old in a strikingly positive spirit. Such destruction was right, proper and long delayed. Now was the time for people to make of the world what they would, independent of received ideas. What Stevens proposed was a truly anarchic individualism, based on an arrogant sense of the self.

Poetry was Stevens's way of demonstrating the potential of the individual to see things as he chose, and in six collections of poems, from *Harmonium* (1923) to *The Auroras of Autumn* (1950), he performed, as Helen Vendler notes, an apparently inexhaustible series of experiments 'in diction, in rhetoric, in syntax, in genre, in imagery, in voice and in meter'.[2] But in spite of the clarity of his response to what others saw as twentieth-century dilemmas and what he saw as twentieth-century opportunities, Wallace Stevens has often seemed a paradoxical figure in American culture. How could a sensuous and intellectual poet and philosopher happily spend most of his life as an executive of the Hartford Life and Accident Insurance Company in Connecticut? Why would Stevens only write poetry in his spare time when no one placed a higher value on poetry and on art in general than he? After all, it was Stevens who argued that art and poetry had never had more to offer than in the post-Romantic period, unsure as it was of how to approach the universe when people no longer believe that God is pantheistically present. It was Stevens who maintained that

> The relation of art to life is of the first importance especially in a skeptical age since, in the absence of a belief in God, the mind turns to its own creations and examines them, not alone from the aesthetic point of view, but for what they reveal, for what they validate and invalidate, for the support that they give.[3]

The paradoxes are explained by Stevens's definition of poetry: the exercise of the imagination working on reality. Poetry can be an interior, daily act; it does not always have to be committed to paper. Stevens was extraordinarily uninterested in seeing his poetry published, but his poetic theory and practice were distinguished and in some senses unique. According to Stevens the mind's own creations – ideas, acts of imagination, poems perhaps – had achieved a utility transcending art. They had become philosophy. 'After one has abandoned a belief in God, poetry is that essence which takes its place as life's redemption,' he claimed.[4] But in spite of his use of religious terminology, poetry, as Stevens saw it, is not an act of faith by which man is automatically redeemed from passing his life in despair and incomprehension; nor is it simply an act of imagination. It requires an effort of will. For if poetry is to take the place of God, all conventional ideas of God have to be consciously abandoned. We must no longer

> Suppose an inventing mind as source
> Of this idea, nor for that mind compose
> A voluminous master folded in his eye.

Instead, it is necessary to

> Become an ignorant man again
> And see the sun again with an ignorant eye
> And see it clearly in the idea of it.[5]

In this last line, which, in its deceptive simplicity of language and its syntactical awkwardness, owes something to Gertrude Stein, Stevens sets forth one of the crucial elements of his philosophy. When we look at something afresh, we must first give it intellectual meaning, for it has none implanted in it by a non-existent creator. Stevens does not believe that everything has an inherent meaning; nor does he believe that one human being can decide meaning for another. (Poetry, therefore, is something one person writes rather than something another person reads.) Everyone must look at the universe for himself, and must make up his own mind. Everyone must be an intellectual.

Stevens is asking a great deal of people, but he has a very high estimate of their capacity for thought and of their equally important capacity for imagination. If objects in the natural universe have no inherent meaning for us to detect, we must invent meaning. Through an act of fiction-making, which is an intentional act of will and an abandoned act of the imagination, we can put whatever construction we choose on, say, the sun. We can all be fiction-makers. We *must* all be fiction-makers or the universe will have no meaning for us. The imagination working on reality is poetry, Stevens tells us. So we can all be poets; that is to say, we all have the poetic perception; we do not all have the capacity for poetic expression.

Stevens is rightly celebrated for one of the period's most memorable and significant cultural dogmas: 'Poetry is the Supreme Fiction.'[6] He makes it clear that by the word fiction he intends more than poetry or even the act of imagination. As only fiction can give reality meaning, and as this meaningful reality has a subjective validity, fiction is, for the individual in question, truth. Fiction equals poetry equals subjective truth. And as in a godless universe there is no other truth than the subjective, fiction equals poetry equals truth. Fiction, poetry and imagination are, by Stevens's definition, primary instruments of arriving at knowledge and understanding. We can use the imagination to impose order on what has seemed to be godless chaos; that order is first created, then perceived. 'See it clearly in the idea of it.'[7]

Stevens suggests that poetry, fiction and the imagination are not luxuries, but necessities. They fill a vacuum created by a world of common sense and natural science, a world which lacks what human beings need to live fully: sensation and the feeling expression of that sensation. For the human being, a feeling creature who needs to give that feeling expression, nothing except poetry deals with and provides that sensation without which human life is incomplete and ultimately meaningless. Stevens's art counters meaninglessness; his theory offers an original method for discovering meaning in the modern universe. Many of Stevens's early poems, collected in *Harmonium* (1923), demonstrate his theory, from the difficult 'Comedian as Letter C' to the more accessible 'Thirteen Ways of Looking at a Blackbird'. They also show what Robert Buttel calls 'the hugely fantastic situation and point of view, and the essential gaudiness of word and metaphor with which Stevens probed to the limits of the imagination's power'.[8] But it is 'Sunday Morning', the poem with which Stevens first attracted significant attention when it appeared in Chicago's *Poetry, A Magazine of Verse* in 1916, which is Stevens's earliest, clearest and perhaps finest demonstration of the theory and practice of the Supreme Fiction. The poem shows a woman in the act of filling the void left by the loss of faith. She uses her mind to reject other people's myths (fictions); she brings her imagination to bear on reality and is ready, at the end of the poem, to create her own fiction.

There are two voices in the poem, sometimes distinct and sometimes fused: Stevens's and the lady's. He can enter into her state of mind, for it has been his. Clearly he is already a heretic, a non-believer, who urges the lady to relinquish her nostalgic longing for 'The holy hush of ancient sacrifice'. He attempts to convince her that she is wrong when she says that in spite of the contentment of a Sunday morning passed in deliberate defiance of traditional religious observance, 'I still feel / The need of some imperishable bliss.' He does not hold out to her the hope of eternity or any kind of afterlife. We have to accept that the world is finite, he says. Death is an expression of the impermanent and changing human condition. Boldly, he does his best to make the fact of death attractive to her. If death is 'sure obliteration', it is also the end of the cycle of life, and that cycle constitutes part of the marvel of the universe. Would we be without the cycle of the day, the moods of morning and of evening too? Does not the lady herself like April's green and also have a desire for June? He is sure she has 'a remembrance of awakened birds' and one of 'the consummation of the swallow's wings'. She loves the high summer of 'new plums and pears' and 'the littering leaves of autumn'. Each age, like each season, has its consolation, be it that of maiden or matron, boy or man. One cannot have all this and not have death, which is integral to the cycle. But the post-Romantic world cannot enthuse about death as destiny when it has no afterlife to look forward to. When Stevens states 'Death is the mother of beauty', he does so with somewhat less success and conviction than, for example, the pantheistic Whitman in 'Out of the Cradle Endlessly Rocking'. However, Stevens at least achieves a reconciliation with the fact of death which is both intellectual and sensory, based as it is on the desirability of having the widest possible range of sensation and experience available to us.

Sensation, not sacrifice, is holy for Wallace Stevens, a sensation which rejects permanence, which rejects anything but itself. He does seem to need a focus for this 'religion' or sensation, however, and he finds that focus in the symbol of the sun. To choose deliberately an alternative 'god' is an effective way of demonstrating his heresy, and the sun, a well-established pagan symbol of the sensuous, is an effective choice. In classical and contemporary times alike, the abandoned, self-glorying exposure of the body to the sun, in dance, in ritual or on a beach is a fact and a symbol. Section VII of 'Sunday Morning' describes an act of devotion to the sun with a bold use of Christian imagery, with what one might even call consistently perverted Christian imagery, for earlier in the poem Stevens adopts Christ as his symbol of mortality and Palestine as the land of false dreams. The chant of Stevens's sun worshippers is 'a chant of paradise'. Instead of God being pantheistically present in nature, the pagans become that pantheistic presence:

> . . . their chant shall enter, voice by voice,
> The windy lake wherein their lord delights,
> The trees, like serafin, . . .

The pagans are at once the heavenly choir, the worshipping congregation and the gods. They are a 'heavenly fellowship'; they have 'dew upon their feet', not unreal stigmata.

In his rejection of traditional Christianity and his concern with the liberated imagination, the consciousness and its possibilities, Stevens seems a typical modern writer. But his emphasis on an imagination reinforced by concentrated intellect and his aggressive, ambitious claims for the power of the imagination set him apart. He is determined to seek meaning and value, and this is the significance of his distinctive voice. He has a positive, contemporary answer to chaos. He believes in the creation of fictions by which we may live; he believes above all in the fiction of poetry, the subjective construct formed by mind, imagination and the matter which they 'interpret' or transform. It is not a question of transcending reality or of escaping into fantasy. In section VIII he emphasizes the fact that *we* are doing the living, that deer walk upon *our* mountains. There is nothing in the sky – no God, no gods. It is a sky of independence and isolation with which we, as fiction-makers, can do as we please. The universe consists of the physical world, possibly 'an old chaos of the sun', animal and vegetable life, and ourselves. There is no doubt who is the master here! Section VIII reasserts our power to make order out of chaos; so does the whole of 'Sunday Morning', and so do Stevens's writings on poetry. If we are creators, and if we can create what we choose, surely we can create order. Fiction can become the new reality. Clearly, we cannot wish away such a reality, such a disorder, as an on-going war; but we can use our imagination to look beyond that war, to create or to focus on something that does give us hope and pleasure. Imagination can save us from despair. It enables us to engage in what the hedonistic Stevens called 'the highest pursuit': 'the pursuit of happiness on earth'.

Of all major American writers of the period, only Stevens is so useful, so pragmatic, preaching individual means to individual ends; only Stevens among major American writers of this period offers a profound yet individually accessible, individually viable philosophy. His American egalitarian assumption of everyman's capacity for fiction-making is matched by his application of built-in obsolescence to ideas. 'It Must Change,' he writes of poetry, which is fiction, which is philosophy.[9] Reality changes, knowledge changes, the imagination has different material to work with; the individual changes too. But Stevens also believes that poetry has a number of immutable characteristics. 'It Must Give Pleasure,' he asserts.[10] The fact of fictionalizing is pointless if it does not improve on the dissatisfactions which create the need to fictionalize. He stresses that 'It Must Be Abstract':[11] man must use his mind and his imagination to make his own philosophical construct – he must not simply fix on one aspect of reality which is acceptable to him. Stevens wants man to stretch his faculties. For Emerson's 'self-reliant' man he substitutes the word 'Giant'.[12] And a giant Stevens's man must be in terms of the self-discipline needed to fictionalize, to change the fictions as the reality changes, to formulate an individual philosophy without help. He is automatically a giant, too, for in a universe with no God he is head and shoulders above any other species.

As 'Sunday Morning' opens, the title in conjunction with the first words set the scene for Stevens's demolition of Christianity. Although it is Sunday morning, in his universe it is a time of 'complacencies', not a general state of complacency – as we see, the lady is not altogether secure – but of leisure, luxury and numerous creature comforts; and one of these comforts suggests the class of the lounging lady. It is the 'peignoir' she wears. It may just be an American dressing gown called by a fancy name; it may be a French import. But education, status and pretension are indicated. She is leisurely, she is sensual; she relishes the pungency of 'late coffee and oranges'; she enjoys looking at 'the green freedom of a cockatoo'. Perhaps she has let her bird out of its cage for a treat, or perhaps she has an exotic rug – African, ethnic – in her room. She is in a state of limbo – dreaming, barely awake – but she is oppressed by the fact that for Christians, though not for her, Sunday morning has 'meaning'. She feels guilty that she is not observing the Sabbath. For her it is just a sunny day, full of bright round orange shapes – we wonder if she is something of a sun worshipper – on which she self-consciously tries to dissipate, with hedonism, the conventional images of the Christian Sunday. But she feels 'the dark encroachment': the presence, the memory of 'that old catastrophe', the Crucifixion. On the one hand, it is a catastrophe because she believes that the western world has wrongly based much of its civilization on the assumption that the son of God died here, and thereby made salvation possible; on the other hand, if God exists and his son did die in that way, she is proving unworthy of the sacrifice. Images of blood and the sepulchre enter her mind. She dreams of Palestine. Everything is coloured with uncertainty for her.

In the second verse she looks without conviction at her alternatives, the pleasures of her sense, 'the comforts of the sun', the 'pungent fruit', the 'bright green wings'. Her sight, her touch, her skin come alive. But is this enough for her? Is she really satisfied by, can she consistently and effectively cherish, 'the balm and beauty of the earth' as if it were heaven? She tries to be certain, but she finds it difficult to concentrate – her imagination and her mind keep wandering to Christianity. She has insufficient imaginative abandon (she does not achieve this fully until sections VII and VIII). Stevens admonishes her. She must not give her bounty – her mind, her life – to the dead (which is how he sees Christ). 'Divinity must live within herself'. She is the God, the giant, the creator of the universe within which she chooses to live. Yet Stevens ends the verse sombrely, fatalistically: 'These are the measures destined for her soul.' She will have to be satisfied with the pleasure this world can offer:

> . . . unsubdued
> Elations when the forest blooms; gusty
> Emotions on wet roads on autumn nights;
> All pleasures and all pains . . .

Here we see a modification of Stevens's optimism; although all sensation can be hers, its measures, beats and treads are ominous in comparison with the comforting soundlessness of the wide and healing waters which can take her, literally and figuratively, to the Holy Land, to Christianity. But if the feeling of religion is comfort, the actuality, according to Stevens, is blood and sepulchre. If Christ existed he was mere man, with a finite life. Stevens does not underestimate the powerful illusion of Christianity which, at this stage in the poem, seems more satisfying than the realities of a self-centred universe, a universe of uncertain advantages, a universe which does not exclude pain and brings strange pleasures, dangers even: 'Emotions on wet roads on autumn nights'. The surface is slippery. Is it preferable to the road to Calvary?

The rest of the poem consists of attempts by the poet, the observer, to trace the ways in which he and the lady can come to accept the idea of earth as heaven and paradise. They do so by the application of imagination. In section III the old classical gods are conjured up. Although they run attractively counter to Christian myth – Jove had an 'inhuman' birth, unlike Christ, and 'No mother suckled him' – Stevens describes the gods, with mocking alliteration, as moody, mythy, muttering, pretentious and tyrannical. Even their followers, the 'hinds', who do not realize they have created the gods but believe they exist, are not satisfied. They replace Jove with 'a star', the Star of Bethlehem, God in man, 'our blood, commingling, virginal, / With heaven'. But this logically progressive myth does not satisfy Stevens. It makes no sense of reality as he perceives it. The Christian cosmology does not seem to him to be satisfying even as myth. He cannot think of the sky, literally or figuratively, as something which separates man from a heaven which he may not reach and which is itself beyond the bounds of imagination. His imagination will only allow him to think of the sky as a part of the physical universe, and that universe is the only paradise he can imagine. He suggests to the lady that if she too can see the sky as part of the world we know, that is to say as part of the world we can imagine (for imagination is truth), then she will see that a godless sky is a friendly sky.

But the concepts of the afterlife and of paradise as imperishable bliss still attract the lady. She does not want to believe that life is finite; she is not sure there is consolation enough in Stevens's assurance that 'Death is the mother of beauty', in his reminder that new and beautiful life springs out of the dust to which we return, his affirmation of the process of nature as something acceptable, as a reason for contentment, as a cause for positive joy. But he insists. If death strews the leaves of sure obliteration, she also watches over and allows the joys of adolescence, generation after generation.

> She makes the willow shiver in the sun
> For maidens who were wont to sit and gaze
> Upon the grass, relinquished to their feet.
> She causes boys to pile new plums and pears
> On disregarded plate. The maidens taste
> And stay impassioned in the littering leaves.

(Disregarded plate, Stevens explained, was fine family silver, rarely used, but used here by the boys to impress their girls.) Now Stevens begins to convince the lady. He makes the inevitable sound so seductive, so appropriate; he makes the death which delays a decent interval seem positively benevolent.

Imagination, then, can convince the lady that the fact of death is inextricable from the fact of life. Death *is* the affirmation of process, and makes the concept of paradise and the afterlife – processes which lead only to stasis – seem ridiculous. Stevens plunders the imagery of the Christian paradise as described in the Bible and in religious tracts and poems to suggest the impossibility of the Christian theory, and demonstrates that the old Christian paradise was in fact dependent on earthly images to evoke what cannot be known or described – or believed. A note of pity for Christianity creeps into Stevens's voice:

> Why set the pear upon those river-banks
> Or spice the shores with odours of the plum?
> Alas, that they should wear our colours there,

He does not even think that Christianity has used the best earthly images and objects of the natural world to express itself. To him the lute, the stringed instrument so celebrated in the Psalms, is insipid.

Having rejected the gods, what can the imagination offer in their place? Section VII at first seems to present some difficulties of interpretation. Is Stevens suggesting or mocking alternatives to Christianity? The sun worship which entails chants of paradise suggests a seeking for something beyond the earth. Or is the stanza an affirmation of the natural world? Is Stevens the hedonist affirming 'orgy'? The stanza becomes clear if we remember that the essential Stevens is the man for whom the imagination is the all-important instrument for making over and ordering the world. Here he is asserting the right of any individual to make of the world what he will. He does not want us to think of these men as disciples of a new religion. On the contrary. He calls them 'the heavenly fellowship / Of men that perish'. He is depicting men who know that they are finite, that they will die as surely as the morning dew will disappear from their feet. He does not describe the supple ring of men as sun worshippers in the traditional sense, for he does not believe in a shared faith. He describes their devotion to the sun as an act of imagination. They see the sun 'Not as a god, but as a god might be'. The men are exercising their capacity for fiction-making; they are fusing their fiction with the occasional need for a focus of celebration and devotion – fusing the glorious and powerful reality of the sun with the imagination which temporarily creates a god for them. Once again, Stevens is deliberately heretical. He affirms 'orgy' as superior to Christianity. The sensuous lady, too, affirms this, for her voice has merged with Stevens's in this verse.

In the last stanza, the poet, the world and the mind of the lady combine to reject the old gods and affirm the power of human beings to make order out of the old chaos if they so choose. 'Old chaos' is a rich phrase for Stevens: it implies both the nonsense which he considered Christianity to be and the notion that the world was not created by God but took the form of the planet earth breaking off from a sun. To live in this world is to be unsponsored, to be free. No one stands behind us, we are responsible neither to God nor to godparents. To Stevens this freedom is inescapable. It is a fact, whether we like it or not – a fact for Stevens, for the lady, for the Giant, for everyone. And our greatest freedom is the freedom to make fiction. The exercise of the enabling imagination can become as natural as the fact that deer walk, quail whistle, berries ripen. It can mature like ripening berries; it can be as complex as the ambiguous undulation of extended wings. We can do what we will with our imagination – we can be formal, casual, we can make our own patterns and movements and shape our own lives against the background of the empty sky. Significantly, the wings Stevens describes in this last stanza are those of pigeons, birds who carry messages. But they are 'casual' pigeons. They are not carrying a message from us or to anyone. Any messages are of our creation, and we carry them within ourselves. They are messages from ourselves to ourselves. Thus Stevens ends by making simple but not conventional use of the natural reality he observes. What nature is and does, people can be and do – walk, whistle, be spontaneous, be calculating, be ambiguous – and we can be and do these things until death, until we go downward to darkness. Stevens's Giant finds himself in a wilderness where everything is possible, not in a Garden of Eden where so much is denied. Stevens's lady now knows that any divinity must lie within herself. She can now say

> . . . 'The tomb in Palestine
> Is not the porch of spirits lingering
> It is the grave of Jesus, where he lay.'

When 'Sunday Morning' first appeared in *Poetry, A Magazine of Verse*, it was in a shortened form of the poem as we know it. The magazine's editor, Harriet Monroe, with Stevens's consent, preferred to publish a poem made up of the following sequence of sections: I, VIII, IV, V, VII. She was concerned to make the poem more decidedly pagan and not to have it end on what she felt was an uncertain note. Section VIII can be seen as predominantly grave in tone, a re-emphasis of the pains as well as the pleasures of sensation, a statement of the inability of the imagination to dispense with ambiguity, an admission of the unpredictable power of the physical universe – new chaos to follow the old. The fact that Stevens accepted the rearrangement might suggest that he did not find the affirmative tone of section VII incompatible with section VIII, that section VIII too is affirmative.

The style of 'Sunday Morning' is characteristically sensuous. Stevens loves alliteration: holy hush, wide water, silent shadows, mythy minds, burning bosom. His is an adjectival style, formally cadenced, syntactically conventional, full of the rich imagery and rhetoric with which he so aptly conveys the content and the passion of his philosophy. Indeed, 'Sunday Morning' is a poem which is passionate with colour, taste and texture. To read it is at once a physical and an intellectual experience. But for all its descriptive richness, for all that we take images away with us – it may be the cockatoo, the supple and turbulent ring of men, the plums and pears, the bough of summer or the winter branch – it is ultimately an abstract poem in which we are less concerned with how it describes something than with what that something signifies.

The fact that Stevens is a lone voice does not diminish his stature. His assertion that paradise can only exist on earth and must be created here is at once challenging and comforting. He is the poet as philosopher-artist, asserting and demonstrating the desirability, the possibility, the necessity of shaping the objective world to the demands of the imagination. He speaks with one of the more optimistic voices of the period.

Notes

1 Wallace Stevens, 'Sunday Morning', *Selected Poems*, London, 1970 (originally published in book form in *Harmonium*, 1923). Quotations from 'Sunday Morning' are taken from this edition and, unless noted otherwise in textual parentheses, from pages 30–4.
2 Helen Vendler, *On Extended Wings: Wallace Stevens' Longer Poems*, Cambridge, Mass., 1969, 10.
3 Wallace Stevens, *Opus Posthumous*, New York, 1957, 159.
4 ibid., 158.
5 Wallace Stevens, 'Notes Toward a Supreme Fiction', *Selected Poems*, op. cit., 99.
6 Wallace Stevens, 'A High Toned Old Christian Woman', ibid., 27.
7 Stevens, 'Notes', ibid., 109.
8 Robert Buttel, *Wallace Stevens: The Making of 'Harmonium'*, Princeton, 1967, 247.
9 Stevens, 'Notes', op. cit., 109.
10 Stevens, 'Christian Woman', ibid., 27.
11 Stevens, 'Notes', ibid., 99.
12 ibid., 105.

Further reading

Beckett, Lucy, *Wallace Stevens*, New York and London, 1974.
Bloom, Harold, *Wallace Stevens: The Poems of Our Climate*, Ithaca and London, 1976.
Buttel, Robert, *Wallace Stevens: The Making of 'Harmonium'*, Princeton, 1967.
Ehrenpreis, I. (ed.), *Wallace Stevens: A Critical Anthology*, Harmondsworth, 1972.
Vendler, Helen H., *On Extended Wings: Wallace Stevens' Longer Poems*, Cambridge, Mass., 1969.
Stevens, Wallace, *The Necessary Angel*, New York, 1954.
Stevens, Wallace, *Opus Posthumous*, New York, 1957. The third section, Stevens's prose.

6

Ezra Pound (1885-1972)

In a Station of the Metro

The apparition of these faces in the crowd;
Petals on a wet, black bough.

Lustra (1915)

Life and Contacts

Vocat æstus in umbram – Nemesianus Ec. IV.

I

E. P. Ode Pour L'Élection de son Sépulcre

For three years, out of key with his time,
He strove to resuscitate the dead art
Of poetry; to maintain 'the sublime'
In the old sense. Wrong from the start –

No, hardly, but seeing he had been born
In a half savage country, out of date;
Bent resolutely on wringing lilies from the acorn;
Capaneus; trout for factitious bait;

"Ιδμεν γάρ τοι πάνθ', ὅσ' ἐνὶ Τροίῃ
Caught in the unstopped ear;
Giving the rocks small lee-way
The chopped seas held him, therefore, that year.

His true Penelope was Flaubert,
He fished by obstinate isles;
Observed the elegance of Circe's hair
Rather than the mottoes on sun-dials.

Unaffected by 'the march of events',
He passed from men's memory in *l'an trentuniesme*
De son eage; the case presents
No adjunct to the Muses' diadem.

II

The age demanded an image
Of its accelerated grimace,
Something for the modern stage,
Not, at any rate, an Attic grace;

Not, not certainly, the obscure reveries
Of the inward gaze;
Better mendacities
Than the classics in paraphrase!

The 'age demanded' chiefly a mould in plaster,
Made with no loss of time,
A prose kinema, not, not assuredly, alabaster
Or the 'sculpture' of rhyme.

'Hugh Selwyn Mauberley' (1920)[1]

* * *

Ezra Pound is one of those rare figures who would have been a significant figure in contemporary literature had he published no first-rate poetry. He was an excellent critic and a kindly, magisterial friend to numbers of poets. His fine use of language, the creative liberties he took with spelling and typeface can be sampled in letters which must be among the most interesting and idiosyncratic of his time. The experimental Pound refreshed the theory and practice of poetry; he thought and wrote about his age with momentous perception. He spoke with what was quickly recognized as a 'fresh voice'.

Though he was an expatriate who left America for Europe in 1908 and returned under tragic circumstances in 1946, labelled a traitor for broadcasting in favour of Mussolini during the Second World War, and detained as insane at St Elizabeth's Hospital, Washington, D.C. for twelve years, Pound was, in many senses, a profoundly American poet, heir to Whitman's arrogance, to his generosity and to his attempt, characterized by Pound himself in 'To Whistler, American', 'to try to wrench her [America's] impulses to art'.[2] To Whitman's interest in politics he added a passion for history. With commitment and enthusiasm he observed his world, pronounced on it and attempted to reform it. But where Whitman's world was America, Pound's was international. He went beyond Whitman's idiosyncratic fusion of the Bible, American sights and sounds and the occasional foreign word; he mixed the rhythms and accents of Provençal and Italian, Anglo-Saxon, Christian, classical and oriental poetry with his own feeling, his own vision, his own vocabulary. It was what T. S. Eliot called 'the synthetic construction of a style of speech',[3] and the substance of the speech offered a cultural synthesis. 'Make It New' was one of Pound's slogans, but he preached a newness which drew on the best of the past. As he wrote in 1910, 'real time is independent of the apparent and . . . many dead men are our grandchildren's contemporaries, while many of our contemporaries have been already gathered into Abraham's bosom'.[4] The past had shaped and in some senses should continue to shape the present, but the present must give rise to its own forms and ideas.

Pound did dislike unquestioning adherence to the conventional and to the self-indulgent and longwinded romanticism which characterized early twentieth-century poetry. His sense of the need for a refreshed poetry, poetry appropriate to the age, was one of the things which led him to respond enthusiastically to a letter and an invitation he received in 1911, while he was living in London, from Harriet Monroe, a Chicago woman with a strong commitment to aggressively American poetry. She stated that 'some of your recent verse makes me hope that you will be interested in this rather adventurous attempt to give the art of poetry a voice in the land', and asked him to contribute to her magazine for new poetry. He responded that he had faith in an 'American Risorgimento' that 'will make the Italian Renaissance look like a tempest in a teapot', and was quickly made *Poetry*'s 'foreign editor'.[5] Monroe had read his volumes of poems, *Personae* and *Exultations*, on a visit to London in 1909 and had thought it ridiculous that Pound could only find a publisher in England. She had particularly liked a poem of his entitled 'Revolt against the Crepuscular Spirit in Modern Verse'; she too wanted to leave behind the nineteenth-century American tradition of patriotic jingles and dialect poetry. She felt that Pound heralded the death of what his poem called 'thin ephemera' and the birth of what he christened 'titanic spawn'.[6]

In the early years of its life it was Pound who ensured the survival of this significant little magazine, the first in America devoted solely to original poetry, articles on poetry and reviews of collections of poetry.

Despite its admirable editorial policy – 'We promise to refuse nothing because it is too good, whatever the nature of its excellence. We shall read with special interest poems of modern significance, but the most classic subject will not be declined if it reaches a high standard of quality'[7] – the magazine would have been a short-lived phenomenon without Pound. Initially it needed well-known (and therefore non-American) names to draw in readers and subscribers, and it was Pound, in Europe, who collected prestigious contributions from W. B. Yeats, John Masefield, Alfred Noyes and the celebrated Indian poet, Rabindranath Tagore. Additionally – how Monroe's faith in him was rewarded – he introduced to *Poetry* the important new talents of T. S. Eliot, Robert Frost and H. D. (Hilda Doolittle). In return Monroe gave him a regular platform for his own views and poems and space for his protégés (Richard Aldington, Skipwith Cannell, F. S. Flint). For the first eighteen months, until Harriet Monroe was sure of a pool of native talent available to her without going through Pound, *Poetry* was as much his as hers.

But, as Pound's relationship with the magazine showed, he was no mere chauvinist. He did want to discover and to publish first-rate American poetry, but he could not in conscience promote anything but the best poetry, wherever written. He did not have Harriet Monroe's concern that the American public must be slowly educated in a poetry of unfamiliar styles and sometimes radical subject matter; he could not tolerate her occasional censorship in the interests of American taste, or her delaying of the publication of Eliot's 'The Love Song of J. Alfred Prufrock' for five months. He did feel that America as a place and Americans as people offered the potentiality for something new in poetry, and on occasion he even liked to think that the words American and poet were interchangeable.

> 'Mais d'abord il faut être un poète,' as MM. Duhamel and Vildrac have said at the end of their little book, *Notes sur la Technique Poétique*: but in an American one takes that at least for granted, otherwise why does one get born upon that august continent![8]

But for most of the time he was making it clear that he did not believe with Monroe that good art could be made, or could become, acceptable to a majority which wanted 'nonsense', exaggerated emotion, stories and sentiment, which liked Longfellow's 'The Slave's Friend' and 'The Village Blacksmith', Whittier's 'Barbara Freitchie', and such folk poetry offerings as James Whitcomb Riley's 'When the Frost is on the

Punkin'. At times he despaired of an uncerebral country of blandness and prudishness which disliked the mildest satire. 'Could Freud or Jung unfathom such a sink' of repression, inhibition, escapism, narrowness and anti-intellectualism, he wondered.[9] If only Americans could get themselves a classical education! The criticism which a University of Chicago Professor of Classics directed at the 'accuracy' of Pound's creative 'translation' of *Sextus Propertius*, together with a dislike of censorship and a desire to have a freer hand, led Pound to sever his connection with *Poetry* in 1919. But the collaboration had been significant and so was the magazine. *Poetry*'s success encouraged the birth and survival of other and more radical little magazines in America, and Pound was able to place James Joyce's *Ulysses* in one such magazine, the *Little Review*.

Eliot described Pound as 'the animator of artistic activity in any milieu in which he found himself', and paid tribute to Pound's capacity to help writers speak with their own voices. *The Waste Land* was dedicated to Pound, 'il miglior fabbro', and in 1946 Eliot wrote:

> It was in 1922 that I placed before him in Paris the manuscript of a sprawling, chaotic poem called 'The Waste Land' which left his hands, reduced to about half its size, in the form in which it appeared in print. . . . This is irrefutable evidence of Pound's critical genius and unprecedented devotion to the art of Poetry.[10]

Anywhere and anyone poetic interested Pound, and his study of oriental culture led him to help formulate and promote one of the most influential poetic philosophies of his time, imagism, which reflected the spareness, the compression, the linear quality of oriental art. Pound was particularly excited by the short Japanese poem, the hokku (or haiku), which had the qualities of a picture. Such a poem was a graphic symbol, written in characters which visually represented its idea. (Pound believed the Japanese/Chinese written characters were a picture language, 'ideograms'.) It was not possible, in the confines of the unpicturesque western alphabet, to reproduce the hokku; but it was possible to articulate the liberating theory of imagism, which entailed using no superfluous word – no adjective, for instance – which did not reveal something. It meant focusing on an image not as something elaborated but, in Pound's words in *Poetry* for March 1913, as

> an intellectual and emotional complex in an instant of time. . . . It is the presentation of such a 'complex' which gives that sense of sudden liberation; instantaneously that sense of freedom from time and space

> limits; that sense of sudden growth, which we experience in the presence of the greatest works of art.[11]

While imagist poetry is clear and concrete it offers the reader the chance to make his own interpretation. As Pound said of 'In a Station of the Metro': 'In a poem of this sort one is trying to record the precise instant when a thing outward and objective transforms itself, or darts into a thing inward and subjective.'[12] The poem is at once an objective statement – here is the crowd, here is the branch – and a marvellously personal observation – it is only the poet who has seen the metro crowd in this way, or the petals in this way. Imaginatively and realistically Pound puts before us shapes which are both clustered (crowds, flowerheads) and linear (the train, the platform, the bough, the trees). The word 'apparition' gives a sense of the paleness of the faces and the petals, and of the shock of recognition with which Pound makes the connection with the pale petals. The natural objects are adequate in themselves, their relationship is unelaborated, yet they have rich connotations. There is a tenderness here for the faces symbolized in the petals; there is beauty in the mass; there is a provocative suggestion of likeness and unlikeness in noisy urban-industrial society and the quiet pastoral scene. Nothing in this poem is superfluous and everything works with denseness and complexity. The juxtaposition of prepositions and articles, for instance, focuses on the subjects in the picture. We move from 'in' to 'of' to 'in' to 'on', from plural to singular. We are freed from the limits of time and space, though both are utilized: the twentieth-century metro, the rush hour, blossom time. The enclosed unit of the city and the space in which the reader sets the bough (a picture, a country, the countryside, perhaps even a city street or a back garden) are there and are also transcended. The permutations and combinations of this economical poem are manifold. It is what Pound said an imagist poem should be, an intellectual and emotional complex. (It is also, in its cluster imagery, an embodiment of another theory or movement with which Pound became associated, vorticism, which propounded the image, in paint, marble or word, as the 'radiant node or cluster . . . from which, and through which, and into which, ideas are constantly rushing'.[13]) Even such bare words as wet and black are rendered richly evocative and full of meaning. Is the metro crowd seen against dark, shiny trains, a black wall or a black poster? Is the poet trying to communicate a sense of freshness, a sparkle he detected in the crowd? Or is it just a use of texture and colour which highlights the contrast between foreground and background? Such speculation can only leave us marvelling at the way in which Pound, who had originally written a thirty-line poem describing the faces he had seen when he got out of a metro train at La Concorde in 1911, managed, over a period of eighteen months, to produce this fine example of precise, patterned, imagist art, simultaneously compressed and expansive.

If Pound is often and properly remembered for his association with little magazines, with the imagists and the vorticists (the painter Wyndham Lewis, the sculptor Gaudier-Brzeska), his support for such iconoclastic art forms as the music of George Antheil and Eric Satie, and finally for the obsessions with usury and fascism which got between his poetry and his public, he is also and rightly associated with the poem 'Hugh Selwyn Mauberley', which, with T. S. Eliot's *The Waste Land*, is a landmark of modern poetry. Eliot wrote of 'Mauberley', 'It is compact of the experience of a certain man in a certain place at a certain time; and it is also a document of an epoch; it is genuine tragedy and comedy; and it is, in the best sense of Arnold's worn phrase, a "criticism of life".'[14] Both 'Mauberley' and *The Waste Land* reject the dominant romantic fallacy that humanity should be preoccupied with the expression and the development of the self and that the author's feelings should be paramount. Both poems attempt and achieve a revolutionary kind of impersonality in which the poet's presence enhances and does not diminish the fact of the matter: the aridity, unreality and superficiality of twentieth-century urban society (though not of all people – Mauberley and Tiresias are unwilling victims, uncomfortably aware of what F. R. Leavis called 'the miscellaneousness of modern culture, the absence of direction . . . the uncongeniality of the modern world to the artist; and his dubious status there').[15] Tradition – the history of human quests and experiences – and myth – the history of imagination and belief – offer the background ('Mauberley') and the framework (*The Waste Land*) of these 'original' and 'archaeological' poems (Eliot on Pound).[16] Both poems fuse form and theme quite remarkably. Dislocated words indicate dislocation in society; complexity of thought and variety of allusion reflect the accumulated civilization in which the poets live.

Eliot and Pound both make great demands on the reader. They had lost the Georgian poets' vague faith in the instinctive response of a large audience. They treated esoteric issues esoterically. But if they believed that good poetry and serious thought were best aimed at an elite, it was nevertheless the whole of society, the whole of civilization which concerned them and to which they sought to give perspective. There are, of course, differences between the two. Leavis would argue that Pound is not complexly concerned about the soul, that he lacks 'moral, religious and anthropological preoccupations',[17] that he is an aesthete, mainly concerned with art. Certainly Eliot employs the symbolism of certain fertility myths that reputedly formed the pagan origins of the Christian Grail legend to universal effect. *The Waste Land* ends with the Sanscrit word 'Shantih' – the peace which passeth all understanding – repeated three times. His poem has 'religious' associations, an epic quality, a cyclical, seasonal framework and a set of not inaccessible symbols (the river, the waste land itself) which Pound's 'Mauberley' lacks. For all these reasons – and, some would argue, for its art and its profundity – the poem has had greater critical acclaim than Pound's. Pound utilizes mythic allusion in a more restricted way than Eliot, setting one civilization against another. His is a brisker poem, with the air of being less meditative and with the partly pathetic Mauberley as the poem's unifying symbol. But Pound shows a profound concern for the spirit and for the integrity of the individual, as well as for the fate of the artist in the twentieth century. In 'Mauberley' he anticipates Eliot by using his knowledge of history, myth, tradition and his own experience as a poet to set the modern age in sobering perspective. His world is as wasted as Eliot's; indeed the poem is remarkable for the savagery with which it attacks what is and rejects what was.

The savagery is in part a result of Pound's agonized response to the First World War, especially terrible to Pound because it occurred in the cultures and countries which he valued so highly, and which he hoped could interact with America as the two had begun to combine in his poetry. In 'Mauberley' he comes close to rejecting the notion that the old world culture was worth preserving. Why should people die for 'a botched civilization', 'For two gross of broken statues / For a few thousand battered books'? The soldiers had gone into war 'pro domo et pro patria', and had found themselves walking 'eye-deep in hell'. Their rulers had deceived them with 'old men's lies'; they had come home to the same lies and new ones too. Justifiably they were cynical. The references to the wars of classical Greece, to Troy, Ulysses and Agamemnon, act as grim reminders of the kind of world war-heroes of all eras have found when they returned, and of the consistent inhumanity of many men and the tyrannical irresponsibility of most politicians.

Pound comments most explicitly on the disillusion engendered by the war in sections IV and V. The first two sections of the poem show how Pound and his protagonist Mauberley had realized before the war, by the nature of the civilian culture, that the times were out of joint. Critical opinion is divided as to where in the poem as a whole Pound ends and Mauberley begins. John Espey[18] has argued that the whole of Part I of 'Hugh Selwyn Mauberley', from the Ode through Envoi (thirteen sections), deals with Pound and with the contacts of Pound and Mauberley, and that Mauberley himself does not emerge as an individual until Part II of the poem, 'Mauberley' (five sections). But surely Pound's title tells us that he intends us to be reading about Mauberley from the first, and surely he does not intend us to assume, as some critics have, that the poem is entirely autobiographical. He clearly and rightly utilized elements of autobiography, for it was impossible to take himself out of this passionately felt poem about his age and his art. Unlike Pound, however, Mauberley is unable to make up his mind whether to join, to leave or to fight the age in which he lives. Pound has said[19] that he is no more Mauberley than Eliot is J. Alfred Prufrock; it is as befits a worthy protagonist that Mauberley is both sensitive and talented, and Pound is effectively concerned that if such a man went under. . . . Pound is also perhaps writing out, thinking through and burying a terrible vision of himself as he might have been had he been all Mauberley: he might have committed himself to the path of aestheticism, he might have ignored reality. Thus he entitles the first poem an ode ('E. P. Ode', also 'epode') on the choice of the location of his own sepulchre. His choice in the poem is London, though, as William Carlos Williams[20] pointed out, Pound is writing equally of a culture and a generation which polluted rivers and gave handsome endowments to the Metropolitan Museum of Art. Pound speaks for and to those who have had enough of what Lucy Beckett calls 'fashionable raptures or quick financial returns or phoney drawing-room reputations',[21] those who are turning their backs on futility, stagnation and superficiality in national life, be it American or English. Such a society was a place for death, not for life. It defined for Pound what he did not want, and thus the epigraph, which translates as 'the heat calls us into the shade'.

In the person of Mauberley Pound sets up a more accommodating, less idealistic, less iconoclastic person than himself, who, by section X, convinces himself that he can remain in society and yet dissociate himself from it. Unlike Pound, he is not a poet who adventurously seeks to change the world. Unlike Mauberley, it was not Pound's style to be, like the poet in section I, 'Bent resolutely on wringing lilies from the acorn'. This is not a picture of Pound, but of a poet who is half realist, half pre-Raphaelite, seduced by the sirens of the age and the status quo. Section I gives the possible history of a promising poet whose career in some sense mirrors Pound's. For instance, from 1908 to 1911 Pound was in London; his birthplace, America, could, physically and culturally, be seen as 'half-savage'; he admired Flaubert's ability to find and use the *mot juste*. But Pound was not slow to see the genius of Flaubert. His was no emotional, uncritical commitment to traditional poetry, to 'the sublime / In the old sense'. He did fish by 'obstinate isles' (the reference is to the bulldog spirit, English inflexibility), but the always restless, always experimental Pound was not seduced by England or by its literature. On the contrary, rarely has a writer been more conscious of change and of contemporaneousness as a principle of literature. And, as the whole of 'Mauberley' demonstrates, this intensely political individual was not unaffected by the march of events.

The opening section of the poem can of course be seen as Pound's version of the kind of dismissive epitaph society might choose for his gravestone, but it can also be seen as Mauberley writing about one of his contacts, Ezra Pound. Mauberley, in a spirit of self-justification, paints Pound as slow to be true to his Flaubertian muse, as a man who failed to make his mark, as meeting the traditional death of the individual with hubris, struck down by the gods as was Capaneus, who defied Zeus. The uncertain and insufficient Mauberley describes Pound as being seduced by the sirens' song with its message of arrogant self-sufficiency: 'for we know the things that are in Troy'.

The mixture of references to Pound and to Mauberley gives the poem both immediacy and distance. Mauberley takes the edge off propaganda by being less impassioned than Pound; Pound, by giving us the march of events which affected him so much more than Mauberley, suggests Mauberley's limitations and Ezra's rightness. In section II it is perhaps Pound who speaks first and Mauberley who imitates, with less commitment and conviction, what Pound has said. Thus the inverted commas around the 'age demanded' when the phrase appears for the second time. It is in this section that we get the importunate, awkward graceless age of the early twentieth century put before us, an age which loved the wrong substances, shapes and styles. The 'accelerated grimace' – a phrase which aptly suggests increasing speed and increasing horror – is also thought to refer to futurism, which Pound described elsewhere as 'accelerated impressionism'.[22] Pound disliked impressionism, an art form which depended not on the artist but on the appearance of the world. All mimetic art was anathema to him, and thus he dismissed the cinema, which he thought would never get beyond realism, the realistic novel ('prose kinema') and those who judged sculpture by the closeness with which it imitated nature, people who logically wanted not original art but plaster casts from nature. To Pound all the art forms the age valued were mendacities – the lightweight fiction of the period, for instance (Compton Mackenzie and H. G. Wells) – and he attacked writers like Arnold Bennett, who wrote with both eyes on commercial success (see section X, 'Mr. Nixon'). The age was hostile to the subjective, the introspective, to new versions of old truths, to his own unliteral translations, to the subtle echoes in 'Mauberley' of the rhythms of the Latin poet Bion and the French symbolist Théophile Gautier and of the experimental art of François Villon and Henry James. It preferred pointless restatement or photographic realism. It was no more interested in profound change than were its political leaders.

But the section as a whole has a force and a meaning which does not rely on the elucidation of such references. In style it is a provocative mixture of traditional, even formal vocabulary, with variously placed and patterned qualifications: 'not certainly', 'better', 'chiefly', 'not assuredly'. Set against this there is a colloquial movement of the section, with enjambment making for a kind of prose rhythm and the frequent use of the internal comma for a kind of syncopated speech rhythm. The rhymes deal in opposites – grimace and grace, plaster and alabaster, reveries and mendacities. Cultures, images, textures and tones, each evocative of a whole complex of meanings, are set against each other. Pound is at once achieving and asking for interaction and synthesis. Nothing is of itself satisfactory, neither the past nor, in a vacuum, non-mimetic art. As his epic, unfinished series of 'Cantos' was to underline, Pound believed in an art which can draw equally and creatively but never imitatively from the cultures of the past, the phenomena of the present and modern art forms of vitality and integrity. His belief might be traced back to the way in which America derived from and was shaped by old worlds, yet still developed and manifested a new identity. But even in America that synthesis was only occasionally achieved – Thomas Jefferson was Pound's rare political example and Henry James his rarer artistic one. The modern world was even less one of fusion. Pound offered a way of studying that world through the double focus of past and present. The result is a depressingly convincing indictment of modern life, but the acute perception and the art of the indicter give hope.

Notes

1 Ezra Pound, 'At a Station of the Metro' and 'Hugh Selwyn Mauberley', *Collected Shorter Poems of Ezra Pound*, London, 1968 (originally published 1915 and 1920 respectively). All quotations from these poems are taken from this edition and, unless noted otherwise in textual parentheses, from pages 119 and 203–6 respectively.
2 Ezra Pound, 'To Whistler, American', ibid., 25.
3 T. S. Eliot, 'Introduction to Ezra Pound: selected poems, 1928', in J. P. Sullivan (ed.), *Ezra Pound: A Critical Anthology*, Harmondsworth, 1970, 104.
4 Ezra Pound, 'The spirit of romance', in Sullivan, ibid., 37.
5 Harriet Monroe, *A Poet's Life*, New York, 1938, 252, 259–60.
6 Pound, *Collected Shorter Poems*, op. cit., 97.
7 Monroe, op. cit., 252.
8 Ezra Pound, 'A few don'ts by an imagiste', in Sullivan, op. cit., 45.
9 Ezra Pound, 'L'Homme Moyen Sensual', *Collected Shorter Poems*, op. cit., 258.
10 T. S. Eliot, 'Ezra Pound', in Walter Sutton (ed.), *Ezra Pound: A Collection of Critical Essays*, Englewood Cliffs, NJ, 1963, 19.
11 Pound, 'A few don'ts', in Sullivan, op. cit., 41–2.
12 Ezra Pound, 'Vorticism', in Sullivan, ibid., 54.
13 ibid., 57.
14 Eliot, 'Introduction to Ezra Pound', in Sullivan, ibid., 109.
15 F. R. Leavis, 'New bearings in English poetry', in Sullivan, ibid., 124.
16 Eliot, 'Introduction to Ezra Pound', in Sullivan, ibid., 103.
17 Leavis, 'New bearings', in Sullivan, ibid., 125.
18 John J. Espey, *Ezra Pound's 'Mauberley': A Study in Composition*, London, 1955.
19 Quoted in Sullivan, op. cit., 92.
20 William Carlos Williams, 'Excerpt from a critical sketch: a draft of thirty cantos by Ezra Pound', in Sullivan, ibid., 117.
21 Lucy Beckett, *Wallace Stevens*, Cambridge, 1974, 61.
22 Pound, 'Vorticism', in Sullivan, op. cit., 55.

Further reading

Brooker, Peter, *A Student's Guide to Selected Poems of Ezra Pound*, Boston and London, 1979.
Espey, John J., *Ezra Pound's 'Mauberley': A Study in Composition*, London, 1955.
Kenner, Hugh, *The Poetry of Ezra Pound*, Norfolk, Conn., 1951.
Rosenthal, M. L., *A Primer of Ezra Pound*, New York, 1960.

Sullivan, J. P. (ed.) *Ezra Pound: A Critical Anthology*, Harmondsworth, 1970. A marvellous source for Pound, Eliot, Leavis, Williams and others on Pound.
Sutton, Walter (ed.), *Ezra Pound: A Collection of Critical Essays*, Englewood Cliffs, NJ, 1963. Especially Earl Miner, 'Pound, haiku and the image'.

7
Sherwood Anderson (1876-1941)

He was an old man with a white beard and huge nose and hands. Long before the time during which we will know him, he was a doctor and drove a jaded white horse from house to house through the streets of Winesburg. Later he married a girl who had money. She had been left a large fertile farm when her father died. The girl was quiet, tall, and dark, and to many people she seemed very beautiful. Everyone in Winesburg wondered why she married the doctor. Within a year after the marriage she died.

The knuckles of the doctor's hands were extraordinarily large. When the hands were closed they looked like clusters of unpainted wooden balls as large as walnuts fastened together by steel rods. He smoked a cob pipe and after his wife's death sat all day in his empty office close by a window that was covered with cobwebs. He never opened the window. Once on a hot day in August he tried but found it stuck fast and after that he forgot all about it.

Winesburg had forgotten the old man, but in Doctor Reefy there were the seeds of something very fine. Alone in his musty office in the Heffner Block above the Paris Dry Goods Company's store, he worked ceaselessly, building up something that he himself destroyed. Little pyramids of truth he erected and after erecting knocked them down again that he might have the truths to erect other pyramids.

Doctor Reefy was a tall man who had worn one suit of clothes for ten years. It was frayed at the sleeves and little holes had appeared at the knees and elbows. In the office he wore also a linen duster with huge pockets into which he continually stuffed scraps of paper. After some weeks the scraps of paper became little hard round balls, and when the pockets were filled he dumped them out upon the floor. For ten years he had but one friend, another old man named John Spaniard who owned a tree nursery. Sometimes in a playful mood, old Doctor Reefy took from his pockets a handful of the paper balls and threw them at the nursery man. 'That is to confound you, you blithering old sentimentalist,' he cried, shaking with laughter.

The story of Doctor Reefy and his courtship of the tall dark girl who became his wife and left her money to him is a very curious story. It is delicious, like the twisted little apples that grow in the orchards of Winesburg. In the fall one walks in the orchards and the ground is hard with frost underfoot. The apples have been taken from the trees by the pickers. They have been put in barrels and shipped to the cities where they will be eaten in apartments that are filled with books, magazines, furniture, and people. On the trees are only a few gnarled apples that the pickers have rejected. They look like the knuckles of Doctor Reefy's hands. One nibbles at them and they are delicious. Into a little round place at the side of the apple has been gathered all of its sweetness. One runs from tree to tree over the frosted ground picking the gnarled, twisted apples and filling his pockets with them. Only the few know the sweetness of the twisted apples.

The girl and Doctor Reefy began their courtship on a summer afternoon. He was forty-five then and already he had begun the practice of filling his pockets with the scraps of paper that became hard balls and were thrown away. The habit had been formed as he sat in his buggy behind the jaded grey horse and went slowly along country roads. On the papers were written thoughts, ends of thoughts, beginnings of thoughts.

One by one the mind of Doctor Reefy had made the thoughts. Out of many of them he formed a truth that arose gigantic in his mind. The truth clouded the world. It became terrible and then faded away and the little thoughts began again.

The tall dark girl came to see Doctor Reefy because she was in the family way and had become frightened. She was in that condition because of a series of circumstances also curious.

The death of her father and mother and the rich acres of land that had come down to her had set a train of suitors on her heels. For two years she saw suitors almost every evening. Except two they were all alike. They talked to her of passion and there was a strained, eager quality in their voices and in their eyes when they looked at her. The two who were different were much unlike each other. One of them, a slender young man with white hands, the son of a jeweler in Winesburg, talked continually of virginity. When he was with her he was never off the subject. The other, a black-haired boy with large ears, said nothing at all but always managed to get her into the darkness, where he began to kiss her.

For a time the tall dark girl thought she would marry the jeweler's son. For hours she sat in silence listening as he talked to her and then she began to be afraid of something. Beneath his talk of virginity she began to think there was a lust greater than in all the others. At times it seemed to her that as he talked he was holding her body in his hands. She imagined him turning it slowly about in the white hands and staring at it. At night she dreamed that he had bitten into her body and that his jaws were dripping. She had the dream three times, then she became in the family way to the one who said nothing at all but who in the moment of his passion actually did bite her shoulder so that for days the marks of his teeth showed.

After the tall dark girl came to know Doctor Reefy it seemed to her that she never wanted to leave him again. She went into his office one morning and without her saying anything he seemed to know what had happened to her.

In the office of the doctor there was a woman, the wife of the man who kept the bookstore in Winesburg. Like all old-fashioned country practitioners, Doctor Reefy pulled teeth, and the woman who waited held a handkerchief to her teeth and groaned. Her husband was with her and when the tooth was taken out they both screamed and blood ran down on the woman's white dress. The tall dark girl did not pay any attention. When the woman and the man had gone the doctor smiled. 'I will take you driving into the country with me,' he said.

For several weeks the tall dark girl and the doctor were together almost every day. The condition that had brought her to him passed in an illness, but she was like one who has discovered the sweetness of the twisted apples, she could not get her mind fixed again upon the round perfect fruit that is eaten in the city apartments. In the fall after the beginning of her acquaintanceship with him she married Doctor Reefy and in the following spring she died. During the winter he read to her all of the odds and ends of thoughts he had scribbled on the bits of paper. After he had read them he laughed and stuffed them away in his pockets to become round hard balls.

'Paper Pills' from *Winesburg, Ohio* (1919)[1]

* * *

During his lifetime Sherwood Anderson varied the accounts he gave of his family, his birthplace and his upbringing, and the different stories he told demonstrate a rootlessness, a dissatisfaction with self and with society which was echoed in his best work, *Winesburg, Ohio*. A version of Anderson's home town, Clyde, Ohio, Winesburg is also a version of his America.

The year in which *Winesburg, Ohio* appeared – 1919 – was the year of the Treaty of Versailles, which put a formal end to the First World War and organized the postwar distribution of conquered and ceded territory. America, initially reluctant to be involved in what it saw as Europe's war, had only become a combatant in 1917, rallying with enthusiasm and altruism behind President Woodrow Wilson's plan to 'make the world safe for democracy'. But although half a million American lives had been lost in the war, for a variety of reasons – Wilson's ill health, inept American diplomacy and European determination – America found it had little influence over the shape the peace treaty took. She only succeeded, in a separate settlement, in insisting that the bankrupt Europeans pay America her debts; America was now the world's creditor nation. She was not a signatory to the peace, which she rightly saw as punitive. In their greedy reallocation of lands, the Allies were making inevitable future struggles for territory and power. The Treaty of Versailles was utterly at variance with the just and idealistic peace for which Americans had hoped. After this traumatic experience of European war and peace, after this unrewarded loss of life, American involvement in the outside world was swiftly replaced by isolation, extroversion by introversion. The prohibition of alcoholic drink was about to become anachronistic law in a country determined to seek pleasurable escape from wartime restrictions. The Communist party of America was founded that year (the Socialist party was to poll nearly a million votes the following year) and a national steel strike took place. It was a time of turmoil, of radical political and union activity unprecedented in American history. Alcock and Brown flew the Atlantic, but what else in 1919 constituted a quintessentially American achievement? Nothing – and *Winesburg, Ohio* demonstrates the sad search for such achievement and for the values which might lead back to it.

The book was also written as a response and a challenge to what Anderson called

> the most materialistic age in the history of the world, when wars would be fought without patriotism, when men would forget God and only pay attention to moral standards, when the will to power would replace the will to serve and beauty would be well-nigh forgotten

> in the terrible headlong rush of mankind toward the acquiring of possessions. (p. 81)

All you needed was a chicken in every pot and two cars in every garage. Self-indulgence and self-centredness were taking the place of sacrifice and social conscience. It was unfashionable to care about anything. Anderson felt that when people talked about America as 'the great land of opportunity . . . such talk pretty much meant getting on, if possible growing rich, getting to be something in the world. The idea of accumulation of possessions got all mixed up with the idea of happiness.'[2] Anderson's early works had already explored this theme. *Windy McPherson's Son* (1916) described a man who grew up to make a great deal of money but felt little accompanying satisfaction. *Marching Men* (1917), in Francis Hackett's strong but fitting words, described

> the rawest American people, brutal in their callous acceptance of their own ugly and shoddy material condition, flaccid in their personal tastes and futile in their spurts to escape from banality . . . a people barbarous in their solemnity about trivial things and their levity about serious ones . . . anarchistic in their relation to any sustained purpose outside the immediacies of their food and shelter, their women and their progeny.[3]

Anderson himself achieved some financial success – but little else – as a paint manufacturer and a successful advertising man.

Marching Men was a prophetic novel, an early and acute comment on the tyranny inherent in modern industrialism, and *Winesburg* too was to be prophetic. It argued the need for fraternity and the right to individualism, a need and a right soon to be denied by what the book depicted as perhaps an even greater evil than industrialism or materialism: the urge to seek and to show forth an inhibiting, crippling sameness, or 'normalcy', as Warren G. Harding, President from 1921 to 1923 and like Anderson an Ohioan, said in his apt misreading of a speech on 'normality'. *Winesburg* anticipated the intolerance with which Americans reacted to noncomformists during the 1920s. Communists (the Red Scare), blacks (the revived Ku Klux Klan) and immigrants (the Sacco and Vanzetti case) were all victims of the decade. So were many of the unconventional inhabitants of Winesburg.

Anderson was then reacting against what he saw and what he intuitively anticipated. He shared the radical instincts of 'muckraking' journalists and novelists: prior to book publication, extracts from

Winesburg appeared in three 'insurgent' magazines – *The Seven Arts*, *The New Masses*, *The Little Review* (which published his 'Paper Pills'). He had the 'progressive' impulse toward urgent reform. Before chaos came, before the law of the jungle prevailed, he was determined to rediscover and restate the very best in the American spirit, the qualities of innocence, idealism and brotherly love. He was afraid that innocence might have gone forever, even from the simple rural areas of America. His impression was that 'the farmer by the stove is brother to the men of the cities, and if you listen you will find him talking as glibly and as senselessly as the best city man of us all' (p. 71). Idealism and love were as difficult to find in the country as in the city. Only Dr Reefy offers an effective example of American virtue.

Anderson's reforming analysis detected 'a certain tenseness', a febrile quality in American life that was traceable to the fact that

> every one seems to be trying to think nationally and internationally. The old human interest of one man in another seems to have been lost somewhere. People seem more and more to be separating themselves into groups and classes.[4]

The impulse was to avoid or destroy human relationships. He wanted to re-establish them, to get away from issues to people, to American people, to people whose faces seemed full of a 'strange significance'.

> To quote Herman Melville, 'Who has ever fathomed the strangeness and wonder of man?' I get sometimes the illusion that every man and woman I meet is crying out to me. Sometimes a single glance at a human face seems to tell a whole life story, and there have been times, when I walked thus, when I had to go along with bowed head, looking at the sidewalk. I could not bear looking at any more faces.[5]

Anderson wanted to forget about evolution, revolution, about materialism, altruism, pragmatism. To think less, act more. And just as he wanted to get back to people, so he wanted people to reach within themselves to what had been hidden under accumulated layers of social varnish, local, national and lately international preoccupations. He wanted them to be instinctive, even if this instinctiveness could amount to a kind of moral incoherence, even if this instinctiveness might lead to unsocial behaviour, or what America in 1919 would define as odd and unacceptable. People, ordinary people, could rebuild society on the basis of a primitive honesty. Anderson deliberately chose as characters what Maxwell Geismar calls 'average figures of an average American order',[6] who lead inconsequential lives, who are the embodiments of imperfect American standards and actions but who might just return to a purified version of these. No wonder that when the book appeared Hart Crane called *Winesburg* an important chapter in 'the Bible of the American consciousness'.[7]

The rural setting of Winesburg helped remind readers of the pastoral origins of America and of the dreams that went with the Virgin Land – the dream of a chosen, unfallen people who could constitute the human race at its exemplary best, a myth at odds with reality. But it would be wrong to suggest that Anderson affirmed country life *per se*. He emphasized the lesson of that life: be natural, do not force or stunt growth, flourish and give. In Winesburg, where the physical conditions for the agrarian idyll exist, most people are blind to what matters, as Anderson hints in his description of the Winesburg apple orchards. The apples most people eat – the unnaturally large, over-cultivated ones – reflect consumerism and bad taste, the turning away from what is natural; the humble, natural, unpretentious apples – that is, the values that most people overlook and despise – can give them back their innocence. To eat these apples helps resist temptation. It is a kind of reversal of the Garden of Eden; there is an apple people should eat which will guard against evil, which will bring beneficial knowledge, which will allow them to rise. In Anderson's parable God is absent, and so is the biblical fall; he is arguing that people have wilfully abandoned a state of natural goodness, and he is seeking ways of getting back to it.

His treatment of young George Willard, one of the most thoughtful and idealistic characters, demonstrates just how far Anderson was from saying 'back to the farm'. George Willard leaves Winesburg for the city; he wants a more varied life, he longs to work on a better newspaper. But he is not moving from innocence to corruption. First, Winesburg is a microcosm of America: George has already seen cruelty, intolerance, squalor, corruption. Second, he has an inner security, an open-minded strength which stems from his naiveté, from his innocently unjudging though instinctively knowledgeable sense of people, and not from his sense of place or from the spirit of place. Anderson argues that innocence comes from inner openness, and from the loving observation of other people. This is Anderson's way back to goodness.

Although Anderson is often classified as a naturalistic writer who believed that we are governed by our environment and our genetic composition and as a realistic writer who wrote of the reality of an

America sadly strayed from her ideals, in a number of senses he gave the lie to the notion that he was either realist or naturalist. For to some significant degree his people are defined by the attitudes and actions of other people in the community, not by themselves. And far from dealing with the familiar, Anderson uses the rare and strange, the unusual and the unnatural, to suggest the dominant power of mind over matter and environment. He calls *Winesburg* 'The Book of the Grotesque' (p. 21). Initially he uses the word grotesque to describe his belief that some incongruity or other seems to characterize all the men and women he has met. But then, curiously, he suggests that grotesqueness is the product of truth or truths. 'It was his notion that the moment one of the people took one of the truths to himself, called it his truth, and tried to live his life by it, he became a grotesque and the truth he embraced became a falsehood' (p. 25). The connotations of this notion at first seem sombre and naturalistic. Whether the flaw lies in the truth or in the individual embracing that truth, disfigurement seems inevitable. But Anderson is saying that what we need are *common* truths, *shared* values.

The titles of the twenty-five stories in *Winesburg, Ohio* indicate the range of qualities which Anderson sees as dangerously exaggerated: for example, adventure, respectability, sophistication, drink. For Anderson the significant truth is not that of individual philosophy or individual probity but the shared and fundamental truth of love and an accompanying tolerance. Individuality taken to extremes distorts this essential human quality which is as much social as individual. 'In the beginning', says Anderson,

> when the world was young there were a great many thoughts but no such thing as a truth. Man made the truth himself and each truth was a composite of a great many vague thoughts. All about in the world were the truths and they were all beautiful. . . . There was the truth of virginity and the truth of passion, the truth of wealth and of poverty. . . . And then the people came along. Each as he appeared snatched up a dozen of them. (p. 24)

Winesburg is a community full of people who have overdeveloped one 'truthful' aspect of themselves until that aspect has achieved a disproportion which amounts to falsehood. Joe Welling, who likes to talk, has become compulsive and indiscriminate in his speech. Jesse Bentley, a religious man, has come to see himself as the Abraham of his time, ready not only to lead his people out of Canaan but to sacrifice children. Alice Hindman is obsessed by the unfulfilment of spinsterhood. She runs naked in the streets late at night; the rain on her skin is the nearest she comes to a lover's touch.

The grotesque is also present in *Winesburg* in its conventional form as an expression of alienation, of the world seen through a terrifying perspective, and bears out the generalization that the grotesque mode in art and in literature tends to be prevalent in times of radical change and disorientation. The move into the 1920s – from war to peace, internationalism to isolation, sacrifice to hedonism, simplicity to sophistication – was just such a time. The inhabitants of Winesburg are people who out of dissociation, desperation and courage have become eccentric, who are forced into grotesque postures, grotesque acts, grotesque restraints by a society which is unloving and ultraconventional. They suffer from misshapen feelings and psychic deformity. They are thrust into frozen postures of defence. Their inhibitions and their awkwardness are such that Anderson decided not to employ stream of consciousness in the novel, but to use a syntactically ordered but otherwise disordered outpouring of inchoate emotions, thoughts, actions. He wants the kind of release for his characters which the stream of consciousness would suggest, but he cannot pretend they have achieved this liberation. They suffer from both subconscious and conscious inhibition. They shun the truth, avert their eyes, cannot speak or touch at the moment when to do those things would be right, expressive and fulfilling.

If only people loved each other they would be free to look, to speak, to touch; and it is this undemanding, unselfish love which, in 'Paper Pills', Dr Reefy has to offer the girl who has been frightened by the selfishness and the unnaturalness of the young men who have been her suitors. Some of them had 'a strained, eager quality in their voices and in their eyes when they looked at her' – they wanted to marry her for the rich acres of land she had inherited on the death of her father. The one who 'talked continually of virginity' was the most dishonest of them all – she sensed that 'there was [in him] a lust greater than in all the others'. And the suitor who was honest about his intentions, 'a black-haired boy with large ears, [who] said nothing at all but always managed to get her into the darkness, where he began to kiss her' proves a selfish lover – he makes her pregnant and wounds her with bites which are not love bites but lust bites. Anderson's sense that not to love is an act which violates the human condition is expressed with such force that it almost seems exaggerated. The suitor who wants to possess her unlovingly takes on monstrous and diabolical proportions. He becomes a vampire. When the girl meets Dr Reefy, who cares unselfishly, 'it seemed to her that she never wanted to leave him again'. Such is his love that he achieves an uncanny insight into her mind 'without her saying anything'. She has discovered the sweeetness of the twisted apples which the rest of the world rejected. 'Winesburg had forgotten the old man.' The tall dark girl discovers him and learns to 'pay attention' to others. She and the doctor marry.

Later in the book the now widowed Dr Reefy also manages to redeem with love George Willard's unhappy mother. His transforming imagination sees inside the middle-aged, physically decaying woman the girl whom she is reminiscing about. 'He thought that as she talked the woman's body was changing, that she was becoming younger, straighter, stronger' (p. 226).

> 'You dear! You lovely dear! Oh you lovely dear!' he muttered and thought he held in his arms not the tired-out woman of forty-one but a lovely and innocent girl who had been able by some miracle to project herself out of the husk of the body of the tired-out woman. (pp. 227–8)

The words of love he uses are the words she has told him an earlier lover had cried out at the moment of passion. The words, she thought, expressed something she would have liked to achieve in life: tenderness and ecstasy. The wise Dr Reefy can not only see her and love her as she truly is, ignoring the grotesque distortions of gaunt body and neurotic mind that do not express her, he can explain to her why love may have eluded her.

> 'Love is like a wind stirring the grass beneath the trees on a black night,' he had said. 'You must not try to make love definite. It is the divine accident of life. If you try to be definite and sure about it and to live beneath the trees where soft night winds blow, the long hot day of disappointment comes swiftly and the gritty dust from passing wagons gathers upon lips inflamed and made tender by kisses.' (p. 223)

She has tried too hard to force love. As a girl she had paraded through the streets with travelling men, guests at her father's hotel. She had worn loud clothes and had urged them to tell her of life in the cities. Once she startled the town by putting on men's clothes and riding a bicycle down Main Street. Let it happen – you cannot make it happen,

Reefy tells her. It happens to Reefy when the dark girl comes to him for advice; it happens between the widowed Reefy and Mrs Willard. In both cases the love that developed was a result of mutual openness.

Anderson brings the scene between Reefy and Elizabeth Willard down to earth with a bump. A noise outside his office, the fear of being found, makes them spring apart hysterically. On a realistic level Dr Reefy is, of course, abusing his position as a doctor, taking advantage of a patient, a married woman, the local hotel-keeper's wife. He is afraid of exposure. On a more profound level he is being forced to live by his own philosophy: love at its highest, a fusion of the spiritual and the physical, is 'the divine accident of life' (p. 223).

It is certainly not because he is conventional that Anderson shows the relationship stopping short of consummation. Anticipating the mood of the 1920s and of the decades that followed, Anderson feels that sexual repression can do little but harm. Any expression of love, sexual or otherwise, is natural, and what is natural is right. There is no merit in gentility.

Anderson's emphasis on the physical, however, is neither crude nor merely sexual. Like Whitman he believes that touch is rational, not irrational, that the physical senses lead us to knowledge which is as cerebral as it is tactile or visual. His use of the imagery of hands in the first story in the book makes this point strongly. Wing Biddlebaum's sensitive fingers teach him to love nature, to cherish the berries he picks to sell, to care for the pupils whose shoulders he touches with innocently homoerotic hands. Eventually Winesburg makes Wing ashamed of his hands, so unlike 'the quiet inexpressive hands of other men who worked beside him in the fields' (p. 29). He comes to believe that his hands are unnatural, even sexually perverted. He does exaggerate his sensitivity, he does make it grotesque; but Anderson nevertheless affirms the merit of appreciative touch. It is a loving way to harmony with our world and other people.

Dr Reefy is a figure of instinctive wisdom and love, almost a mythic figure – old, with a white beard, huge nose and hands. The jaded white horse seems too small, too inadequate for this large and energetic man. He does in fact wear out the horse and realistically replaces it with a little grey one. The animal world cannot keep up with him. Unlike the other inhabitants of Winesburg, he is not worn down by other people. It makes no difference to him that Winesburg has forgotten him; he can live the marvellously active life of the inquiring mind. He is, even if the community does not know it, its linchpin. He is the doctor, the healer; he elicits confidences and is involved in the telling or the detecting of what lies behind the grotesqueness. At the same time he is, in his own right, an intensely alive individual. Anderson images Dr Reefy's liveliness in physical and in psychological terms. His hands, the tools of his trade – and for Anderson so often the key to the character of the individual – are at once simple, natural and strong. 'When the hands were closed they looked like clusters of unpainted wooden balls as large as walnuts fastened together by steel rods.' In keeping with the myth they are 'unnaturally large'. They are also like an abacus – they are the primitive and therefore admirable measuring instruments with which Reefy works, as doctor and as man.

He scribbles his thoughts on scraps of paper and stuffs them in his pockets where they form naturally into little hard round balls. These balls are like his hands in shape and hardness; they are, in effect, extensions of his hands. Body and mind are one. He is a whole man, round and satisfying; even his pipe is a round cob shape. But Anderson goes further in attributing symbolic significance to Dr Reefy when he has Reefy bombard his friend the nursery man (another natural, apple loving man) with the paper pills, and when he compares Reefy's life to the delicious twisted little apples from the orchards of Winesburg – the round simple fruit which looks like Dr Reefy's knuckles and like the paper pills. Body, mind and natural universe are in harmony in Reefy. The images of circularity and wholeness represent Dr Reefy's life and mind, his fidelity to the encompassing truth of unselfish, insightful, outgoing love. He is no grotesque. He is the perfect man; to eat of the apples which are like the story of his life, to touch his hands, to acquire his wisdom is to rise from the fallen, corrupted state of America and to ascend to innocence, happiness and goodness. Observe, care, listen, help, love, be: this is his philosophy, this is Anderson's message to America. But Reefy does not impose his philosophy on others, and Anderson does not write a propaganda pamphlet. He embodies his ideas in a tale which the reader is at liberty to read, to interpret or to leave alone. Anderson believes in example not in precept, and Reefy throws away the thoughts which he is tempted to elaborate in a system, which he builds into pyramids. He cannot and will not dispense paper pills, Harding's nostrums; when he comes close to formulating a gigantic truth, a panacea (and such self-righteousness leads to grotesqueness, Anderson says), he is saved from falling by the act of observing and listening to the tall dark girl, with whom he falls in love. To Anderson, as to Gertrude Stein, listening is part of loving.

Stein's creative influence is apparent in 'Paper Pills', particularly in the repetition of slightly varied phrases: twisted apples, twisted little apples, gnarled apples, gnarled twisted apples, twisted apples, little hard round balls, paper balls, hard balls, round hard balls. Thus attention is focused on the complete integrity of Dr Reefy's life. It could be said that what Stein does for words normally seen as ordinary, Anderson does for people usually seen as nothing special. He makes us savour them and see them in a new light.

It is not insignificant that the unifying character in the book, the only confidant of many people in Winesburg, the heir to the rejected Dr Reefy, is young George Willard, the reporter: the investigator, the listener and the truth-teller. At the end of the book George and his girl make love for the first time in a way which is marked by a spirit of giving rather than taking. George becomes fully loving – a rounded individual, independent and other-regarding. He too is made whole by love as the dark girl made Dr Reefy whole. It was not new to preach redemption by love, love which can be physical or spiritual or both; but it was bold to do so in 1919. It was never more timely than in Anderson's tough, harsh, thoughtless, selfish and self-indulgent America.

Notes

1 Sherwood Anderson, *Winesburg, Ohio*, ed. Malcolm Cowley, London, 1967 (originally published 1919). All quotations from *Winesburg, Ohio* are taken from this edition and, unless noted otherwise in textual parentheses, from pages 35–8.
2 Sherwood Anderson, 'A writer's conception of realism', in Dexter Perkins (ed.), *The Theory of the American Novel*, New York, 1970, 294.
3 Francis Hackett, 'To American workingmen', in Ray Lewis White (ed.), *The Achievement of Sherwood Anderson: Essays in Criticism*, Chapel Hill, 1966, 26.
4 Anderson, 'A writer's conception of realism', in Perkins, op. cit., 289.
5 ibid., 290–1.
6 Maxwell Geismar, *The Last of the Provincials, 1915–25*, Boston, 1949, 234.
7 Quoted in Irving Howe, *Sherwood Anderson*, Stanford, 1966, 111.

Further reading

Howe, Irving, *Sherwood Anderson*, Stanford, 1966.
Rosenfeld, Paul, Introduction to *The Sherwood Anderson Reader*, Boston, 1947.

Trilling, Lionel, 'Sherwood Anderson', *The Liberal Imagination*, New York, 1951.

White, Ray Lewis (ed.), *The Achievement of Sherwood Anderson: Essays in Criticism*, Chapel Hill, 1966.

White, Ray Lewis (ed.), *The Merrill Studies in Winesburg, Ohio*, Columbus, Ohio, 1971.

8

Sinclair Lewis (1885–1951)

When Carol had walked for thirty-two minutes she had completely covered the town, east and west, north and south; and she stood at the corner of Main Street and Washington Avenue and despaired.

Main Street, with its two-storey brick shops, its storey-and-a-half wooden residences, its muddy expanse from concrete walk to walk, its huddle of Fords and lumber wagons, was too small to absorb her. The broad, straight, unenticing gashes of the streets let in the grasping prairie on every side. She realized the vastness and the emptiness of the land. The skeleton iron windmill on the farm a few blocks away, at the north end of Main Street, was like the ribs of a dead cow. She thought of the coming of the Northern winter, when the unprotected houses would crouch together in terror of storms galloping out of that wild waste. They were so small and weak, the little brown houses. They were shelters for sparrows, not homes for warm laughing people. . . .

She glanced through the fly-speckled windows of the most pretentious building in sight, the one place which welcomed strangers and determined their opinion of the charm and luxury of Gopher Prairie – the Minniemashie House. It was a tall lean shabby structure, three storeys of yellow-streaked wood, the corners covered with sanded pine slabs purporting to symbolize stone. In the hotel office she could see a stretch of bare unclean floor, a line of rickety chairs with brass cuspidors between, a writing desk with advertisements in mother-of-pearl letters upon the glass-covered back. The dining-room beyond was a jungle of stained tablecloths and catsup bottles.

She looked no more at the Minniemashie House.

A man in cuffless shirt-sleeves with pink arm-garters, wearing a linen collar but no tie, yawned his way from Dyer's Drug Store across to the hotel. . . .

Dyer's Drug Store, a corner building of regular and unreal blocks of artificial stone. Inside the store, a greasy marble soda-fountain with an electric lamp of red and green and curdled-yellow mosaic shade. Pawed-over heaps of toothbrushes and combs and packages of shaving-soap. Shelves of soap-cartons, teething-rings, garden seeds, and patent medicines in yellow packages – nostrums for consumption, for 'women's diseases' – notorious mixtures of opium and alcohol, in the very shop to which her husband sent patients for the filling of prescriptions.

From a second-storey window the sign 'W. P. Kennicott, Phys. & Surgeon', gilt on black sand.

A small wooden motion-picture theatre called 'The Rosebud Movie Palace'. Lithographs announcing a film called 'Fatty in Love'.

Howland & Gould's Grocery. In the display window, black, overripe bananas and lettuce on which a cat was sleeping. Shelves lined with red crepe paper which was now faded and torn and concentrically spotted. . . . The Bon Ton Store – Haydock & Simons's – the largest shop in town. The first-storey front of clear glass, the plates cleverly bound at the edges with brass. The second storey of pleasant tapestry brick. One window of excellent clothes for men, interspersed with collars of floral piqué which showed mauve daisies on a saffron ground. Newness and an obvious notion of neatness and service. Haydock & Simons. Haydock. She had met a Haydock at the station; Harry Haydock; an active person of thirty-five. He seemed great to her, now, and very like a saint. His shop was clean!

Axel Egge's General Store, frequented by Scandinavian farmers. In the shallow dark window-space heaps of sleazy sateens, badly woven galateas, canvas shoes designed for women with bulging ankles, steel and red glass buttons upon cards with broken edges, a cottony blanket, a granite-ware frying-pan reposing on a sun-faded crepe blouse.

Sam Clark's Hardware Store. An air of frankly metallic enterprise. Guns and churns and barrels of nails and beautiful shiny butcher knives.

Chester Dashaway's House Furnishing Emporium. A vista of heavy oak rockers with leather seats, asleep in a dismal row.

Billy's Lunch. Thick handleless cups on the wet oilcloth-covered counter. An odour of onions and the smoke of hot lard. In the doorway a young man audibly sucking a toothpick.

The warehouse of the buyer of cream and potatoes. The sour smell of a dairy.

The Ford Garage and the Buick Garage, competent one-storey brick and cement buildings opposite each other. Old and new cars on grease-blackened concrete floors. Tyre advertisements. The roaring of a tested motor; a racket which beat at the nerves. Surly young men in khaki union overalls. The most energetic and vital places in town.

A large warehouse for agricultural implements. An impressive barricade of green and gold wheels, of shafts and sulky seats, belonging to machinery of which Carol knew nothing – potato-planters, manure-spreaders, silage-cutters, disc-harrows, breaking-ploughs.

A feed store, its windows opaque with the dust of bran, a patent medicine advertisement painted on its roof.

Ye Art Shoppe, Prop., Mrs. Mary Ellen Wilks, Christian Science Library open daily free. A touching fumble at beauty. A one-room shanty of boards recently covered with rough stucco. A show-window delicately rich in error: vases starting out to imitate tree-trunks but running off into blobs of gilt – an aluminium ash-tray labelled 'Greetings from Gopher Prairie' – a Christian Science magazine – a stamped sofa-cushion portraying a large ribbon tied to a small puppy, the correct skeins of embroidery-silk lying on the pillow. Inside the shop, a glimpse of bad carbon prints of bad and famous pictures, shelves of phonograph records and camera films, wooden toys, and in the midst an anxious small woman sitting in a padded rocking-chair. . . .

The post-office – merely a partition of glass and brass shutting off the rear of a mildewed room which must once have been a shop. . . .

The State Bank, stucco masking wood.

The Farmer's National Bank. An Ionic temple of marble. Pure, exquisite, solitary. A brass plate with 'Ezra Stowbody, Pres't'. . . .

In all the town not one building save the Ionic bank which gave pleasure to Carol's eyes; not a dozen buildings which suggested that, in the fifty years of Gopher Prairie's existence, the citizens had realized that it was either desirable or possible to make this, their common home, amusing or attractive. . . . She escaped from Main Street, fled home.

She wouldn't have cared, she insisted, if the people had been comely. She had noted a young man loafing before a shop, one unwashed hand holding the cord of an awning; a middle-aged man who had a way of staring at women as though he had been married too long and too prosaically; an old farmer, solid, wholesome, but not clean – his face like a potato fresh from the earth. None of them had shaved for three days.

'If they can't build shrines, out here on the prairie, surely there's nothing to prevent their buying safety razors!' she raged

She fought herself: 'I must be wrong. People do live here. It can't be as ugly as – as I know it is! I must be wrong. But I can't do it. I can't go through with it.'

She came home too seriously worried for hysteria; and when she found Kennicott waiting for her, and exulting, 'Have a walk? Well, like the town? Great lawns and trees, eh?' she was able to say, with a self-protective maturity new to her, 'It's very interesting.'

Main Street (1920)[1]

* * *

Sinclair Lewis's novel *Main Street*, which quickly sold over a million copies and was translated into a dozen languages, is a significant novel in a number of ways. Lewis's biographer claimed that 'no reader was indifferent to Main Street; if it was not the most important revelation of American life ever made, it was the most infamous libel upon it.'[2] It was acclaimed by critics as writing so powerful that it was thence forward impossible to walk down any Main Street – and all American towns had a street of that name – without recalling and affirming Sinclair Lewis's description of 'the unsparing apologetic ugliness'. It was hailed as life by social and political commentators, as an authentic American story based on the acute observation of people and of social and cultural habits. Indeed, Lewis wrote in a foreword to the novel:

> This is America – a town of a few thousand. . . . The town is, in our tale, called 'Gopher Prairie, Minnesota.' But its Main Street is the continuation of Main Streets everywhere. The story would be the same in Ohio, or Montana, in Kansas or Kentucky or Illinois, and not very differently would it be told in Up York State or in the Carolinian hills. (p. iv)

Some went so far as to call *Main Street* a tragedy of crassness, hypocrisy and inchoate idealism. The novel 'proved' that social life in the American town was hollow, that moral life was shaky, that privacy was impossible. It called in question the quality of civilized life in the American heartland, the Middle West, that 'empire' of wheat and corn and dairies 'which feeds a quarter of the world' (p. 29), and reputedly the home of the Middle American, the typical American. It even addressed the future of civilization in a world dominated by America, as Lewis made savagely explicit.

> Main Street is the climax of civilization. That this Ford car might stand in front of the Bon Ton Store, Hannibal invaded Rome and Erasmus wrote in Oxford cloisters. What Ole Jensen the grocer says to Ezra Stowbody the banker is the new law for London, Prague, and the unprofitable isles of the sea; whatsoever Ezra does not know and sanction, that thing is heresy, worthless for knowing and wicked to consider. (p. iv)

It was fashionable in late nineteenth- and early twentieth-century America to pour scorn on the way of life which, before the post-Civil War revolution in industrial and urban growth, had been dominant in America: life on the farm, in the village and in particular in the small American town. The small town might have a library and an amateur dramatic society, a band even; but what were these compared with the museums, the theatres and orchestras of the city? Small town people were supposed to have less education and less artistic sensibility than city folk. Their whole outlook was indicted as narrow and restrictive; it frowned upon change, initiative and beauty. It demanded that in what they wore and said, in what they ate and drank, in how they decorated their houses and in where they went for their holidays, everyone should be like everyone else in the community.

In *Main Street* Lewis explores this legend of small town life through the critical eyes of Carol Kennicott, a girl from the twin cities of Minneapolis and St Paul, a girl of some culture and artistic tendencies, who has married a doctor from Gopher Prairie, Minnesota. She only has to walk down Main Street on her first day in town to know the legend is fact. 'Oozing out from every drab wall, she felt a forbidding spirit which she could never conquer.' Her impulse is to run.

Carol Kennicott's reaction was Lewis's; he ran from the small town in which he grew up, Sauk Centre, Minnesota, the model for Gopher Prairie. Nor was he alone. By 1920 America was nearing the end of a self-conscious transition from a rural society to one in which the great city was the norm and the goal. By 1920, for the first time in history, more than half of all Americans lived in cities, and there were signs of a growing preoccupation with the relative merits of city and country. In addition to *Main Street* two other indictments of such rural communities as Gopher Prairie appeared in 1920 – Zona Gale's *Miss Lulu Bett* and

Floyd Dell's *Moon-Calf*. *Main Street* also derived from Lewis's response to Sherwood Anderson and, more particularly, to Edgar Lee Masters, who, in his collection of poems, *Spoon River Anthology* (1915), painted a series of pictures not only of a mean and narrow existence in a small town in Illinois but also of the mutual incomprehension that can exist between husbands and wives (his Mr and Mrs Benjamin Pantier afford a good example of this).

Main Street offers a frank and moving account of a marriage in which each partner's expectations of the other are disappointed, a marriage in which, in spite of 'biology and mystery', there is a good deal of physical incompatibility. Will Kennicott is naturally lusty; Carol proves somewhat frigid and achieves a separate room. To the perceptive H. L. Mencken:

> Here is the essential tragedy of American life, and if not the tragedy, then at least the sardonic farce; the disparate cultural development of male and female, the great strangeness that lies between husband and wife when they begin to function as members of society. . . . To Will Kennicott, as to most other normal American males, life remains simple; do your work, care for your family, buy your Liberty Bonds, root for your home team, help to build up your lodge, venerate the flag. But to Carol it is far more complex and challenging. She has become aware of forces that her husband is wholly unable to comprehend.[3]

Gopher Prairie only reinforces her belief in the necessary and transforming power of the forces of beauty and culture. She sees a town crying out for improvement, and wants to take it on herself to lead a campaign of re-educating the people, rebuilding Main Street; she wants to introduce exotic food and serious reading. He is satisfied with things as they are, and does not think it appropriate that the doctor's wife should so aggressively and brazenly attempt to take over and make over the town in which, after all, she is a newcomer.

Carol's abilities do not match her ambitions; she finds it difficult to make friends, let alone converts, and her schemes of renovation are grandiose and impractical. She wants a theatre – the town needs public restrooms. When Gopher Prairie makes clear its disapproval of her friendly relationship with her maid, her sympathy with the local socialist, her friendship with the best-read person in town, who happens to be the clerk in the draper's shop, she makes a dramatic move, rejecting the town that has rejected her. She enacts a trial separation from her huband, taking her child and moving to Washington, D.C., where she earns an independent living as a clerk in the Bureau of War Risk Insurance, and where no one is at all concerned with how 'radical' she may or may not be. She is allowed to live her own life. But in Washington Carol learns some home truths, truths with which Lewis tempers his indictment of Gopher Prairie. In Washington, too, there is a kind of conformity. In her office she experiences 'an endurance of monotonous details' (p. 421) – dictating and filing. If the city allows privacy, it also engenders anonymity and loneliness, which Carol comes to find as oppressive as the permanent presence of neighbours in her home in Gopher Prairie. Nor is Washington the liberal Mecca it seems. Carol realizes that 'always she was to perceive in Washington (as doubtless she would have perceived in New York or in London) a thick streak of Main Street' (p. 423). But if this makes Gopher Prairie look better than on her first walk down Main Street, it makes the general American condition look worse. There is, it seems, no escape from the stultifying environment, from small-minded people, from ugliness. Not, at any rate, for the individual like Carol Kennicott, who lacks the ultimate confidence and independence to throw off either the obligatory material conformity of the bright 1920s or the old social conformity of the small, unprogressive community which finds ways of making difference and isolation untenable and of negating political and social emancipation.

Sadly, the rebelling Carol, who had so rightly hated Main Street on first sight, is turned into a wife and mother who has to affirm it or perish. *Main Street* has as its subtitle 'The Story of Carol Kennicott', and it is indeed the story of how she is made to relinquish the passionate independence and revolutionary zeal with which she came to Gopher Prairie, the story of how she is made to accede and to conform. Her submission is an accurate reflection of a time when peer pressure was to be paramount. The pressures on Carol are obvious at the end of the day on which she first sees Main Street, returns home and, with what Lewis describes as 'self-protective maturity', responds to her husband's 'exulting' question – 'Well, like the town?' – with 'It's very interesting.' Though she does not realize it, she is obviously prepared to settle for half; on this first day, one of the ordinary, disappointing citizens of Gopher Prairie she had met the previous evening at the station, Harry Haydock, seems 'great to her, now, and very like a saint. His shop was clean!'

Carol is uncompromisingly harsh in her private assessment of what meets her eye on her first walk down Main Street. Lewis is giving strong expression to his alarm at the sights, sounds and smells, the second-rate ethos of Middle America. This America pays lip-service to art with stucco masking wood and with sanded pine slabs purporting to symbolize stone, but by and large it is smugly careless of its appearance. The windows of the Minniemashie House are 'fly-speckled' and the floor is bare and unclean. The dining room is 'a jungle of stained table-cloths'. The marble soda fountain in Dyer's Drug Store is greasy; the heaps of toothbrushes and combs and the packages of shaving soap bear the marks of being pawed over. In the grocery store window a cat sleeps on the display of overripe bananas and rotting lettuce. When the town is alive, it is crassly and crudely so, and nowhere more than in Billy's Lunch: 'Thick handleless cups on the wet oilcloth-covered counter. An odour of onions and smoke of hot lard. In the doorway a young man audibly sucking a toothpick.' Even the dairy – the dairy, in the Middle West! – smells sour. Only guns and cars, machinery and hardware, indices of violence and speed and utility, are shiny and polished. Worst of all, Gopher Prairie's 'touching fumble at beauty', the Art Shoppe, which doubles as the Christian Science Library. It offered for sale:

> vases starting out to imitate tree-trunks but running off into blobs of gilt – an aluminium ash-tray labelled 'Greetings from Gopher Prairie' . . . a stamped sofa-cushion portraying a large ribbon tied to a small puppy . . . bad carbon prints of bad and famous pictures.

Carol is kind to call this a 'touching fumble at beauty', when it is a pathetic display of bad taste. But she is desperate to find something right, something that will help her forget the stultifying reality of Gopher Prairie. What consoles her most is the symbol of all venality and materialism and of the conformity which springs from materialism: 'The Farmer's National Bank. An Ionic temple of marble. Pure, exquisite, solitary.' The name of the President is significant – he is a Mr Stowbody – the man who gathers to himself people's money and sometimes their lives too. Carol herself is, of course, not responding to his name but to the Ionic architecture – Old World beauty, but better than none. She does not particularly care for the style or the stock of the Bon Ton Store, but it is such a relief to find clear glass windows bound with shining brass that her imagination transforms the clothes in the window to 'excellent clothes for men' and can even stomach the hideous 'collars of floral piqué which showed mauve daisies on a saffron ground'. Neatness and service are now almost like art forms to her, and she tries to make her imagination work in a similar way on the people she sees: 'She wouldn't have cared, she insisted, if the people had been comely . . . "surely there's nothing to prevent their buying safety razors!" she raged.' Her rage is as much at herself, at being forced back on such superficial things for such cold comfort, as it is at them. But her attempt to compromise is depressing. It is clear that she is in danger of succumbing to the 'Village Virus' – a phrase Lewis once thought of using as the book's title, and which is summed up by a character later in the book as 'the germ which – it's extraordinarily like the bookworm – infects ambitious people who stay too long in the provinces' (p. 159).

Lewis is concerned not to seem one-sided in his attitude to Gopher Prairie, and so he presents, arriving on the same train that brings Carol to the town, a young Swedish girl, Bea Sorenson. The largest place she has ever been to is Scandia Crossing, population 67, and her perspective is that of the farm girl to whom Gopher Prairie is a big city and Main Street like Fifth Avenue. To Bea the fly-speckled Minniemashie House is a grand hotel, 'awful high'; Carol's 'man in cuffless shirt-sleeves with pink arm-garters, wearing a linen collar but no tie' becomes 'a fine big gentleman in a new pink shirt with a diamond and not no washed-out blue denim working shirt'. A crude 'electric lamp of red and green and curdled-yellow mosaic shade' is to the awe-struck Bea 'a great big lamp with the biggest shade you ever saw – all different kinds of coloured glass stuck together'; and as for the greasy soda fountain which Carol so despises – 'suppose a fella took you *there*!' thinks Bea, breathlessly. Bea sees dandy buttons; Carol sees red glass and steel on a cracked card. 'Swell people,' says Bea. 'I must be wrong. People do live here,' agonizes Carol. Carol writes off 'Fatty in Love' at the motion-picture house; pictures every week, exults Bea (p. 43). But though Bea's naiveté is not without charm, her viewpoint is not to be trusted. She exaggerates – her criteria are size, quantity, brightness and anything that is not Scandia Crossing. She makes the perspective of Carol, who has also come hopefully to Gopher Prairie, seem not cruel but accurate.

Lewis sets Carol's impression against a second perspective, that of her husband, Will Kennicott, who loves Gopher Prairie as it is. Where Bea wears rose-coloured spectacles and Carol uses a hypersensitive lens, Will takes slightly blurred, sepia pictures of Gopher Prairie, and woos Carol with them. To Will Gopher Prairie should be taken calmly, tolerantly. It is capable of improvement, but improvement must be slow and natural, not overnight and imposed. If Gopher Prairie's citizens had all been like Will, Carol might, she sometimes thinks, have been content;

but he tolerates other people's intolerance, his occasional dullness seems to reinforce their unadulterated dullness, their forced camaraderie colours his genuine heartiness. More often than not, Gopher Prairie prevents Carol from seeing Will as he is, a good and simple man. 'I'm all the science there is here,' he tells her. He can get up and get home at unearthly hours, deliver babies in appalling conditions as long as 'I have you here at home to welcome me.' 'You're all the things I see in a sunset when I'm driving in from the country' (p. 393). His is an American success story; he has his dream, and he has his reality.

But the message of *Main Street* comes from the place, not the people. It is Main Street that first confronts Carol with her sense of the quality of life in Gopher Prairie, and it is that street which stays with the reader, which seems to conjure up and enshrine the America of 1920. This is partly because Lewis made sure that his powerful description of the street occurred early on, and also because he set it in deliberate contrast to the novel's equally powerful opening, an evocation of the past.

> On a hill by the Mississippi where Chippewas camped two generations ago, a girl stood in relief against the cornflower blue of Northern sky. She saw no Indians now; she saw flour-mills and the blinking windows of skyscrapers in Minneapolis and St. Paul. Nor was she thinking of squaws and portages, and the Yankee fur-traders whose shadows were all about her. She was meditating upon walnut fudge, the plays of Brieux, the reasons why heels run over, and the fact that the chemistry instructor had stared at the new coiffure which concealed her years. . . .
>
> A girl on a hilltop . . . a rebellious girl. (p. 7)

We first see Carol, then, in the context of American history and adventure. We are reminded of the courageous and adventurous people who created a society out of a wilderness; we remember the idealism of the early Americans, who wanted to shine as a lighthouse beacon to the world, to build a 'city on a hill', a new Jerusalem. Carol is not even conscious of her inheritance here, it is so much a part of her. This hopeful, adventurous, ardent, ambitious girl is all that is left of the spirit which wanted to make a brave new world, and she immediately senses that Main Street threatens that spirit. 'The broad, straight, unenticing gashes of the streets' and its huddle of Fords frightened her. Middle Westerners had gouged out for themselves a structure which defaced the majestic prairie. The continent had been violated and the continent was taking revenge. Nature had turned the windmill into a skeleton;

'the grasping prairie' was moving in on the town. Carol 'thought of the coming of the Northern winter, when the unprotected houses would crouch together in terror of storms galloping out of that wild waste'. Lewis is writing metaphorically; Gopher Prairie is really in danger of being false, in its ugliness, to the beauty and promise of the continent – of being false, in its pettiness and inertia, to the American ideals of generosity and initiative. How poorly Gopher Prairie compared with the shanty towns of the frontier which had vigour, which despised complacency. There should have been no place, in the American Experiment, for complacency, yet Gopher Prairie, like all American small towns, would be satisfied with updated, tawdry versions of what it already was.

Lewis drums into us the harsh reality of Main Street. Unlike Carol, we cannot see it in a glorious sunset at the end of the novel, partly because Lewis does not want us to but also because his special talent as a writer is to capture the real scene, the group, the still life, not to paint romantic pictures. He surely is, as E. M. Forster[4] pointed out, the first American photographic novelist – and sometimes a movie-maker too, for his still life is suddenly animated as a banana visibly decays a little more or a human figure moves into the picture. The pictures give the human figure definition, and vice versa. The young man sucking a toothpick is defined by Billy's Lunch; the anxious woman in the padded rocker is explained by the barely viable Art Shoppe. What carries conviction in Main Street is what we feel Lewis can, as it were, corroborate rather than imagine – what he has seen, smelt and felt. Forster described Lewis as a marvellous documentary photographer who does not arrange, or rearrange, but who registers a significant scene on his lens. His quick eye catches the man yawning his way across the street, the shapeless canvas shoes designed for women with thick ankles, the mildewed post office and 'a granite-ware frying pan reposing on a sun-faded crepe blouse'. All small town America is here.

Of all preceding fiction about small town and rural America, Lewis liked best Hamlin Garland's *Main-Travelled Roads* (1891), and *Main Street* owes a debt to Garland's theory of a sincere literature, a literature of verities. The 'veritist', wrote Garland, 'aims to be perfectly truthful in his delineation of his relation to life, but there is a tone, a color, which comes unconsciously into his utterance, like the sobbing stir of the muted violins beneath the frank clear song of the clarionet – and this tone is one of sorrow that the good time moves so slowly to approach.'[5] Lewis's highly successful realistic novel ends on just such a note of sorrow: 'I may not have fought the good fight,' Carol admits (p. 447). She has not been true to the piercing vision she had of an environment which must at all costs be changed. She cannot bear to see Gopher Prairie as it really is. A few weeks after arriving in the town she tells herself, 'In city shops she was merely A Customer. . . . Here she was Mrs. Doc. Kennicott, and her preferences in grapefruit and melons were known.' A few weeks later, 'as she never entered it, the Minniemashie House ceased to exist for her' (p. 66). This is the realistic Lewis's picture of a complex romantic who wants to change the way Americans live and think, who is capable of a sensitivity greater than anyone else's in the community but who is defeated by her own limitations of intellect, by determined local opposition and by a pressure to conform which she cannot continue to resist. Increasingly she has to romanticize in order to survive. The transforming power of the imagination helps her to ignore the unbearable photographic reality. How else could Carol return to Gopher Prairie as she does at the end, and allow herself to take the back seat in her husband's car, along with another woman. In order to come to terms with it, she has to see Gopher Prairie as good; and she acts on her new 'vision' with a vengeance.

> 'I'll sit back with Ethel,' she said, at the car.
>
> It was the first time she had called Mrs. Clark by her given name; the first time she had willingly sat back, a woman of Main Street.
>
> 'I'm hungry. It's good to be hungry,' she reflected, as they drove away. . . .
>
> 'Let's all go to the movies tomorrow night. Awfully exciting film,' said Ethel Clark.
>
> 'Well, I was going to read a new book, but – All right, let's go,' said Carol. (p. 445)

And so Carol, whose definition of fulfilment is now 'to be hungry', goes off to the Rosebud Movie Palace, along with millions of Americans for whom culture would consist of what Hollywood had to offer; and that, more often than not, was third-rate slapstick, mild titillation or moral melodrama.

Carol imagines herself not only in the role of regular citizen but in that of submissive wife, and she plays the role to perfection. The last thing we see her do is to pat Kennicott's pillow and turn down the sheets. 'I have kept the faith,' she persists in saying, as she does it, and refers to her daughter as 'a bomb to blow up smugness' (pp. 446–7). But as Lewis so remarkably demonstrates in his picture of Main Street, it is the visual image which tells the truth. And it is pictures rather than ideas which keep Carol sane. In a conscious act of will and imagination, a Stevensesque act of fiction-making, she turns her first impression of Main Street on its head.

> Her active hatred of Gopher Prairie had run out. She saw it now as a toiling new settlement. She saw Main Street in the dusty Prairie sunset, a line of frontier shanties. . . . She saw Gopher Prairie as her home, waiting for her in the sunset, rimmed round with splendour. (pp. 438–9)

Notes

1 Sinclair Lewis, *Main Street*, London, 1973 (originally published 1920). All quotations from *Main Street* are taken from this edition and, unless noted otherwise in textual parentheses, from pages 37–42.
2 Mark Schorer, *Sinclair Lewis: An American Life*, London, 1961, 269.
3 H. L. Mencken, 'Consolation', in Mark Schorer (ed.), *Sinclair Lewis: A Collection of Critical Essays*, Englewood Cliffs, NJ, 1962, 18.
4 E. M. Forster, 'Our photography: Sinclair Lewis', ibid., 95–9.
5 Hamlin Garland, *Crumbling Idols*, Cambridge, Mass., 1966, 43–4.

Further reading

Hilfer, A. C., *The Revolt from the Village*, Chapel Hill, 1969.
Lynd, Robert and Helen, *Middletown: A Study in American Culture*, New York, 1929. Fascinating contemporary study of 'average' America.
Schorer, Mark, *Sinclair Lewis: An American Life*, London, 1961.
Schorer, Mark (ed.), *Sinclair Lewis: A Collection of Critical Essays*, Englewood Cliffs, NJ, 1962. Contains two especially perceptive essays: Walter Lippmann, 'Sinclair Lewis', and E. M. Forster, 'Our photography: Sinclair Lewis'.

9
Jean Toomer (1894–1961)

Houses are shy girls whose eyes shine reticently upon the dusk body of the street. Upon the gleaming limbs and asphalt torso of a dreaming nigger. Shake your curled wool-blossoms, nigger. Open your liver lips to the lean, white spring. Stir the root-life of a withered people. Call them from their houses, and teach them to dream.

Dark swaying forms of Negroes are street songs that woo virginal houses.

Dan Moore walks southward on Thirteenth Street. The low limbs of budding chestnut trees recede above his head. Chestnut buds and blossoms are wool he walks upon. The eyes of houses faintly touch him as he passes them. Soft girl-eyes, they set him singing. Girl-eyes within him widen upward to promised faces. Floating away, they dally wistfully over the dusk body of the street. Come on, Dan Moore, come on. Dan sings. His voice is a little hoarse. It cracks. He strains to produce tones in keeping with the houses' loveliness. Cant be done. He whistles. His notes are shrill. They hurt him. Negroes open gates, and go indoors, perfectly. Dan thinks of the house he's going to. Of the girl. Lips, flesh-notes of a forgotten song, plead with him. . . .*

Dan turns into a side-street, opens an iron gate, bangs it to. Mounts the steps, and searches for the bell. Funny, he cant find it. He fumbles around. The thought comes to him that some one passing by might see him, and not understand. Might think that he is trying to sneak, to break in.

Dan: Break in. Get an ax and smash in. Smash in their faces. I'll show em. Break into an engine-house, steal a thousand horse-power fire truck. Smash in with the truck. I'll show em. Grab an ax and brain em. Cut em up. Jack the Ripper. Baboon from the zoo. And then the cops come. 'No, I aint a baboon. I aint Jack the Ripper. I'm a poor man out of work. Take your hands off me, you bull-necked bears. Look into

* Ellipsis appears in original text.

my eyes. I am Dan Moore. I was born in a canefield. The hands of Jesus touched me. I am come to a sick world to heal it. Only the other day, a dope fiend brushed against me – Don't laugh, you mighty, juicy, meat-hook men. Give me your fingers and I will peel them as if they were ripe bananas.'

Some one might think he is trying to break in. He'd better knock. His knuckles are raw bone against the thick glass door. He waits. No one comes. Perhaps they havent heard him. He raps again. This time, harder. He waits. No one comes. Some one is surely in. He fancies that he sees their shadows on the glass. Shadows of gorillas. Perhaps they saw him coming and dont want to let him in. He knocks. The tension of his arms makes the glass rattle. Hurried steps come towards him. The door opens.

'Please, you might break the glass – the bell – oh, Mr. Moore! I thought it must be some stranger. How do you do? Come in, wont you? Muriel? Yes. I'll call her. Take your things off, wont you? And have a seat in the parlor. Muriel will be right down. Muriel! Oh Muriel! Mr. Moore to see you. She'll be right down. You'll pardon me, won't you? So glad to see you.' . . .

Mrs. Pribby retreats to the rear of the house. She takes up a newspaper. There is a sharp click as she fits into her chair and draws it to the table. The click is metallic like the sound of a bolt being shot into place. Dan's eyes sting. Sinking into a soft couch, he closes them. The house contracts about him. It is a sharp-edged, massed, metallic house. Bolted. About Mrs. Pribby. Bolted to the endless rows of metal houses. Mrs. Pribby's house. The rows of houses belong to other Mrs. Pribbys. No wonder he couldn't sing to them. . . .

Dan goes to the wall and places his ear against it. A passing street car and something vibrant from the earth sends a rumble to him. That rumble comes from the earth's deep core. It is the mutter of powerful underground races. Dan has a picture of all the people rushing to put their ears against walls, to listen to it. The next world-savior is coming up that way. Coming up. A continent sinks down. The new-world Christ will need consummate skill to walk upon the waters where huge bubbles burst. . .* Thuds of Muriel coming down. Dan turns to the piano and glances through a stack of jazz music sheets. Ji-ji-bo, JI-JI-BO!

'Hello, Dan, stranger, what brought you here?'

Muriel comes in, shakes hands, and then clicks into a high-armed seat under the orange glow of a floor-lamp. Her face is fleshy. It would tend to coarseness but for the fresh fragrant something which is the life of it.

* Ellipsis appears in original text.

Her hair like an Indian's. But more curly and bushed and vagrant. Her nostrils flare. The flushed ginger of her cheeks is touched orange by the shower of color from the lamp.

'Well, you havent told me, you havent answered my question, stranger. What brought you here?'

Dan feels the pressure of the house, of the rear room, of the rows of houses, shift to Muriel. He is light. He loves her. He is doubly heavy.

'Dont know, Muriel – wanted to see you – wanted to talk to you – to see you'. . . .

'Lets talk about something else. I hear there's a good show at the Lincoln this week.'

'Yes, so Harry was telling me. Going?'

'To-night.'

Dan starts to rise.

'I didnt know. I dont want to keep you.'

'Its all right. You dont have to go till Bernice comes. And she wont be here till eight. I'm all dressed. I'll let you know.' . . .

Muriel, leading Bernice who is a cross between a washerwoman and a blue-blood lady, a washer-blue, a washer-lady, wanders down the right aisle to the lower front box. Muriel has on an orange dress. Its color would clash with the crimson box-draperies, its color would contradict the sweet rose smile her face is bathed in, should she take her coat off. She'll keep it on. Pale purple shadows rest on the planes of her cheeks. Deep purple comes from her thick-shocked hair. Orange of the dress goes well with these. . . . Dan is ushered down the aisle. He has to squeeze past the knees of seated people to reach his own seat. He treads on a man's corns. The man grumbles, and shoves him off. He shrivels close beside a portly Negress whose huge rolls of flesh meet about the bones of seat-arms. A soil-soaked fragrance comes from her. Through the cement floor her strong roots sink down. They spread under the asphalt streets. Dreaming, the streets roll over on their bellies, and suck their glossy health from them. Her strong roots sink down and spread under the river and disappear in blood-lines that waver south. Her roots shoot down. Dan's hands follow them. Roots throb. Dan's heart beats violently. He places his palms upon the earth to cool them. Earth throbs. Dan's heart beats violently. He sees all the people in the house rush to the walls to listen to the rumble. A new-world Christ is coming up. Dan comes up. He is startled. The eyes of the woman dont belong to her. They look at him unpleasantly. From either aisle, bolted masses press in. He doesnt fit. The mass grows agitant. For an instant, Dan's and Muriel's eyes meet. His weight there slides the weight on her. She braces an arm against the brass rail, and turns her head away. . . . The house snaps dark. The curtain recedes upward from the blush of the footlights. Jazz overture is over. The first act is on.

Dan: Old stuff. Muriel – bored. Must be. But she'll smile and she'll clap. Do what youre bid, you she-slave. Look at her. Sweet, tame woman in a brass box seat. Clap, smile, fawn, clap. Do what youre bid. Drag me in with you. Dirty me. Prop me in your brass box seat. I'm there, am I not? because of you. He-slave. Slave of a woman who is a slave. I'm a damned sight worse than you are. I sing your praises, Beauty! I exalt thee, O Muriel! A slave, thou art greater than all Freedom because I love thee.

'Box-Seat' from *Cane* (1923)[1]

* * *

In its experimental form and often surrealistic technique, in its evocative awareness of the complexity of black America, Jean Toomer's *Cane* (1923) was one of the period's most important pieces of writing. A sequence of stories, poems, vignettes and plays, *Cane* was one of the first works to appear in the movement that came to be known as the Harlem Renaissance, that assertive time when a number of black American writers in search of identity looked back to Africa with curiosity and burgeoning Afro-Americanness and wrote with pride and dedicated defiance on black difference from white America. The writers of this renaissance treated problems of racial identity and racial stereotypes with unprecedented freedom. They attempted to assert not only that blackness is beautiful but that the masses of the black people, the 'folk', with their folk songs, folk legends and folkways, had dignity and perhaps even enshrined the special merits of the race.

All black American literature is in a sense related to the fact of slavery, and to the appalling discrimination which continued to prevail in American race relations and particularly in the South after the Civil War ended in 1865. In its early days, the so-called Reconstruction policy brought a brief period of effective enfranchisement for the former slaves in which the southern whites, already subject to martial law (enforced by occupying northern forces and often by black militia), became even more passionately entrenched in racist postures. There followed a period in which the whites regained effective political control in the South, and 'Jim Crow' legislation – separate facilities for black and white, luxurious for the white, primitive for the black – came into being. Black reactions were twofold. There were those who supported the ideas of Booker T. Washington, president of the Tuskegee Normal and Industrial Institute. Washington believed that the black must quietly demonstrate his right to be treated as a human being, by such utilitarian means as personal hygiene – the gospel of the toothbrush – diligence in work, high productivity, cheerfulness and modesty. He must be willing to cast down his bucket where he is and get on with the job, looking for long-term rewards for his race, not for immediate rewards for himself. Such conduct would breed grudging and eventually wholehearted admiration, and full recognition of the Negro's equal humanity and equal ability would follow. Separate but equal as the fingers of one hand was Washington's millennial slogan. At the turn of the century an alternative philosophy manifested itself, that of W. E. B. Du Bois, a more militant individual: militant, however, not so much on behalf of all Negroes as on behalf of the 'talented tenth', who, by demonstrating in themselves that a minority of intelligent Negroes could do anything intelligent whites could do, would also demonstrate how nonsensical was racial discrimination. Du Bois feared that Booker T. Washington's limited educational philosophy – his effective discouragement of higher education – would deprive the race of the possibility of such a 'talented tenth'.

The First World War provided the impetus for the awakening of a sense of black culture in whites and blacks alike. The war had offered an economic stimulus for southern blacks to work in northern industries, and there they enjoyed greater freedom and higher rewards than ever before. Black servicemen, many of whom stayed in New York when they were shipped home from France, had also tasted a kind of equality during the war. Optimistically, blacks moved in numbers to the nation's capital. Toomer saw them moving towards dominance in such areas as

> Seventh Street [which] is a bastard of Prohibition and the War. A crude-boned soft-skinned wedge of nigger life breathing its loafer air, jazz songs and love, thrusting unconscious rhythms, black-reddish blood into the white and whitewashed wood of Washington. (p. 39)

And there was a black dimension, indeed a black impetus, to the Jazz Age, embodied in such all-black musicals, as *Shuffle Along* (1921) and in such black musicians as King Oliver, Louis Armstrong and Duke Ellington, who played in prohibition nightspots. In an age of excess and abandon, black dancing and music – hip, limber, hot – seemed to express what white Americans were looking for. If not equal, blacks were at least complementary, and certainly exciting. Eugene O'Neill demonstrated an interest in blacks in *The Emperor Jones* (1921), a sensitive treatment of a black American Pullman porter who, with some success, utilizes the techniques of white capitalism to secure his dictatorship of a West Indian island. In *All God's Chillun Got Wings* (1924) O'Neill deals with racial intermarriage, while Sherwood Anderson's novel *Dark Laughter* (1925) contrasts the natural richness of Negro life with the sterility of white America in the 1920s. Jean Toomer was reputed to have had some influence on the last two works.

Most of the writers of the Harlem Renaissance – Langston Hughes, Countee Cullen, Sterling Brown, Arna Bontemps and Zora Neale Hurston – lived and worked out of Harlem. They formed a black literary community. Toomer, however, was never really part of this community and was not formed by it; but by a mixture of cultural accident and cultural timeliness, he was in the forefront of the decade's examination of black identity. His background helps explain him somewhat. He was the grandson of Pinckney B. S. Pinchback, who, in the brief early period of Reconstruction, was acting Governor of Louisiana. Some time after losing office, Pinchback and his daughter moved to W Street, a prosperous white suburb of Washington, D.C., where Toomer was born. The family fortune quickly decayed; the Toomers moved first to New York and then back to a poorer, black neighbourhood in Washington. Toomer was bewildered and unsettled by the rapid change of environment. Physically rootless and culturally dissociated, he wandered from college to college, studying agriculture at the University of Wisconsin and at the Massachusetts College of Agriculture and spending a brief time at the American College of Physical Training in Chicago. His inveterate attendance at public lectures in whatever city he found himself gave him a wide and eclectic knowledge, and it was through such lectures that he developed an interest in literature, especially in Anderson and the imagists and in Robert Frost and Carl Sandburg (a rural folk poet and an urban folk poet: he may well have seen himself as an amalgam of the two in *Cane*). He also became interested in the ideas of Waldo Frank, a social revolutionary who had attacked the white establishment in *Our America* (1919). It was probably at a lecture given in Chicago by the radical lawyer Clarence Darrow that Toomer was 'converted' to atheism, and at this time too he 'discovered' sociology. For a while Toomer continued to wander – selling cars, teaching physical education, doing settlement work. He began to give lectures himself – to shipyard workers on sociology, for instance.

This was a restless, rootless American life, which suddenly blossomed into the marvellous *Cane*, when, with his head full of ideas and beginning to feel that a literary identity might be his, Toomer went to Sparta, Georgia, as head of an industrial and agricultural school for Negroes. In addition to his burgeoning interest in writing, he also developed an interest in his own culture. 'Loving . . . the Negro group', he wrote at this time,

> has stimulated and fertilized whatever creative talent I may contain within me. A visit to Georgia last fall was the starting point of almost everything of worth that I have done. I heard folk-songs come from the lips of Negro peasants. I saw the rich dusk beauty that I had heard many false accents about, and of which . . . 'till then, I was somewhat skeptical. And a deep part of my nature, a part that I had repressed, sprang suddenly to life and responded to them. Now, I cannot conceive of myself as aloof and separated.[2]

So, from feeling alienated and without a culture, Toomer found one and belonged. Yet *Cane* is not quite what his statement of new-found identity would suggest. If it is a celebration of black ways and types, it is also a criticism of these things. Though it makes us smell cane and see cotton, taste 'dark purple ripened plums' (p. 12) and touch the sweet gum tree, it also makes us aware that this is a land where climate and setting dictate an uncanny indolence. The sky seems too lazy to pursue the setting sun.

Most of all the sugar cane communicates Toomer's vision of his race. It connotes a hard reality, if a sweet and sensuous one too; it involves laborious toil and has a kind of built-in suffocation. It is Toomer's image of what it is to be a southern black: to live a life which is economically marginal but in many ways satisfying.

> All around the air was heavy with the scent of boiling cane. A large pile of cane-stalks lay like ribboned shadows upon the ground. A mule, harnessed to a pole, trudged lazily round and round the pivot of the grinder. Beneath a swaying oil lamp, a Negro alternately whipped out at the mule, and fed cane-stalks to the grinder. A fat boy waddled pails of fresh ground juice between the grinder and the

boiling stove. Steam came from the copper boiling pan. The scent of the cane came from the copper pan and drenched the forest and the hill that sloped to factory town, beneath its fragrance. It drenched the men in circle seated around the stove. (p. 29)

Cane does not paint life in the South as a pastoral idyll. Nor does it suggest that all northern Negroes can find their identity by going to the South. Indeed, the Toomer surrogate in *Cane*, Ralph Kabnis, the northerner precariously holding down a teaching position in a southern school, is a tragic figure. He finds the black folk songs full of a 'weird chill' (p. 81). They terrify him as much as the presence of the Ku Klux Klan. What consolation do the blacks of the South offer him as they sing, fatalistically, of a

White-man's land.
Niggers, sing.
Burn, bear black children
Till poor rivers bring
Rest, and sweet glory
In Camp Ground. (p. 81)

The Booker T. Washington-figure in the Kabnis story, the southerner preacher Mr Hanby, finds Kabnis too dissolute; the blacks find him not one of them, just a stuck-up northern nigger whom they would like to lynch. A compassionate black, a carpenter, can find Kabnis a home but can offer him no real security, no real understanding, no joy, no sense of belonging, no salvation, only a sense of difference and fear. The most powerful figure in this sombre story is that of Father John, who lives in a cellar beneath the carpenter's shop. This primitive black totem, who does not teach and rarely speaks, is an object of reverence to an essentially superstitious people. But what is holy to the southern black seems pagan and threatening to Kabnis. Father John is 'a black hound spiked to an ivory pedestal' (p. 113). In effect he holds the black back; he is as good as a white man's nigger.

Cane has a three-part structure. The first section, set in Georgia, focuses on what Darwin Turner calls 'stories about women whose behaviour and thought contrasts with the expectations and demonstrations of society'.[3] This focus may have been intended to balance the last section of the book, which returns to Georgia for the male-oriented story of the tragic Kabnis (who is so distraught by the fact that he cannot identify with his race that he starts back down the evolutionary ladder with only sex and drink to occupy him). Certainly Toomer is not offering us that sociological generalization of the black woman as the dominant force in black society, who both creates and compensates for the fecklessness and rootlessness of her man. But Toomer did view himself, in his Georgia experience, as a man who suddenly saw things in their proper perspective – and one of these things was male sexuality, something whose urgency and potency had worried him as an adolescent, but which now seemed more than complemented and justified by black female sexuality. 'The genius of the South' was 'Blood-hot eyes and cane-lipped scented mouth' (p. 13). Georgia meant the sanctifying of sensuality; and section one of *Cane* is in part a paean to this sensuality, which seemed to Toomer to make unconventional 'virtue' of conventional 'vice'. The white woman who has two black children is hallowed for her unashamed impulses. Carma, the woman as strong as a man, whose husband kills because of her infidelity, is urged to take more lovers. Fernie May Rose – the instinctive whore – is hymned by Toomer as holy. We pity Esther when the black preacher rejects her body; we do not blame Louisa when her white and black lovers bring about each other's death.

So there is a balance between the flamboyant celebration of women and women's liberation at the beginning of the book and the picture of the plight of the intellectual male at the end. The middle section brings the two elements together in a series of stories, some set in Washington and some in Chicago, in which we see blacks out of the deep South trying to adjust to themselves, to each other and to what is likely to be the kind of society and setting that most blacks will increasingly find themselves in. The stories pose the same question. Can black virtues withstand separation from the South? Why, for instance, cannot John speak of his love to Dorris as he wants to?

> Dorris. John sees her. Her hair, crisp-curled, is bobbed. Bushy, black hair bobbing about her lemon-colored face. Her lips are curiously full, and very red. Her limbs in silk purple stocking are lovely. John feels them [in his imagination]. Desires her. Holds off. (p. 51)

Why is Paul unable to express his desire for the responsive Bona? Why does Rhobert fixate on material possession? Why is he so introverted and isolated? 'Rhobert wears a house, like a monstrous diver's helmet on his head. . . . Rods of the house like antennae of a dead thing, stuffed, prop up in the air' (p. 40).

They are all trying to make sense of a society which is too bourgeois, too frenetic. They are responding to the restrictiveness of the urban environment, which is in every sense less open. There are formal, forbidding rows of houses instead of the casual, dispersed shacks; there are stuffy theatres instead of fresh cane fields, artificial art instead of natural song. There is the urge to conform and to prove something. 'Money burns the pocket, pocket hurts.' Shirts balloon, Cadillacs zoom, observes Toomer (p. 39). Do not prove – just be, he admonishes. His own Georgia experience made him so secure in his identity that subsequently he was able to say that 'from my own point of view I am naturally and inevitably an American. I have strived for a spiritual fusion analagous to the fact of racial intermingling.'[4] He thus felt able, for the most part, to ignore race as a subject in his writings. (Numbers of unplaced novels and stories dealt with such subjects as mysticism and Gurdjieff's fusion of mind, body and soul through meditation and mental exercise.) But he recognized that most people in the 1920s, white and black, and the uprooted black in particular, had problems of identity, lacked his own sense of security. It is this extreme sense of insecurity, expressed so effectively through Dan and Muriel (grotesques who remind us of Sherwood Anderson) and in images of the surreal, that Toomer is out to capture in the central section of *Cane*. Paradoxically, Toomer's own security in part accounts for his subsequent failure as a writer. Complacency does not breed great literature. When he wrote *Cane* he was near enough to the insecurity he had just left to combine celebration and compassionate insight in fine proportions. He was, at that moment, acutely conscious of black reality, physical and psychological. He felt he had full access to the black psyche, for he was, himself, at this time 'cane-lipped' (p. 13).

In *Cane* Toomer intends both to evoke and to transcend race. Cane becomes a metaphor for all human relationships. 'Time and space have no meaning in a canefield,' he writes (p. 11); and it is clear in 'Box-Seat' that Toomer can at once convey what is black and what is universal. Dan is a black preacher, with all that entails – a sense of revivalism, a sense of revelation, the capacity to plead and to be didactic and to move. 'I am Dan Moore. I was born in a canefield. The hands of Jesus touched me. I am come to a sick world to heal it.' He has black rhythm: 'Ji-ji-bo, JI-JI-BO!' He imagines things in terms of blackness: the houses in which the black girls live become all-black structures; the street where the black girls live has a 'dusk body'. He has black political consciousness: 'A continent sinks down', the 'new-world [black] Christ is coming up'. Muriel is a strikingly attractive black woman. Her hair 'curly and bushed and vagrant', the pale purple shadows on the planes of her cheeks, her orange dress bespeak her vitality. A schoolteacher in the city of Washington, she is a complex person. Like a disciple of Booker T. Washington, she knows her place, and like a follower of W. E. B. Du Bois, she has arrived and has status. She is also any girl of any colour wondering just how far she should go with her lover. On the one hand, she wants to blame him for being a 'timid lover, brave talker', on the other, she is afraid he might rape her. And perhaps she wants him to. They excite each other at Mrs Pribby's, and in the theatre she thinks, 'He makes me feel queer. Starts things he doesnt finish' (p. 62). Her thoughts are characteristic of the uncertainty of the relations between the sexes when each is unsure of what is going on in the other's mind. She longs not to see him because he irritates her. At the same time, she meditates 'If I love him, can I keep him out? Well then, I dont love him. Now he's out. Who is that coming in?' (p. 62). She is imagining intercourse with Dan as she sees him coming into the vaudeville theatre. He too is aroused. While she is asking him 'why don't you get a good job and settle down?' he is thinking: 'Same old line. Shoot it at me sister. Hell of a note, this loving business. For ten minutes of it you've got to stand the torment of an intolerable heaviness' (p. 59). But they exchange platitudes which have nothing to do with their strong physical awareness of each other. Dan thinks and speaks for all men in his position – disliking what the woman is, but finding her physically irresistible – when he says: 'Drag me in with you. Dirty me. Prop me in your brass box seat. . . . He-slave.' He cannot help himself, though he is disgusted at Muriel's behaviour in the theatre. She is bourgeois, she is inhibited, she is a slave to convention, she is everything he despises.

But if there are things in 'Box-Seat' to which the concept of colour is irrelevant, there are things to which the concept of colour is vital, in both content and effect. There is the image of the narrator himself, the dreaming nigger, who wants blacks to dream of a new, God-given world, just as the whites had done in seventeenth-century America. He adjures himself in terms assertive of race to revivify the lives of those passive blacks who are withering away. He speaks to them and to himself when he says, 'Shake your curled wool-blossoms, nigger. Open your liver lips to the lean, white spring.' He is the average black who has to cope with a world in which the police are always trying to pin a crime on him. He is the above-average spokesman for the submerged, repressed race on the American continent, who hears from a streetcar a subterranean threat, as from the 'underground railway' which had taken blacks to freedom before the abolition of slavery – who has a sense of blacks rising, in every sense, social, political and religious. The blacks are the rooted people, salt of the earth, the savour, the saviour, the new strength of America. They, the buried people, will be resurrected, will resurrect. Towards the end of the extract Dan affirms the 'soil-soaked fragrance' of the portly Negress sitting next to him. The black woman – his revelation in the South – here represents a positive and admirable life force.

> Through the cement floor her strong roots sink down. They spread under the asphalt streets. Dreaming, the streets roll over on their bellies, and suck their glossy health from them. Her strong roots sink down and spread under the river and disappear in blood-lines that waver south.

Waver – because the Negro's destiny must be played out where the power is.

It is by an affirmation of this woman and of the dismal plight and outcast status of his race that Dan frees himself from Muriel. At the conclusion of a boxing match between two dwarfs (part of the vaudeville entertainment), Muriel shrinks as one of the dwarfs offers her, as a matador offers a bull's ear, a rose which is stained with his nosebleed. The ugly mood of the crowd forces her to take it. She cannot at first see the kinship between the stunted black race and the dwarf: have nots both. When the realization is forced on her, she 'sees black', says Toomer. She sees, but we know she is going to do her best to forget what she sees. 'JESUS WAS ONCE A LEPER!' shouts Dan, and his passion for Muriel leaves him. 'He is as cool as a green stem that has shed its flower' (p. 66).

It is vital that Toomer should choose a circus-like freak show for the denouement of 'Box-Seat'. He wants to sustain the grotesqueness of the story, and he does not simply want to set Dan's assertion of common humanity against Muriel's diffidence and elitism (she dislikes, even fears, the dense mass of people in the theatre and in the world outside). Toomer wants support for Dan from the audience, from the race. For instead of preaching a sophisticated New Negro, which was what the Harlem Renaissance did, Toomer preaches the primitive old one, the old one seen and analysed and presented from a fresh, frank and validating perpective. Toomer dislikes traditional black passivity; he dislikes old taboos and superstitions (and Muriel has bourgeois ones – this or that cannot be done or else . . .). He loves the black ability to move and to be moved, the sense of compassion and community, the physical assertiveness, the spontaneity, the outpouring of religious fervour. He wants an educational system which incorporates these qualities, not one which, as in Muriel's case, does its best to exclude them. He sees the Negro in the 1920s at the point of opportunity and definition. He is at once trying to get away from the stereotypes and to recognize the element of truth in them. Thus he chooses the black mammy, the image of placidity and quiescence, whose eyes show her to be unconscious of her potential, as the symbol of the revolution.

There are touches not only of surrealism in 'Box-Seat' but of the absurd (the disappearing bell) and of comic-strip pop art. 'In . . . [my] right hand will be a dynamo – In . . . [my] left, a god's face that will flash white light from ebony. I'll grab a girder and swing it like a walking-stick,' fantasizes Dan, towards the end of the story (p. 65). A Cubist picture springs out in the paragraph beginning 'People came in slowly'. Toomer creates overlapping planes of blue, crimson, rose, purple and orange as Muriel comes into the theatre and takes her seat. Expressionism – which entails communication of inner experience through the free representation of objective facts – is present too. Dan, the lusty man, the black man whom whites see as more animal than human, the reformer conscious of threatening the black middle class, feels that to others he is 'Jack the Ripper. Baboon from the zoo', and retaliates in kind. 'Give me your fingers and I will peel them as if they were ripe bananas.' But most of all, Toomer uses surrealistic imagery, imagery which expresses the workings of the subconscious mind, which juxtaposes incongruous and startling objects, which transfers the qualities usually associated with one person or object to another. Thus Dan's subconscious responds to inhibition and restriction and conformity by seeing chairs bolting themselves to people, houses bolting themselves to their inhabitants and vice versa:

> There is a sharp click as she [Mrs. Pribby] fits into her chair and draws it to the table. The click is metallic like the sound of a bolt being shot into place. . . . The house contracts about him. It is a sharp-edged, massed, metallic house. Bolted. About Mrs. Pribby. Bolted to the endless rows of metal houses. Mrs. Pribby's house. The rows of houses belong to other Mrs. Pribbys. No wonder he couldn't sing to them.

The steel bullet of Mrs Pribby's eye is a surrealistic image, and so is that of Christ re-entering a nightmarish world of disordered elements and trying, in Toomer's image, 'to walk upon the waters where huge bubbles burst'. Almost everything that Dan imagines has a surrealistic dimension. Even the portly Negress turns into a tree; her roots then become breasts which the streets suck. The anti-realism beneath the realistic surface and the shocking incongruities of 'Box-Seat' startle us into questioning what we see, how we see and how we interpret; they jolt us into recognition of the experimental art with which Toomer so successfully explores and expresses the processes and layers of consciousness.

'"Box-Seat" muddles me to the last degree,' wrote W. E. B. Du Bois.[5] Not surprisingly. How could the talented Toomer prefer Dan and the dwarf to Muriel and Mrs Pribby? Du Bois's theory prevented him from seeing that in Dan Moore Toomer has created a character who almost makes revolution, even bloody revolution, seem desirable – a sensitive, sensuous man capable of a controlled fantasy life, capable of creating and using symbols through which he can exalt and deflate himself, reformist, race proud. Dan Moore and Toomer, too, live life with all their faculties. While they have a freedom of mind and mood and movement not inaccurately associated with blacks, and while their style and perception and imagination and expression derive from blackness and a response to blackness, they are men and artists as well as black men and black artists. In the black literature of the period no other writer and no other character spoke so effectively for the black man and for the black as a man.

Notes

1 Jean Toomer, *Cane*, ed. Darwin T. Turner, New York, 1975 (originally published 1923). All quotations from *Cane* are taken from this edition and, unless noted otherwise in textual parentheses, from pages 56–63.
2 Quoted in Turner, Introduction to *Cane*, xvi.
3 ibid., xxi.
4 ibid., xvi.
5 W. E. B. Du Bois, 'The younger literary movement', in Frank Durham (ed.), *The Merrill Studies in 'Cane'*, Columbus, Ohio, 1971, 42.

Further reading

Durham, Frank (ed.), *The Merrill Studies in 'Cane'*, Columbus, Ohio, 1971.

Franklin, John Hope, *From Slavery to Freedom*, New York, 1956.
Huggins, Nathan, *The Harlem Renaissance in American Letters*, New York and Oxford, 1971.
Turner, Darwin T., Introduction to *Cane*, New York, 1975.

10

H. L. Mencken (1880–1956)

Has it been duly marked by historians that the late William Jennings Bryan's last secular act on this globe of sin was to catch flies? A curious detail, and not without its sardonic overtones. He was the most sedulous flycatcher in American history, and in many ways the most successful. His quarry, of course, was not *Musca domestica* but *Homo neandertalensis*. For forty years he tracked it with coo and bellow, up and down the rustic backways of the Republic. Wherever the flambeaux of Chautauqua smoked and guttered, and the bilge of Idealism ran in the veins, and Baptist pastors dammed the brooks with the sanctified, and men gathered who were weary and heavy laden, and their wives who were full of Peruna and as fecund as the shad (*Alosa sapidissima*) – there the indefatigable Jennings set up his traps and spread his bait. He knew every country town in the South and West, and he could crowd the most remote of them to suffocation by simply winding his horn. The city proletariat, transiently flustered by him in 1896, quickly penetrated his buncombe and would have no more of him; the cockney gallery jeered him at every Democratic national convention for twenty-five years. But out where the grass grows high, and the horned cattle dream away the lazy afternoons, and men still fear the powers and principalities of the air – out there between the corn-rows he held his old puissance to the end. There was no need of beaters to drive in his game. The news that he was coming was enough. For miles the flivver dust would choke the roads. And when he rose at the end of the day to discharge his Message there would be such breathless attention, such a rapt and enchanted ecstasy, such a sweet rustle of amens as the world had not known since Johann fell to Herod's ax.

There was something peculiarly fitting in the fact that his last days were spent in a one-horse Tennessee village, and that death found him there. The man felt at home in such simple and Christian scenes. He liked people who sweated freely, and were not debauched by the refinements of the toilet. Making his progress up and down the Main street of little Dayton, surrounded by gaping primates from the upland valleys of the Cumberland Range, his coat laid aside, his bare arms and hairy chest shining damply, his bald head sprinkled with dust – so accoutred and on display he was obviously happy. He liked getting up early in the morning, to the tune of cocks crowing on the dunghill. He liked the heavy, greasy victuals of the farmhouse kitchen. He liked country lawyers, country pastors, all country people. He liked the country sounds and country smells. I believe that this liking was sincere – perhaps the only sincere thing in the man. His nose showed no uneasiness when a hillman in faded overalls and hickory shirt accosted him on the street, and besought him for light upon some mystery of Holy Writ. The simian gabble of the cross-roads was not gabble to him, but wisdom of an occult and superior sort. In the presence of city folks he was palpably uneasy. Their clothes, I suspect, annoyed him, and he was suspicious of their too delicate manners. He knew all the while that they were laughing at him – if not at his baroque theology, then at least at his alpaca pantaloons. But the yokels never laughed at him. To them he was not the huntsman but the prophet, and toward the end, as he gradually forsook mundane politics for more ghostly concerns, they began to elevate him in their hierarchy. When he died he was the peer of Abraham. His old enemy, Wilson, aspiring to the same white and shining robe, came down with a thump. But Bryan made the grade. His place in Tennessee hagiography is secure. If the village barber saved any of his hair, then it is curing gall-stones down there to-day. . . .

If the fellow was sincere, then so was P. T. Barnum. The word is disgraced and degraded by such uses. He was, in fact, a charlatan, a mountebank, a zany without shame or dignity. His career brought him into contact with the first men of his time; he preferred the company of rustic ignoramuses. It was hard to believe, watching him at Dayton, that he had traveled, that he had been received in civilized societies, that he had been a high officer of state. He seemed only a poor clod like those around him, deluded by a childish theology, full of an almost pathological hatred of all learning, all human dignity, all beauty, all fine and noble things. He was a peasant come home to the barnyard. Imagine a gentleman, and you have imagined everything that he was not. What animated him from end to end of his grotesque career was simply ambition – the ambition of a common man to get his hand upon the collar of his superiors, or, failing that, to get his thumb into their eyes. . . . What moved him, at bottom, was simply hatred of the city men who had laughed at him so long, and brought him at last to so tatterdemalion an estate. He lusted for revenge upon them. He yearned to lead the anthropoid rabble against them. . . .

Hour by hour he grew more bitter. What the Christian Scientists call malicious animal magnetism seemed to radiate from him like heat from a stove. From my place in the courtroom, standing upon a table, I looked directly down upon him, sweating horribly and pumping his palm-leaf fan. His eyes fascinated me; I watched them all day long. They were blazing points of hatred. They glittered like occult and sinister gems. Now and then they wandered to me, and I got my share, for my reports of the trial had come back to Dayton, and he had read them. It was like coming under fire.

Thus he fought his last fight, thirsting savagely for blood. All sense departed from him. He bit right and left, like a dog with rabies. He descended to demagogy so dreadful that his very associates at the trial table blushed. His one yearning was to keep his yokels heated up – to lead his forlorn mob of imbeciles against the foe. That foe, alas, refused to be alarmed. It insisted upon seeing the whole battle as a comedy. Even Darrow, who knew better, occasionally yielded to the prevailing spirit. One day he lured poor Bryan into the folly I have mentioned: his astounding argument against the notion that man is a mammal. I am glad I heard it, for otherwise I'd never believe in it. There stood the man who had been thrice a candidate for the Presidency of the Republic – there he stood in the glare of the world, uttering stuff that a boy of eight would laugh at! The artful Darrow led him on: he [Bryan] repeated it, ranted for it, bellowed it in his cracked voice. So he was prepared for the final slaughter. He came into life a hero, a Galahad, in bright and shining armor. He was passing out a poor mountebank. . . .

Bryan, in his malice, has started something. . . . Heave an egg out of a Pullman window, and you will hit a Fundamentalist almost everywhere in the United States to-day. They swarm in the country towns, inflamed by their *shamans*, and with a saint, now, to venerate. They are thick in the mean streets behind the gas-works. They are everywhere where learning is too heavy a burden for mortal minds to carry, even the vague, pathetic learning on tap in little red schoolhouses. They march with the Klan, with the Christian Endeavor Society, with the Junior Order of United American Mechanics, with the Epworth League, with all the rococo bands that poor and unhappy folk organize to bring some light of purpose into their lives. They have had a thrill, and they are ready for more.

'In Memoriam, W.J.B.', from *Prejudices, Fifth Series* (1926)[1]

* * *

H. L. Mencken, journalist, literary critic and savage satirist, once wrote of his work:

> There is something delightful about getting an idea on paper while it is still hot and charming, and seeing it in print before it begins to pale and stale. My happiest days have been spent in crowded press-stands, recording and belaboring events that were portentous in their day, but are now forgotten. These recordings usually died with the events.[2]

But his piece on the veteran American politician William Jennings Bryan, published the day after Bryan's death, has rightly survived as an important piece of writing for political and cultural historians and for literary critics. Not only does it represent, at their most effective, Mencken's acidulous style and the eclectic American language he used so dextrously; it pictures the hardening polarization of ideals and values in American life in the third decade of the century, a polarization summed up by the proceedings at Dayton, Tennessee, and by Mencken's reaction to them. Free speech was set against censorship, the intellect against the emotions, the agnostic against the fundamental Christian, science against religion, North against South, East against West. Almost all of the great Mencken's classic targets, as he categorized them in *A Mencken Chrestomathy*, were in range at Dayton: 'Homo Sapiens, types of men, religion, morals, death, Crime and punishment, Government, Democracy, Americans, the South, History, Statesmen, American Immortals, Odd Fish, Economics, Pedagogy, Psychology, Science, Quackery.'[3] 'In Memoriam: W.J.B.' also offers an unsurpassed example of that American journalism which, in its mixture of the formal and the colloquial, is an art form in itself. None was more appropriate to a time when communications – car, plane, radio, silent movie, increasingly used telephones and increasingly available national newspapers – were reshaping America.

The occasion for Mencken's essay was the 'Monkey' trial of Tennessee schoolteacher John T. Scopes on the charge of teaching the theory of evolution in the high school system in Dayton, Tennessee. Bryan, who had effectively retired from active politics in 1916, had turned his attention to religion and morals; and in tract and book, on the lecture platform and in the pulpit, he had become the country's foremost exponent of Fundamentalism, a creed which taught that every word in the Bible was literally true. Thus the account of Creation in Genesis – by God, in seven days – was not to be questioned. Human beings were not descended from monkeys, and thus Darwin and all who circulated his theory of evolution were doing devil's work. Bryan had been largely responsible for framing the Tennessee anti-evolution statute which made it illegal to teach 'any theory that denies the story of the divine creation of man as taught in the Bible and to teach instead that man has descended from a lower order of animals',[4] and he had helped to get it on the statute books. The Dayton case was the first time the right to teach about evolution in the schools had been tested in the courts, and it was a set-piece trial, for the American Civil Liberties Union had put up John Scopes to test the law. Scopes, a physical education instructor temporarily substituting for the biology teacher, admitted after the trial that though he was using a textbook which dealt with evolution, he could not remember whether he had used that section of the book in class! Mencken was one of hundreds of reporters and thousands of spectators who converged on Dayton in the hot summer which drove the trial out of the courthouse onto the slightly cooler lawns outside. The trial thus became an intensely public spectacle, with prosecutors and defenders virtually rubbing shoulders with salesmen hawking monkey souvenirs along Main Street and with pretty girls wearing badges inscribed 'you can't make a monkey out of me'. Mencken reported the trial for the *Baltimore Evening Sun* (his journalistic alma mater), for his own magazine, the *American Mercury* – marvellously hospitable to new ideas and new writing – and also for the radio station, WGN Chicago. The trial proceedings were broadcast over all America's radio stations; the movie newsreel cameras were present too. It was the first time the literal truth of the Old Testament, and by implication the New, had been so widely and so publicly called into question. A good deal was at stake, for many Christians who could reconcile Darwinism and Christianity felt that to 'teach' evolution was to undermine ethical traditions and widely held religious beliefs, and might open the door to all kinds of unsuitable subjects in school curricula. Equally, many of those who disagreed with Darwin felt obliged to champion freedom of speech. Everything that Bryan, the South and the West, rural America and traditional Christianity stood for seemed to be on trial; everything that Mencken, the North and the

East, the city and independent thought represented seemed either threatening or threatened. The national debate was on.

Bryan came to Dayton to defend the statute; and although on legal grounds he won the case, his ability to defend his faith was terribly punished. History was made: a vast American audience witnessed, through the media, the public annihilation of a human being (McCarthy and Nixon were to follow). The annihilator was Clarence Darrow, a Chicago civil rights lawyer, an agnostic and a contributor to Mencken's *American Mercury* who, a few months before the trial, had published a piece there on the irrational appeal of salesmanship. He, Darrow, dealt in the rational, the specific, the empirically verifiable. It was apt and ironic that the newfangled city man crucified the Nebraska country boy, for Bryan had argued at the end of the nineteenth century that rural America and the Midwest in particular were about to be 'crucified' by Wall Street and the restrictive eastern monetary policy on a 'Cross of Gold', as his most famous speech phrased it.

It was as a country boy, speaking for and to country people, that Bryan came to fame, and became a midwestern folk hero. Originally a journalist for the *Omaha World-Herald* – an appropriately evangelistic title – Bryan served as a mesmeric Chautauqua orator (Chautauqua was a summer school, adult education programme) and then went into politics. He was unexpectedly adopted as the Democratic candidate for President in Chicago in 1896, where, as a Nebraska delegate, he eloquently and charismatically advocated the free coinage of silver, plentiful in the West, to redeem the country from East Coast capitalism. Although he lost the election and never became President, he remained a striking and admired figure in Democratic politics, and was tolerated if not liked by the Republicans. He led the Democratic party until 1912, and became for a short while Woodrow Wilson's Secretary of State. Bryan's supporters defended his apparently inconsistent policies – one moment he was for imperialism, the next against it – by arguing, with some justice, that he was an emotional man, easily swayed by other people in matters where he was less than sure of himself. He was too willing to take advice – in all matters except religious ones, where he was inflexible. As for his religion, they argued, that was 'a good faith too blindly held and too uncritically applied'.[5]

But it did not matter to Mencken that the faith was good, that Bryan was an honest man; what was any faith, any credo but hostile to progress. Intellectual flabbiness and a lack of critical faculty damned Bryan for him. Bryan was a 'clod', a 'zany', a 'charlatan', a mere actor who mouthed panaceas and platitudes. Mencken doubted he believed them, but dubbed him a fool if he did. And for Mencken stupidity was no less a sin than dishonesty, and perhaps more so. He was a man who spoke for the intellect with the intellect. Bryan's success in public life – three times a presidential candidate and always attracting a large following – was for Mencken extraordinary proof that

> we live in a land of abounding quackeries. . . . I have witnessed, in my day, the discovery, enthronement and subsequent collapse of a vast army of uplifters and world-savers, and am firmly convinced that all of them were mountebanks. We produce such mountebanks in greater number than any other country, and they climb to heights seldom equalled elsewhere.[6]

Bryan was not unique. Mencken was appalled.

Such was Mencken's hostility to everything that Bryan represented that he put the worst possible interpretation on whatever Bryan did or said or seemed. Mencken attributed a kind of obscene ingratiation to Bryan's clothing: 'the preposterous country shirt that he wore – sleeveless, and with the neck cut very low'. He could not admit to any sincerity in the man.

> What animated him from end to end of his grotesque career was simply ambition – the ambition of a common man to get his hand upon the collar of his superiors, or, failing that, to get his thumb into their eyes.

Bryan was using the Scopes trial for petty reasons:

> What moved him at bottom was simply hatred of the city men who had laughed at him so long, and brought him at last to so tatterdemalion an estate. He lusted for revenge upon them. He yearned to lead the anthropoid rabble against them.

Both charges were almost certainly untrue: principle – belief in the simple life and the virtues of simple people – rather than ambitious and vindictive calculation was the hallmark of Bryan's political life. His 'malice' was apparent only to Mencken.

The virulence of Mencken's reaction to Bryan indicates how crucial, how close to home for him and for the intellectuals he represented were the issues and the ramifications of the Scopes trial. To Mencken the trial embodied the age-old split in America between fine political theory (the liberties of the people to write, read, teach and speak) and hypocritical political practice (Bryan's attempt to restrict these freedoms and his tyranny over the mob), between intellectual advance and the anti-intellectual assertion that God's infinite wisdom and man's finite capacity were clearly set out in the Bible, between the progressive, experimental life of the city and the unchanging, stagnant life of the country, between speculative, radical North and complacent, conservative South. Tennessee was part of a South which Mencken christened the 'Bible Belt', a region with no terms of reference except debilitating Christian myth, a place where people walked, talked, ate and slept religion. Culturally it deserved to be nicknamed 'the Sahara of the Bozart' (Beaux Arts), for since the Civil War, Mencken contended, the South had not produced a single orchestra, a single painting or a single public building of distinction.

Mencken saw no merit in natural things. For him man was by definition the creature who pushed his faculties and the universe to their limits. The simplicity and innocence which Bryan liked in people and with which he interpreted scripture – like many Fundamentalists he believed he could calculate the year, month and day of Creation – infuriated Mencken, who believed in education, cultivation and sophistication. When he looked at Bryan and his followers he despaired of America, and consequently attacked their simplicity with all the abusive power at his disposal, well displayed in the second paragraph of the essay. Not that Mencken saw much more in the typical northerner, a have-not, than in the typical southerner, a smelly yokel. The bourgeoisie was apathetic and mediocre: Mencken coined the word 'Booboisie' to describe that class. What he deemed President Harding's carelessness and President Coolidge's vacuity were barely superior to Bryan's Fundamentalism.

If life *was* more bearable in America than elsewhere, it was still remarkably unsatisfactory. Democracy blundered along; culture continued lowbrow. The passing show, however, provided entertainment. For Mencken, the role Bryan played, the figure he cut, the fact of the trial and the bizarre yet culturally inevitable spectacle that it presented were at once symptomatic of the despairing fun to be derived from almost everything in American life and of the dangers implicit in the kind of Middle American constituency which a Mississippi Valley folk hero-cum-revivalist statesman could command in spite of being made a laughing stock, perhaps because he was intellectually discredited. The simple majority viewpoint had to be reckoned with. Bryan and his followers were a threat to the quintessential American ideas of liberty and progress and were not to be underestimated. If 'Jennings' was 'the most sedulous fly-catcher in American history' – uncouth, credulous, mouth wide open, preferring the company of gaping rural ignoramuses to Woodrow Wilson's cabinet, from which he had resigned in 1915 – he had also left behind him what Mencken saw as a legacy of evil: a host of faithful Fundamentalist followers, unacceptably literal, unacceptably simple, eager for purpose and direction, dangerously subject to mob oratory. They were Klansmen in the making, and so numerous on the ground that 'Heave an egg out of a Pullman window' and you will hit one. Mencken had some cause for concern. Fundamentalism had made modest gains after the war, strengthened by popular anger against Germany (associated with 'modernist' religion) and by the post-Russian Revolution 'Red Scare' in America (atheism was linked with communism). The times *were* isolationist and anti-intellectual.

Bryan too had been profoundly affected by the mood of the 1920s. Though he believed in the people, though he edited a newspaper called *The Commoner* and was known as 'The Great Commoner', he found himself anachronistic in the period. He continued to champion political and economic reform in a period of Republican conservatism, prohibition in an age of hedonism and Fundamentalism in an age of scientific and technological achievement. The man who believed in the ballot box, the anti-intellectual who believed that wisdom was intuitive, who put heart above head and instinct above education, who, in the words of a not unsympathetic commentator, 'interpreted the voice of the ballot box as the voice of God',[7] found it hard to stomach the shallow indulgences of the 1920s. He found himself hoist with the petard of the Protestant ethic, believing as he did that success was a demonstration of goodness.

Given increasingly to introspection in the 1920s Bryan seems to have anticipated disaster at the trial. He had even wanted to avoid the subject of evolution.

> I am not sure that it is the question of evolution that is involved – the right of the people speaking through the legislature, to control the schools which they create and support is the real issue as I see it. The right of the State to have jurisdiction over its schools, the right of the people through the school board to decide what might be taught.[8]

And he had begun to wonder whether man might have 'brute' tendencies.

> He [man] is either restrained by the consciousness of the ties of kinship and feels toward him as a brother, or he hunts for prey with the savage loathing of a beast. . . . I believe that the fundamental question that the people of the world have got to ask and answer is whether man is to be a brother or a brute.[9]

Before the trial Bryan had delivered a widely circulated lecture on 'The Menace of Darwinism', and even in that lecture it was evident that he was taking seriously the concept of the survival of the fittest, Herbert Spencer's social corollary to Darwinism. If there were any truth in Spencer's theory, what respect could one have for a God who allowed the strongest, the most adaptable to prevail? Where was God's compassion in all this? If virtue was rewarded and evil punished, was weakness evil? Was goodness merely strength and survival?

Mencken caught the confusion, the onset of anguish in Bryan's voice: 'What was once a bugle blast' (a silver tongue, journalists had once punned), 'had become reedy and quavering.' A slight lisp had become more pronounced. Mencken saw Bryan's inability to control himself. Under Darrow's questioning Bryan found himself denying that man is a mammal and 'he repeated it, ranted for it, bellowed it in his cracked voice'. Bryan was on the verge of madness, thought Mencken, for he knew that he was trapped, unable to prove what he believed. 'He bit right and left, like a dog with rabies.' His eyes were 'occult and sinister gems'. Mencken captured the distress Bryan tried so hard to hide as he moved towards his fatal admission, conceding that when the Bible said the world had been created in six days, it did not necessarily mean that a 'day' was twenty-four hours long; it might be a million years. As William Leuchtenberg aptly comments, 'thus Bryan, whose position was grounded on the conviction that the Bible must be read literally, had himself interpreted the Bible', thereby destroying the case for Fundamentalism.[10]

There is an excessiveness, a kind of madness in Mencken's own denunciation of Bryan. Perhaps because he feared that America was the Bryan – the simpleton, the smug one – among the nations, that Bryan was, as the *Chicago Tribune* called him in 1920, 'the normal American citizen'.[11] The outrageous manner in which Mencken stated his case against Bryan was characteristic. Aggressive iconoclasm was his forte and his philosophy; character assassination was habitual with him. He saw words as weapons, and he believed in using to the full the unique characteristics of the American language. His witty and learned book, *The American Language* (1919), remains authoritative. As George Douglas says:

> In Mencken's mind the freedom to play with language, to mingle the talk of a streetcar conductor or an ice wagon driver with that of a professor of classics is a distinctly American prerogative and distinctly American achievement. He would have agreed with George Orwell that one of the best features of the American language is that it can be used freely without crossing any class barriers.[12]

No one demonstrated better than Mencken the flexibility and the eclecticism of the language. The first part of a sentence would be couched in elegant and formal prose using conventional language and conventional images; the second part would provide a deflationary contrast by introducing another kind of image, another kind of language, a contrasting cadence. The first sentence of the essay provides a good example: 'Has it been duly marked by historians that the late William Jennings Bryan's last secular act on this globe of sin was to catch flies?' What a devastating anti-climax, with its comic image of Bryan pumping his palm leaf fan and a savage image of him on his death-bed, mouth open. 'He was born with a roaring voice and it had the trick of inflaming half-wits' is another example of a sentence which starts us off in one direction and delivers us in another. A fine instance of Mencken's ingenuity with the tones and shades of language and vocabulary comes in his description of Bryan's stump speeches. He makes the scene sound like a shoot, with Bryan in search of game; he also makes it sound like an American revivalist camp meeting. He recalls America's German immigrant stock of which he, Mencken, was a part, and by the devastating if malicious biblical parallel he chooses, he beats at their own game the American Christians who pepper their conversations with religious references. He reminds us, in his reference to the flivver, the small car of the period, that this extraordinary scene was enacted in the 1920s.

> There was no need of beaters to drive in his game. The news that he was coming was enough. For miles the flivver dust would choke the roads. And when he rose at the end of the day to discharge his Message there would be such breathless attention, such a rapt and enchanted ecstasy, such a sweet rustle of amens as the world had not known since Johann [Mencken's affectionate Germanic term for John the Baptist] fell to Herod's ax.

In Mencken's skilful hands any undermining of rhetoric was an undermining of Bryan the orator, and any Christian references undermined Christianity. So too Mencken used the mode and images of folklore to undercut Bryan and his credulous followers: 'If the village barber saved any of his hair, then it is curing gall-stones down there to-day.'

In vocabulary and style Mencken mixed the formal, the learned and the colloquial. Thus we have 'sedulous' set against 'flycatcher', 'bilge' against 'idealism', 'baroque theology' against 'alpaca pantaloons', 'inscrutable gods' against 'the smell of cabbage burning'. A saint and some shamans are found 'thick in the mean streets behind the gas-works'. Having emphasized images of the cowboy – 'out where the grass grows high, and the horned cattle dream' – Mencken concludes: 'out there between the corn-rows he [Bryan] held his old puissance to the end'.

Mencken taunts Bryan and his followers by maliciously likening them to apes and other animals – thus suggesting the validity of Darwin's thesis. We see Bryan tracking truth 'with coo and bellow', Bryan with 'bare arms and hairy chest' surrounded by other 'gaping primates', and the whole 'anthropoid rabble' indulging in the 'simian gabble of the cross-roads'.

'In Memoriam: W.J.B.' is a clever, savage, comic, marvellously observed, brilliantly dense piece, with every word precisely chosen and placed. The piece is as much a revelation of Mencken as of Bryan, and a revelation of how to exploit the rich resources of an eclectic and innovative language. (Douglas points out that as with the composition of the American people, not every word comes out of the same bin.)[13] All this and a passionate eloquence too. Bryan was 'deluded by a childish theology, full of an almost pathological hatred of all learning, all human dignity, all beauty, all fine and noble things,' writes Mencken.

Mencken's hostility to Bryan and his advocacy of Darwinism was predictable from his literary preferences. He liked such varied realistic writers as Sherwood Anderson, Sinclair Lewis and James Branch Cabell; he valued most highly Theodore Dreiser, whose novel, *An American Tragedy*, published the year of the Scopes trial, constituted a fictional exploration of the survival of the fittest. He also liked – paradoxically – the Illinois poet Vachel Lindsay, who, unlike Mencken, wanted to bring art to the people and who attempted to write in a style which retained art whilst achieving a kind of popular comprehensibility. Mencken's Bryan essay seems to have been written with Lindsay's fine poem, 'Bryan, Bryan, Bryan, Bryan' (1916), in mind. Bryan, huntsman or prophet, asks Mencken; 'In a coat like a deacon, with a black Stetson hat,' writes Lindsay. Like P. T. Barnum, the circus impresario, fumes Mencken; 'All the funny circus silks / Of politics unfurled,' applauds Lindsay. Mencken's 'simian gabble' is Lindsay's 'truths eternal in the gab and tittle-tattle', and he elaborates the 'childish theology' of Mencken as 'the ultimate fantastics / Of the far western slope / And of prairie schooner children'. Bryan the charlatan, asserts Mencken; Bryan the magician, chants Lindsay.

> He brought in tides of wonder, of unprecedented splendor,
> Wild roses from the plains, that made hearts tender . . .
> Bartlett pears of romance that were honey at the cores,
> And torchlights down the streets, to the end of the world.[14]

Lindsay regrets but accepts as inevitable the defeat of what Bryan stood for. The sophisticated Republican political machine was too much for the simple man. Mencken rejoices in the defeat, but is not sure it is decisive enough. His essay conveys his belief in the continuing dialectic between one man's vision of America and another's, and his sense of the undiminishing polarizations in American life.

Bryan's defeat did not sound the death knell of what he represented, though it diminished him for numbers of people. Darrow's skill did not turn Christians into agnostics, though it made many think again. The Scopes trial settled nothing; it was a moment in American life when two strong and opposed realities dramatically confronted each other and proved irreconcilable. It was clear that the twentieth century, materialistic, scientific, sceptical, sophisticated, was not going to have things all its own way.

Notes

1 H. L. Mencken, *Prejudices, Fifth Series*, New York, 1926. All quotations from 'In Memoriam: W.J.B.' are taken from this edition and, unless noted otherwise in textual parentheses, from pages 64–74.
2 H. L. Mencken, *A Mencken Chrestomathy*, New York, 1962, vii.
3 ibid., ix–xvi.
4 Lawrence W. Levine, *Defender of the Faith: William Jennings Bryan, The Last Decade, 1915–25*, New York, 1965, 326.
5 ibid., 365
6 Mencken, *A Mencken Chrestomathy*, op. cit., vii.
7 Levine, op. cit., 224.

8 ibid., 331.
9 ibid., 243.
10 William E. Leuchtenberg, *The Perils of Prosperity, 1914–32*, Chicago, 1958, 222–3.
11 Quoted in Levine, op. cit., 218.
12 George H. Douglas, *Henry Louis Mencken: Critic of American Life*, Hamden, Conn., 1978, 64.
13 ibid., 65.
14 Vachel Lindsay, *Collected Poems*, New York, 1962, 96–105.

Further reading

Douglas, George H., *Henry Louis Mencken: Critic of American Life*, Hamden, Conn., 1978. Illuminating analysis of Mencken's style.
Kemler, Edgar, *The Irreverent Mr. Mencken*, Boston, 1950.
Levine, Lawrence W., *Defender of the Faith: William Jennings Bryan, The Last Decade, 1915–25*, New York, 1965.
Lindsay, Vachel, 'Bryan, Bryan, Bryan, Bryan', *Collected Poems*, New York, 1923.
Mencken, H. L., *A Mencken Chrestomathy*, New York, 1949.

11

F. Scott Fitzgerald (1896–1940)

I stayed late that night, Gatsby asked me to wait until he was free, and I lingered in the garden until the inevitable swimming party had run up, chilled and exalted, from the black beach, until the lights were extinguished in the guest-rooms overhead. When he came down the steps at last the tanned skin was drawn unusually tight on his face, and his eyes were bright and tired.

'She didn't like it,' he said immediately.

'Of course she did.'

'She didn't like it,' he insisted. 'She didn't have a good time.'

He was silent, and I guessed at his unutterable depression.

'I feel far away from her,' he said. 'It's hard to make her understand.'

'You mean about the dance?'

'The dance?' He dismissed all the dances he had given with a snap of his fingers. 'Old sport, the dance is unimportant.'

He wanted nothing less of Daisy than that she should go to Tom and say: 'I never loved you.' After she had obliterated four years with that sentence they could decide upon the more practical measures to be taken. One of them was that, after she was free, they were to go back to Louisville and be married from her house – just as if it were five years ago.

'And she doesn't understand,' he said. 'She used to be able to understand. We'd sit for hours—'

He broke off and began to walk up and down a desolate path of fruit rinds and discarded favors and crushed flowers.

'I wouldn't ask too much of her,' I ventured. 'You can't repeat the past.'

'Can't repeat the past?' he cried incredulously. 'Why of course you can!'

He looked around him wildly, as if the past were lurking here in the shadow of his house, just out of reach of his hand.

'I'm going to fix everything just the way it was before,' he said, nodding determinedly. 'She'll see.'

He talked a lot about the past, and I gathered that he wanted to recover something, some idea of himself perhaps, that had gone into loving Daisy. His life had been confused and disordered since then, but if he could once return to a certain starting place and go over it all slowly, he could find out what that thing was. . . .*

. . . One autumn night, five years before, they had been walking down the street when the leaves were falling, and they came to a place where there were no trees and the sidewalk was white with moonlight. They stopped here and turned toward each other. Now it was a cool night with that mysterious excitement in it which comes at the two changes of the year. The quiet lights in the houses were humming out into the darkness and there was a stir and bustle among the stars. Out of the corner of his eye Gatsby saw that the blocks of the sidewalks really formed a ladder and mounted to a secret place above the trees – he could climb to it, if he climbed alone, and once there he could suck on the pap of life, gulp down the incomparable milk of wonder.

His heart beat faster and faster as Daisy's white face came up to his own. He knew that when he kissed this girl, and forever wed his unutterable visions to her perishable breath, his mind would never romp again like the mind of God. So he waited, listening for a moment longer to the tuning-fork that had been struck upon a star. Then he kissed her. At his lips' touch she blossomed for him like a flower and the incarnation was complete.

Through all he said, even through his appalling sentimentality, I was reminded of something – an elusive rhythm, a fragment of lost words, that I had heard somewhere a long time ago. For a moment a phrase tried to take shape in my mouth and my lips parted like a dumb man's, as though there was more struggling upon them than a wisp of startled air. But they made no sound, and what I had almost remembered was uncommunicable forever.

The Great Gatsby (1925)[1]

* * *

Fitzgerald wrote that in his early adult life 'I saw the improbable, the implausible, often the "impossible", come true.'[2] But even while his

* Ellipses appear in the original text.

own short and dazzling career was taking its amazing shape in the early and mid 1920s, he sensed that the dark phenomenon of violence was around the corner. To him the age was one of excess, in which neurosis, suicide, insanity and murder in speak-easies underlay the accelerating observance of hedonism. His experience and perception of the hollowness of what he christened the 'Jazz Age' informed *The Great Gatsby*; so did his close study of the colourful and appalling corruption of Arnold Rothstein, a financier with one foot in Wall Street and the other in the underworld, and Edward M. Fuller, an eminent broker of mysterious origin and the first man to commute by air from Long Island to the Atlantic City racecourse.

But though there are elements of Rothstein and Fuller in Gatsby, and though Gatsby's financial and sexual morals are, like the decade's, fairly relaxed, he is more apart from the decade than of it. Not for Gatsby the Black Bottom or the Charleston. He dances an oldfashioned foxtrot with Daisy; he holds aloof from his own parties, merely observing the things which for other people constituted the essence of the 1920s: the cocktails, the syncopation of music and movement, the self-satisfied songs of the period – 'Ain't we got fun'. It is to Gatsby's credit that he does not, that he wants to build on his profound and 'heightened sensitivity to the promises of life'. *The Great Gatsby* is an acid and accurate picture of the modes and mores, the people and pleasures of the Jazz Age, with its 'Seize-the-Day' philosophy, so unlike Gatsby's marvellous affirmation of the richness of life in a smile that also conveys 'eternal reassurance' (p. 32). His difference and his death condemn the decade.

In the character of Jay Gatsby, Scott Fitzgerald creates a quintessential American dreamer, a man of great imagination, inordinate ambition, extraordinary hope and 'romantic readiness' (p. 2). These are the qualities which make him 'great', which set him apart from and above his contemporaries. Unquestionably Gatsby is corrupt. His wealth is derived from such shady operations as bootlegging. One of his associates 'fixed' the World's Series in 1919, and Gatsby carries the taint of public practice into private life to the extent of saying about his relationship with Daisy Fay, 'I'm going to fix everything just the way it was before.' He helps organize the sale of fraudulent securities, and it seems he has been involved in one of the biggest scandals of the 1920s, the Teapot Dome affair, in which enormous profits were made by the secret and illegal sale of oil-rich public land to private operators. But in the context of a society of cruel, aimless, cynical and superficial people, such corruption seems relatively insignificant. And it has, in Fitzgerald's eyes, a kind of justification in that Gatsby's ruthless amassing of wealth and its ostentatious employment is all with the view of achieving what his contemporaries would regard as ridiculous, naive and impossible, and what Fitzgerald regards as admirable and all too rare in a period which has no ideals beyond material satisfaction. Gatsby wants to wipe out the four-year-old marriage between the girl he loved and lost, Daisy Fay, and her husband, Tom Buchanan. He wants not merely to bring about a divorce but to obliterate what has happened, to change the course of history, to achieve the impossible. Even his sympathetic friend, Nick Carraway, the novel's narrator, tells him it is impossible. '"I wouldn't ask too much of her," I ventured. "You can't repeat the past."' At this point in the chapter we share Nick's reservations; by the end of the novel we have come to share his realization that Gatsby's impossible determination is the one thing left in America commensurate with that continent's capacity to engender belief in a limitless possibility. Fitzgerald has made the imperfect Gatsby the carrier of that pristine dream of excellence and perfectibility which, myth has it, and reality a little too, the American continent inspired in the early settlers. For all that Gatsby's dream is flawed in its corrupt modes and its inadequate embodiment, for all that it involves a perversion of the traditional values of stable marriage and ethical business practice, it demonstrates a sensitivity to the possibilities of life on the American continent that precedes Gatsby's meeting with Daisy Fay – at seventeen he was responding to 'hint[s] of the unreality of reality' (p. 65) – and which transcends his relationship with her. The first line of the novel's epigraph – 'Then wear the gold hat, if that will move her' (p. i) – almost suggests that Gatsby's ends justify his means.

Gatsby's imaginative demand of Daisy reflects the original, ambitious response of 'Americans' to America: nothing less than that the past (the Old World, Daisy's marriage) should be discarded and history begin anew. As the historian Daniel J. Boorstin has so eloquently commented:

> America has been a land of dreams. A land where the aspirations of people from countries cluttered with rich, cumbersome, aristocratic, ideological pasts can reach for what once seemed unattainable. Here they have tried to make dreams come true. The American Dream was the most accurate way of describing the hopes of men in . . . a country where the impossible was thought only slightly less attainable than the difficult.[3]

But by the 1920s only Gatsby sees America with the seventeenth-century explorers' eyes as a land of fresh promise and infinite possibility. It is Gatsby who comes nearest to embodying the American spirit so aptly defined by Frederick Jackson Turner as

> that coarseness and strength combined with acuteness and inquisitiveness; that practical, inventive turn of mind, quick to find expedients; that masterful grasp of material things, lacking in the artistic but powerful to effect great ends; that restless, nervous energy; that dominant individualism, working for good and for evil, and withal, that buoyancy and exuberance which comes with freedom.[4]

In memorializing Gatsby's uniqueness as the last frontiersman and dreamer, Fitzgerald indicts a society which can neither accommodate nor comprehend such a man. In setting up a vulgar and unethical man as relatively if not absolutely good, the best man of his time in fact – 'Gatsby turned out all right' (p. 2) and 'you're worth the whole damn bunch put together' (p. 103), says Nick Carraway, whose words carry great force because he 'reserves judgment' (p. 1) and is a self-consciously honest man – Fitzgerald is deliberately showing how far short of its original promise America has fallen. If Gatsby's list of self-improving resolves is closely modelled on Benjamin Franklin's eighteenth-century rules for self-improvement, it also demonstrates a falling off in the intensity and purity of the resolves. Franklin's industry becomes 'No wasting time at Shafters'. Cleanliness becomes 'Bath every other day' (p. 116). Similarly Gatsby takes as his early ideal what Nick calls a 'pioneer debauchee' (p. 66), Dan Cody, who sounds like an amalgam of the frontier heroes Daniel Boone and William Cody (Buffalo Bill), but who is a paler version of them. Dan Cody makes his millions in the Nevada silver mines and becomes a playboy. His restlessness and adventure take the form of cruising the world in his yacht. Like Cody, all the novel's major characters, at home in eastern cities and in the pleasure-seeking twentieth century, are in fact westerners by birth; but, with the exception of Gatsby, they are debilitated approximations of that mythically sturdy, self-reliant and straightforward breed. The utilitarian covered wagon, the prairie schooner, carrier of dreams, symbolic of a new life, appears in the story in the debased form of the car, the ostentatious symbol of mobility, independence and status, a source of envy and an instrument of death. The pastoral dimension of the American Dream is savagely imaged by Fitzgerald in its twentieth-century form as a wasteland between Long Island and New York, 'a fantastic farm where ashes grow like wheat into ridges and hills and ash gray men swarm up with leaden spades' (p. 15). The most idyllic pastoral image in the novel is the comic and incongruous one of Nick's imagining a flock of sheep coming down Fifth Avenue.

The gods in this America are those of a gross materialism and a compulsive consumerism. There is no vision, no divine personality informing the commandments printed out in advertisements and on hoardings. The preacher-God in the novel, who has sight but no 'vision', is Dr T. J. Eckleburg, an oculist's advertisement whose eyes 'look out of no face but instead from a pair of enormous yellow spectacles which pass over a non-existent nose' (p. 15). His vacuous visage dominates the Valley of Ashes. Even Gatsby is secular to the extent that he worships at the altar of Daisy's dock – he looks across Long Island Sound at its green light with what Edwin Fussell calls 'trembling piety'[5] – but he is by no means an irreligious man. Indeed, he has the confident belief in God and God's special relationship with America which the continent inspired in the early settlers. Gatsby looks at his America as the Puritans had done, as God's deliberately planned new world which revealed His intentions; and the conclusion that Gatsby draws from his America is not to do with Puritan concepts of duty and responsibility but with the conviction that 'he must be about His Father's business, the service of a vast, vulgar and meretricious beauty' (p. 65). There are echoes here of the materialistic interpretation put by Bruce Barton in *The Man Nobody Knows* (1925) on Christ's words, 'Wist ye not that I must be about my Father's business';[6] but Gatsby's business incorporates vision as well as venality.

Of the showy 1920s then, but apart from them; a rags-to-riches hero who has unscrupulously worked his way to the top, but a man of serious purpose, no sybarite, who seeks material wealth as a means to an end, not as an end in itself. His blatant lies about his past –

> 'I am a son of some wealthy people in the Middle West – all dead now [they were poor and alive]. I was brought up in America but educated at Oxford because all my ancestors have been educated there for many years. It is a family tradition.'
>
> He looked at me [Nick] sideways . . . he was lying

– his wild pink suits, his contrived vocabulary ('old sport'), his undiscriminating hospitality (he hardly knows who comes to his parties, who swims, who stays in the guest rooms), his oppressively opulent car – 'a rich cream color, bright with nickel, swollen here and there in its monstrous length with triumphant hat-boxes and supper-boxes and tool-boxes, and terraced with a labyrinth of wind-shields that mirrored a dozen suns . . . a sort of green leather conservatory [inside]' – are acceptable means justified by an acceptable end, the idealistic business of the son of the Father, the business of fulfilling the promise inherent in Creation and in the American continent (pp. 42–3). He has made money and moved into the rich society of Long Island in the hope that somehow he will contrive to meet Daisy Fay, who lives there and whom he had known and loved in Louisville, Kentucky, before the war took him away from America. He imagines that the perfection of the relationship can be re-created and sustained.

But no one and nothing in America can match the vitality of Gatsby's dream. He is an idealist struggling to find the ideal in the midst of the real, and meeting a disappointment which he refuses to believe is inevitable. He believes in manifest destiny, in the will to succeed, in money, but all fail him. Daisy too. She is undeniably fascinating, but she lacks the capacity to imagine or will the radical re-creation of her life. She is as insubstantial as the ballooning white dresses she wears, as shallow as her white powder. As she says, 'God, I'm sophisticated' (p. 12), and sophistication for Fitzgerald is an index to the decade's false values. Poignantly, Daisy recognizes her limitations in the scene where she admires the shirts which Gatsby shows her, shirts 'piled like bricks in stacks a dozen high' but representing so much more than affluence.

> He took out a pile of shirts and began throwing them, one by one, before us, shirts of sheer linen and thick silk and fine flannel, which lost their folds as they fell and covered the table in many-colored disarray. While we admired he brought more and the soft rich heap mounted higher – shirts with stripes and scrolls and plaids in coral and apple-green and lavender and faint orange, with monograms of Indian blue. Suddenly, with a strained sound, Daisy bent her head into the shirts and began to cry stormily.
>
> 'They're such beautiful shirts,' she sobbed, her voice muffled in the thick folds. 'It makes me sad because I've never seen such – such beautiful shirts before.' (p. 61)

In their own way, Gatsby's shirts are part of his sense of wonder at what men can make, money can buy and he can have. But if his sense of wonder transforms the material, material things and real people deflate the wonder he seeks, as we see in Chapter 6.

It is in Chapter 6 that Fitzgerald lays before us the flaws in Gatsby's America and in the universe which Gatsby seeks to create (it is here, too, that Gatsby opens himself to Nick, re-creating verbally the past he hopes literally to re-enact). Chapter 5 described how Gatsby met Daisy again at Nick's, and at the beginning of Chapter 7 we see that Gatsby's open house is a thing of the past, and that tight-lipped, inhospitable servants make it possible for Daisy to come over discreetly in the afternoons. This idyllic privacy is, in fact, an indication of the failure of Gatsby's imaginative strategy, a strategy which culminates in the party he gives for her in Chapter 6. All Daisy likes is the pretty sight of a movie director kissing *at* his star's cheek under a plum tree. Daisy responds to surface. Her lack of depth and passion leads her to flinch from the real emotion and the profound inner vitality which Gatsby's life-style struggles to express. (Only Nick and one other wise guest, Owl Eyes, ever see Gatsby as the great showman, the purveyor of riotous dreams that he is.) Daisy can only see Gatsby's way of life as an emblem of his gaudy taste, not as the romantic, extravagant way he had brought their lives together again. 'She didn't like it,' he tells Nick, and recalls an earlier moment when he had realized that to make the dream real was, by definition, to make the dream vanish. 'He knew that when he kissed this girl, and forever wed his unutterable visions to her perishable breath, his mind would never romp again like the mind of God.' But he is man as well as platonic son of God. He desires Daisy; only she seems remotely to embody his dream, and the dream *is* of heaven on earth. Yet to enter into a relationship with her is to hear no longer the tuning-fork that had been struck on a star. To spend his life with Daisy is to deny his vision that 'the blocks of the sidewalks really formed a ladder and mounted to a secret place above the trees – he could climb to it, *if he climbed alone*, and once there he could suck on the pap of life, gulp down the incomparable milk of wonder' (my italics). Cruelly, the dream, which promises the attainment of the unattainable and which derives its idealistic thrust from that promise, is ultimately self-denying.

'The unprecendented American opportunities have always tempted us to confuse the visionary with the real', comments Daniel Boorstin;[7] and Nick Carraway wonders if Gatsby finally recognizes his confusion of the two and abandons his dream of earthly perfection. Would Gatsby abandon his ideal when his wild, careful plans for its realization fall apart? He dies a curious death, shot in his swimming pool by a man who believes Gatsby has run over his wife (Daisy was driving, and

Gatsby kept quiet to protect her), and deserted by Daisy; but does he die disillusioned? Surely not. Chapter 6 suggests that Gatsby had an early sense of the unbridgeable disparity between the real and the ideal and that from the first his great hope defied that sense. His rational self had discounted disillusionment in advance, making a distinction between what he calls 'just personal' (Daisy) and what he longs for as ideal (p. 101). Occasionally the real and the ideal fuse for him, and he experiences rapture. 'At his lips' touch she blossomed for him like a flower and the incarnation was complete.' Nick speculates that when Daisy decided to stay with Tom, Gatsby was led to despair not merely of the personal but of the ideal too, that for the first time Gatsby seriously questioned the promise of the universe. 'He must have looked up at an unfamiliar sky through frightening leaves and shivered as he found what a grotesque thing a rose is' (p. 108) – and how fickle a Daisy, who would compliment a man on being like a rose. Certainly Gatsby is chastened as never before. But on reflection Nick changes his mind, and at the end of the story asserts his belief that Gatsby retained a sense of the wonder of America and continued to dream. The last paragraph of the novel depicts Gatsby as a boat beating against the current, an image which belies Gatsby's disillusionment even if it admits Nick's defeat.

The American Dream, with its emphasis on incorruptible innocence, profound simplicity and freshness of vision, has connotations of the naive and the childlike too; and Fitzgerald's language at the end of Chapter 6 emphasizes that in some ways Gatsby is like a child. His 'fantasy' of climbing a staircase to heaven suggests not only Jacob's ladder but also Jack's beanstalk and Peter Pan's flight; even the action of his mind is likened to a romp, and his concept of bliss and fulfilment to suckling at the breast. But Fitzgerald is also at pains to emphasize both the adult ambition and the metaphysical purity of Gatsby's dream with such words as 'unutterable' and 'incomparable'. (Nature affirms too: 'there was a stir and bustle among the stars' to which only Jay Gatsby responds.) Such words give the measure of Fitzgerald's affirmation of the Gatsby who more than compensates for the self-made millionaire who believes money can help buy satisfaction.

We are left in no doubt of how isolated Gatsby is in the America of the 1920s. Even Nick, who can so movingly reiterate or translate what Gatsby has to say to him (he may even make Gatsby a little more eloquent than he really is – 'I gathered,' says Nick – though we must believe that if the imagery is not entirely Gatsby's, the earnest Nick is choosing words which give the essence of Gatsby's revelation), cannot subscribe to Gatsby's faith in people and place. Nick is well qualified to understand Gatsby for he himself has an occasional sense of what the American Dream is about. As he drives to New York from Long Island he recognizes that 'the city seen from the Queensboro Bridge is always the city seen for the first time, in its first wild promise of all the mystery and all the beauty in the world' (p. 45). But he has too lively a perception of the evil the city allows and engenders to sustain his response to a token of the mysterious, the beautiful, to a hint of the possible incarnation of the ideal. He cannot believe in such things; he cannot abandon himself to what lies behind Gatsby's articulation of his ideal; he shrugs it off as 'appalling sentimentality'. He cannot bring himself to reproduce the words in which Gatsby expresses himself; thus '. . .'. To him Gatsby's is the voice of an irretrievable, irrelevant past, a voice which reminds him of 'an elusive rhythm, a fragment of lost words'.

If Nick cannot affirm Gatsby's dream, it is indeed, and tragically, 'uncommunicable forever'. It dies with him. And so, perhaps, does the fine idea of America as a society obsessed with, in J. H. Raleigh's words, 'the wonder of life and driven by the urge to make that wonder actual'.[8] An exemplary race of visionary individuals was giving way to a society from which an idealistic sense of purpose was conspicuously absent. Gatsby had stood out against artificial values and had lived for original ones; Gatsby had mixed passion and principle; Gatsby was an idealist and that, in both literal and metaphoric terms, led to his death.

Notes

1 F. Scott Fitzgerald, *The Great Gatsby*, New York, 1953 (originally published 1925). All quotations from *The Great Gatsby* are taken from this edition and, unless noted otherwise in textual parentheses, from Chapter 6, pages 73–4.

2 F. Scott Fitzgerald, 'The Crack-Up', in *The Crack-Up with other Pieces and Stories*, Harmondsworth, 1965, 39.

3 Daniel J. Boorstin, *The Image, or What Happened to the American Dream*, Harmondsworth, 1961, 241.

4 Frederick Jackson Turner, 'The significance of the frontier in American history', in Ray Allen Billington (ed.), *Frontier and Section: Selected Essays of Frederick Jackson Turner*, Englewood Cliffs, NJ, 1961, 61.

5 Edwin Fussell, 'Fitzgerald's brave new world', in Arthur Mizener (ed.), *F. Scott Fitzgerald: A Collection of Critical Essays*, Englewood Cliffs, NJ, 1963, 48.

6 Quoted in William E. Leuchtenberg, *The Perils of Prosperity, 1914–32*, Chicago, 1958, 189.
7 Boorstin, op. cit. 242.
8 J. H. Raleigh, 'F. Scott Fitzgerald's *The Great Gatsby*', in Mizener, op. cit., 102.

Further reading

Boorstin, Daniel J., *The Image, or What Happened to the American Dream*, New York, 1961. Especially Chapters 5 and 6.

Fitzgerald, F. Scott, *The Crack-Up*, New York, 1945. Autobiographical essays.

Mizener, Arthur (ed.), *F. Scott Fitzgerald: A Collection of Critical Essays*, Englewood Cliffs, NJ, 1963. Contains three other useful essays in addition to Raleigh's.

Mowry, George (ed.), *The Twenties: Fords, Flappers and Fanatics*, Englewood Cliffs, NJ, 1963.

Piper, Henry Dan (ed.), *Fitzgerald's 'The Great Gatsby': The Novel, the Critics, the Background*, New York, 1970. Especially essays by Piper, Lloyd Morris and John H. Randall III.

12
Ernest Hemingway (1899–1961)

'I'm thirty-four, you know. I'm not going to be one of these bitches that ruins children.'

'No.'

'I'm not going to be that way. I feel rather good, you know. I feel rather set up.'

'Good.'

She looked away. I thought she was looking for another cigarette. Then I saw she was crying. I could feel her crying. Shaking and crying. She wouldn't look up. I put my arms around her.

'Don't let's ever talk about it. Please don't let's ever talk about it.'

'Dear Brett.'

'I'm going back to Mike.' I could feel her crying as I held her close. 'He's so damned nice and he's so awful. He's my sort of thing.'

She would not look up. I stroked her hair. I could feel her shaking.

'I won't be one of those bitches,' she said. 'But, oh, Jake, please let's never talk about it.'

We left the Hotel Montana. The woman who ran the hotel would not let me pay the bill. The bill had been paid.

'Oh, well. Let it go,' Brett said. 'It doesn't matter now.'

We rode in a taxi down to the Palace Hotel, left the bags, arranged for berths on the Sud Express for the night, and went into the bar of the hotel for a cocktail. We sat on high stools at the bar while the barman shook the Martinis in a large nickelled shaker.

'It's funny what a wonderful gentility you get in the bar of a big hotel,' I said.

'Barmen and jockeys are the only people who are polite any more.'

'No matter how vulgar a hotel is, the bar is always nice.'

'It's odd.'

'Bartenders have always been fine.'

'You know,' Brett said, 'it's quite true. He is only nineteen. Isn't it amazing?'

We touched the two glasses as they stood side by side on the bar. They were coldly beaded. Outside the curtained window was the summer heat of Madrid.

'I like an olive in a Martini,' I said to the barman.

'Right you are, sir. There you are.'

'Thanks.'

'I should have asked, you know.'

The barman went far enough up the bar so that he would not hear our conversation. Brett had sipped from the Martini as it stood, on the wood. Then she picked it up. Her hand was steady enough to lift it after that first sip.

'It's good. Isn't it a nice bar?'

'They're all nice bars.'

'You know I didn't believe it at first. He was born 1905. I was in school in Paris, then. Think of that.'

'Anything you want me to think about it?'

'Don't be an ass. *Would* you buy a lady a drink?'

'We'll have two more Martinis.'

'As they were before, sir?'

'They were very good.' Brett smiled at him.

'Thank you, ma'am.'

'Well, bung-o,' Brett said.

'Bung-o!'

'You know,' Brett said, 'he'd only been with two women before. He never cared about anything but bull-fighting.'

'He's got plenty of time.'

'I don't know. He thinks it was me. Not the show in general.'

'Well, it was you.'

'Yes. It was me.'

'I thought you weren't going to ever talk about it.'

'How can I help it?'

'You'll lose it if you talk about it.'

'I just talk around it. You know I feel rather damned good, Jake.'

'You should.'

'You know it makes one feel rather good deciding not to be a bitch.'

'Yes.'

'It's sort of what we have instead of God.'

'Some people have God,' I said. 'Quite a lot.'

'He never worked very well with me.'

'Should we have another Martini?'

The barman shook up two more Martinis and poured them out into fresh glasses.

'Where will we have lunch?' I asked Brett. The bar was cool. You could feel the heat outside through the window.

'Here?' asked Brett.

'It's rotten here in the hotel. Do you know a place called Botin's?' I asked the barman.

'Yes, sir. Would you like to have me write out the address?'

'Thank you.'

We lunched upstairs at Botin's. It is one of the best restaurants in the world. We had roast young sucking pig and drank *rioja alta*. Brett did not eat much. She never ate much. I ate a very big meal and drank three bottles of *rioja alta*.

'How do you feel, Jake?' Brett asked. 'My God! what a meal you've eaten.'

'I feel fine. Do you want a dessert?'

'Lord, no.'

Brett was smoking.

'You like to eat, don't you?' she said.

'Yes,' I said. 'I like to do a lot of things.'

'What do you like to do?'

'Oh,' I said, 'I like to do a lot of things. Don't you want a dessert?'

'You asked me that once,' Brett said.

'Yes,' I said. 'So I did. Let's have another bottle of *rioja alta*.'

'It's very good.'

'You haven't drunk much of it,' I said.

'I have. You haven't seen.'

'Let's get two bottles,' I said. The bottles came. I poured a little in my glass, then a glass for Brett, then filled my glass. We touched glasses.

'Bung-o!' Brett said. I drank my glass and poured out another. Brett put her hand on my arm.

'Don't get drunk, Jake,' she said. 'You don't have to.'

'How do you know?'

'Don't,' she said. 'You'll be all right.'

'I'm not getting drunk,' I said. 'I'm just drinking a little wine. I like to drink wine.'

'Don't get drunk,' she said. 'Jake, don't get drunk.'

'Want to go for a ride?' I said. 'Want to ride through the town?'

'Right,' Brett said. 'I haven't seen Madrid. I should see Madrid.'

'I'll finish this,' I said.

Downstairs we came out through the first-floor dining-room to the street. A waiter went for a taxi. It was hot and bright. Up the street was a little square with trees and grass where there were taxis parked. A taxi came up the street, the waiter hanging out at the side. I tipped him and told the driver where to drive, and got in beside Brett. The driver started up the street. I settled back. Brett moved close to me. We sat close against each other. I put my arm around her and she rested against me comfortably. It was very hot and bright, and the houses looked sharply white. We turned out on to the Gran Via.

'Oh, Jake,' Brett said, 'we could have had such a damned good time together.'

Ahead was a mounted policeman in khaki directing traffic. He raised his baton. The car slowed suddenly pressing Brett against me.

'Yes,' I said. 'Isn't it pretty to think so?'

The Sun Also Rises (1926)[1]

* * *

A number of critics have made comparisons between Ernest Hemingway's *The Sun Also Rises* (1926) and T. S. Eliot's *The Waste Land* (1922). Where Eliot has London as the waste land, it is said, Hemingway has Paris. The characters in both works are banal, unnatural; they are men and women of paltry appetites. Sterility, emptiness and fragmentation abound. But the parallel obscures some of the significant merits of Hemingway's novel: for example, the remarkable, vernacular accessibility which Hemingway achieves, the new norm of behaviour he suggests and the language which matches it. As Leslie Fiedler[2] points out, the use of anti-rhetoric by anti-heroes is appropriate, and so, in a world of non-relation, is minimal syntax and the non-committal conjunction. Hemingway's novel is also noteworthy for its powerful suggestion, rare in the literature of the 1920s, that if, on the whole, life goes on so terribly, it also goes on unterribly and sometimes wonderfully. Hemingway affirms the existence of physical and spiritual territory of some substance and some satisfaction.

The 'botched civilization'[3] which preoccupied Pound, the generation older than himself who had made a mess of things, were not Ernest Hemingway's prime preoccupations. He was more concerned with his own generation, the 'lost generation' – the phrase forms the epigraph to *The Sun Also Rises* and, according to Hemingway, was taken from Gertrude Stein ('You are all a lost generation').[4] She originally used the phrase to a mechanic who botched his work on the ignition of her Ford, and she then used the phrase to describe Hemingway and men of his age who had been in the First World War, a generation which lacked respect and drank too much. She liked the sound and sense of the phrase, and went on using it in conversation. Hemingway had been an ambulance driver in the war, and had been seriously wounded at the Italian front; it was the effect of his observation of suffering and the construction which he put upon the war as a whole which led him to adopt Stein's phrase and create an ethic and an aesthetic, both well demonstrated in *The Sun Also Rises*, his first important novel. Prior to that he had won recognition for a fine collection of short stories, published in 1924, and for his parody of Sherwood Anderson and Gertrude Stein in *The Torrents of Spring* (1926).

Hemingway used a second epigraph for his novel: a text from Ecclesiastes.

> One generation passeth away, and another generation cometh, but the earth abideth forever. . . . The sun also ariseth, and the sun goeth down, and hasteth to the place where he arose. The wind goeth toward the south, and turneth about unto the north. It whirleth about continually, and the wind returneth again according to his circuits. . . . All the rivers run into the sea; yet the sea is not full; unto the place from when the rivers come, thither they return again. (p. iv)

It aply expressed some of the few things that Hemingway affirmed: earth, sun, wind, river – nature not, as in Wallace Stevens's case, transformed by imagination, but nature as it is, varied and beautiful, cyclically reliable, a challenge and a solace, and at its best untainted by corrupting man.

Although Hemingway was an intermittent expatriate who lived in Europe from 1919 to 1929, and spent a good deal of his later life in Europe and Africa travelling and hunting, it would be wrong to see his work as a straightforward rejection of American culture and the American way of life. In common with Scott Fitzgerald and Gertrude Stein, Hemingway had indissoluble if regretful ties with American myth, in his case the myth of an enacted pastoral. Political philosophers such as Thomas Jefferson and nineteenth-century writers such as

Thoreau had posited that a simple life, lived in close and observant contact with nature, preferably with one's hands literally in the soil, made for goodness, and that it was the American's destiny to act out this truth. The theory, and to a much lesser extent the practice, never died out. Hemingway himself compulsively sought the outdoor life; and in his character Nick Adams, hero of *In Our Time* (1924) and many other stories, he created an American whose passion was the natural world, who returned there in time of stress and whose morality was respect for that world.

But *The Sun Also Rises* transcends any feeling Hemingway had for America, any theory he had about that country. It is a novel about modern man, whose values and standards had been shattered by the brutal and disillusioning spectacle of the slaughter of the First World War and by the territorial carve-up which followed. To Hemingway it seemed that modern man had lost belief in anything and in everything – in God, country and politicians, in the just war or the good peace, in conventional morality or traditional assumptions of progress. His was a generation without a sense of purpose, without a sense of historical process. For this generation there was no point in planning, in hoping, in looking to the future. As a friend of Jake Barnes says to him in a conversation about William Jennings Bryan, 'let us not pry into the holy mysteries of the hen coop with simian fingers' (p. 122). It didn't matter which came first, the chicken or the egg. It was no longer possible to be a humanist or an optimist or a religious man. Only a few things might still prove reliable, might still be understood and mastered and enjoyed: a sense of place, the present moment, one's self, physical things and perhaps a friend or two. And it mattered to be loyal to the few precious things one could affirm, be it self or a commitment to others. Sexuality and sensuality were high on the list of pleasures, but took second place to that mixture of controlled feelings, graceful actions and the confrontation of danger and meaninglessness which is courage.

In *The Sun Also Rises* Hemingway puts together a group of people whose lives would almost seem to justify suicide, characterized as they are by impotence, irretrievable bankruptcy, shell shock, promiscuity, pointless death, pointless life and rampant alcoholism. They live crippled lives, enacted in an almost entirely commercial society. And where that society is not already commercial, the touring expatriates, American and British, are making it so, as they discover unspoilt spots like Pamplona and Burguete, and begin to spoil them with their bad conduct and their intrusive behaviour. But, more to the point, they find and create pleasure and even meaning in their individual lives and in their friendships. They come to live by a secular theology. They are bound together by a code which keeps the logical corollary of total disbelief, nihilism, at bay. All that can be done in a world in which there is no God, no immanent meaning in Creation and none in the world man has made is artificially to construct a series of 'principles' which give some kind of shape and sense to life. Some of the tenets of this 'theology' seem a little strange: do not follow a woman around if she does not want you, be a good drunk, hold your liquor like a man even if you are a woman, speak a private code, cadge drinks and accommodation but do not accept money. Brett Ashley lets Count Mippipopolous pay her bills, but she will not let him give her money to go away for the weekend with him.

Such rules and distinctions may seem petty – but the people who make them are not, and they find such rules help to make sense of senselessness. They are not conventionally good or moral people – though at their best they are capable of great loyalty and great self-sacrifice – nor are they positive, for to be positive would suggest an optimism that is illogical for cynics. But when the occasion presents itself they take their pleasure, and, in their understated way, they even articulate what they believe in and stand up for it. They do well against what Hemingway sees as great contemporary odds. Believing the world is 'about' nothing, all they want and need to know – and it is a great deal – is, in Jake Barnes's words, 'how to live in it' (p. 148).

Hence the code, which not everyone can keep. Some of the group slip the bonds voluntarily (Robert Cohn, Brett's lover, decides he prefers more conventional society) and others involuntarily (Brett's fiancé, Mike Campbell, is alcoholic and unreliable). Brett makes excessive demands on Jake's friendship; Jake, on occasion, forgets his primary commitment to courage, 'grace under pressure'. But for those who take the code seriously, as Brett and Jake do, there are gains. One of these is the heightened sense of place which comes to those for whom place is a rare certainty; another is the frank friendship and understanding between those who uphold the code and who are prepared to suffer in order to do so. The scene between Jake and Brett at the end of the novel is a fine example of this.

On the way to the annual bullfights in Pamplona, where they are to be joined by a number of friends, the narrator Jake Barnes, Paris correspondent for an American newspaper, and his novelist friend Bill Gorton decide to make a detour to Burguete, for they are both keen fishermen and Jake knows of some good trout streams in the area.

Their mutual sense of the unadulterated beauty of the Spanish countryside is reinforced by their mutual, silent conviction that life has little to offer except such landscape and such compatibility. Not even the code (so often difficult to sustain) is better. They concentrate hard on what they see (Robert Cohn, who accompanies them part of the way on the bus and who is to prove dramatically unable to keep the code, is appropriately asleep).

> After a while we came out of the mountains and there were trees along both sides of the road, and a stream and ripe fields of grain, and the road went on, very white and straight ahead, and then lifted to a little rise, and off on the left was a hill with an old castle, with buildings close around it and a field of grain going up to the walls and shifting in the wind. I was up in front with the driver and I turned around. . . . Bill looked and nodded his head. (p. 93)

The fishing trip is a good example of finding a reliable source of pleasure, of securing that pleasure, taking it and – wonderfully satisfying in a usually purposeless universe – even being able to plan for it. Jake and Bill's journey through the mountains to the inn, their accommodation at the inn, their careful purchase of rods and tying of flies, their hike from the inn to the stream are deliberate and pleasurable preliminaries to the fishing itself. Hemingway does not attempt to explain the joy of fishing; indeed he almost makes us wonder why it should be pleasurable. There is extreme sensation when Jake puts the wine to cool in the river: 'It was so cold my hand and wrist felt numbed.' There is much cruelty: 'He was a good trout, and I banged his head against the timber so that he quivered out straight.' The ritual is like that of an undertaker or an embalmer: 'I laid them out, side by side . . . three trout on a layer of ferns, then another layer of ferns, then three more trout, and then ferns. . . . They looked nice in the ferns' (pp. 119–20). Hemingway is not saying that trout fishing is nice because it is cruel and cold and clinical, or that it is killing with some sanctification which comes, paradoxically, from the natural setting and the ritual. Nor is he explicitly celebrating fly fishing as an art form. In a meaningless universe pleasure cannot be explained, only described; and so Hemingway describes Jake and Bill fishing, eating, drinking, talking, sleeping. It does not really matter why it is good; after all, Hemingway's definition of morality was something one felt good after. The pleasure is unmistakeable, the beauty clear, if partly perverse, and Hemingway endows the experience with a validating simplicity and innocence.

Artificial as it is, it is as near to nature as man can come. 'This is country' is the simple way Bill comments on the experience (p. 117), while Jake is so at peace here that he can sleep easily, though sleep is something which normally evades him. Bill and Jake sound as if they are Huck Finn and Jim in an idyllic moment on the Mississippi.

> The nights were cold and the days were hot, and there was always a breeze even in the heat of the day. It was hot enough so that it felt good to wade in a cold stream, and the sun dried you when you came out and sat on the bank. We found a stream with a pool deep enough to swim in. (p. 125)

When we set such a passage against the last paragraphs of the novel, it is at first tempting to assume that Hemingway, unlike Anderson and Lewis, is preaching pure pastoralism. Everything that is good beside the trout stream seems less good in the city. The heat of the sun in Madrid is oppressive, the cold is unnatural, the companionship strained. In the urban hotel bar the glasses are coldly beaded by artificial refrigeration; here it is a cocktail with olives (what a contrived role for the natural olive), not the straight, good wine which Jake and Bill have been drinking out of leather bottles. Here it is jittery conversation and too much talk altogether, not the happy silence of the river bank, the sense of people who are comfortable with each other. Here are two people who care for each other, who sit close and rest against each other, and yet are ill at ease and discontented. But a country setting would have made no difference. (Nor would crossing the Atlantic. Europe is no better and no worse than America; it is just more colourful.) People matter more than places; Jake and Bill are able to be happy in the city. In Hemingway's theory environment cannot transform; it is simply there, to be savoured, and Jake and Brett, in conscious and appreciative observance of the code, savour the bar's ambience, its convenient and sophisticated trappings.

This scene and the ending which it provides for the novel contain many things which the code affirmed as more important than contact with nature and a life of almost primitive simplicity. In the fashionable setting of the Spanish capital's bar, Brett and Jake are united as, in Arthurian days, the Knights of the Round Table. With this difference: there is no grail to pursue, simply a limited number of precepts to enact and uphold – such precepts as loyalty, courage, stoicism. The code's insistence on the satisfying reality of what is works in that it distances them from what hurts: Jake's impotence (the result of a war wound) and the physical frustration he feels when he is with Brett, whom he loves; Brett's reluctant decision to leave Romero, the young bullfighter, the courageous man *par excellence* whose grace under pressure is his fascination for her but which the code insists she must not diminish. But the code does not and cannot affect Brett's and Jake's fundamental unhappiness.

First Brett and then Jake manage to affirm the code against great odds in this scene. Temperament and the war have made loyalty to anyone and anything difficult for Brett. War killed her first husband and sent her to work as a volunteer in an English hospital where she met not only the convalescent Jake but fell in love with a man who died of dysentery. She has become promiscuous and cannot remain faithful to her fiancé, Mike Campbell, though she knows this distresses a man already thrown seriously off balance by the war. Two particular cases of unfaithfulness have made her adherence to the code even less satisfactory. First, she has an affair with Robert Cohn, a sentimental and romantic man who will not break cleanly (part of the code) with Brett when she has finished with him; Cohn acts hurt, petulant, confused and, as Mike says, follows Brett around like a bloody steer. Second, she has just had that affair with Romero which threatened one of the crucial sources of support for the code, the courageous act – in this case bullfighting, which showed the confrontation of death as an art form.

> Romero's bull-fighting gave real emotion, because he kept the absolute purity of line in his movement and always quietly and calmly let the horns pass him close each time. . . . Romero had the old thing, the holding of his purity of line through the maximum of exposure, while he dominated the bull by making him realize he was unattainable. (p. 168)

Such bullfighting has been Jake's model of courage for many years; he has introduced Brett, Mike, Bill and Robert Cohn to his vision of the code's enactment. Brett reacts to Jake's explanation of the bullfighter's art with total comprehension: 'She saw why she liked Romero's capework', she had 'never seen him do an awkward thing'. He is grace, consistency and courage. But he is also 'looks' (pp. 167–8). 'Oh, isn't he lovely,' Brett says. 'And those green trousers' (p. 165). 'My God, he's a lovely boy. . . . And how I would love to see him get into those clothes. He must use a shoe-horn' (p. 177). For her to pursue and enslave Romero, to sap his energy, his concentration, his purity of line are in effect wilfully to topple the code's idol; and thus to undercut the pure quest for absolute courage is the cardinal sin in the group's secular theology. In seducing Romero Brett strikes out at her own survival – can she live with herself as the bitch of bitches? – and at the mortified Jake's. How, in the light of this triple betrayal, can Jake continue to be loyal to Brett?

The question is complicated by the fact that Jake himself has infringed his appreciative affirmation of Romero's pure courage. Jake not only first introduces Brett to Romero but continues to bring them together though he knows where the relationship is leading. First, the group toasts Romero in the Hotel Montoya, where they are all staying.

> Just then Montoya [the hotel keeper] came into the room. He started to smile at me [Jake], then he saw Pedro Romero with a big glass of cognac in his hand, sitting laughing between me and a woman with bare shoulders at a table full of drunks. He did not even nod. (p. 177)

Montoya, who for years has acknowledged Jake as the only foreigner in Pamplona with 'aficion' – knowledgeable about bullfighting, intuitive and passionate in his appreciation of the art – and who has given Jake privileged access to the friendship of the bullfighters, is disgusted. Jake has betrayed him as much as Brett has betrayed Jake. And Jake quickly compounds his infraction of the code a few hours later, when he and Brett see Romero in a cafe. Brett begs Jake to ask Romero to join them for a drink. She says she is in love with Romero; she admits she is acting like a bitch. And yet Jake 'looked across the table. Pedro Romero smiled. He said something to the other people at his table, and stood up. He came over to our table' (pp. 184–5). Jake has become Brett's procurer.

In the novel's final scene she reproves and retrieves herself, she regains and reaffirms the code. 'I should have asked, you know,' she says, overtly referring to the fact that she had not believed Romero was only nineteen, but meaning in fact (the reader has to expand Hemingway's terseness on occasion): I should have asked myself what I was doing; I should have thought and talked it through, with myself, with him; I should have remembered the code. The glib terms in which she describes the act of sending Romero away are, in their own way, moving and right, for these people do not allow themselves to talk sentimentally or to talk much at all. As Jake says, 'You'll lose it if you talk about it.' All Brett says is, 'You know I feel rather damned good, Jake.' Understatement intensifies rather than diminishes her action, her poignancy. It is an attempt to be light, but the intensity comes out in her repetition of words and syntax in the next statement and in her savage, diminishing, deflating self-congratulation at the end: 'You know it makes one feel rather good deciding not to be a bitch.' But this not just a scene in which Brett Ashley comes home. It is a scene in which she shows a growth not only in self-knowledge but in knowledge and understanding of Jake. Through her love for Romero and her loss of Romero she now knows what the impotent Jake feels. At the beginning of the novel back in Paris, when Jake wanted to kiss her, she would not give him that small pleasure, not for his sake but for hers.

> Her head was down.
>
> 'Don't touch me,' she said. 'Please don't touch me.'
>
> 'What's the matter?'
>
> 'I can't stand it.'
>
> 'Oh, Brett.'
>
> 'You mustn't. You must know. I can't stand it. . . . I simply turn all to jelly when you touch me.' (pp. 25–6)

Don't get drunk, Brett keeps telling Jake in the scene in the bar in Madrid. Why not? He is a good drunk, and drinking is something he and Brett and the gang do all the time. Here it is her way of saying, I wish you did not have sorrows to drown; I know you are drinking to forget, not for pleasure; I want to show you that I understand and that, as a friend, I care. It is her way of saying 'don't cry'. Brett has never been more in love (than with Romero), never more shaky (in herself), never less selfish (with Jake); and it is the suffering which the return to the code entails that has made her capable of compassion.

Jake Barnes is a figure of much poignancy in this last section of the novel, which gives the lie to the notion that the Hemingway hero is a hard-boiled nay-sayer. He has a veneer of poise and of the matter-of-fact, but his words and actions conceal an emotion for Brett as powerful as hers for Romero. He too needs to repent – of his conduct in Pamplona, of putting personal loyalty to Brett above loyalty to the ideal of courage, of picking a fight with the outsider, Robert Cohn, simply because he was jealous that Cohn had slept with Brett and because Cohn had called attention to Jake's excessive compliance with Brett's excessive demands (he had called Jake a pimp). Jake has to come to terms with his reluctance to leave the solace of France and confront a Spain of painful memories (and thus exhibit grace under pressure); he has to admit his disinclination to play the 'true' friend and hear Brett tell of her decision to leave Romero. He is conscious of a number of lapses into self-pity. Sometimes he can be ironic about his injury. 'Undressing, I looked at myself in the mirror of the big armoire beside the bed. That was a typically French way to furnish a room. . . . Of all the ways to be wounded. I suppose it was funny' (p. 30). But more often 'he felt like crying. . . . It is awfully easy to be hard-boiled about everything in the daytime, but at night it is another thing' (p. 34). Everything conspires to remind him of what he is missing.

> 'Oh, Jake,' Brett said, 'we could have had such a damned good time together.'
>
> Ahead was a mounted policeman in khaki, directing traffic. He raised his baton. The car slowed suddenly pressing Brett against me.
>
> 'Yes,' I said. 'Isn't it pretty to think so?'

As the policeman – who looks not unlike a soldier in his khaki uniform – raises his baton, Jake is reminded of his own impotence and of the war which was its cause. 'Pretty' is an inadequate word, deliberately inadequate and inappropriate: it conceals the kind of emotions the code does not allow to be expressed. It does not describe what we know he feels for Brett, and yet given that this feeling can never find satisfactory physical expression, there is a kind of hollowness, a kind of superficiality to the scene which Jake feels and which the word 'pretty' expresses with excruciating aptness. Once again, Jake Barnes has his injury in perspective. He knows it is pointless to dwell on his physical limitations; he also knows that while sexual potency permits sensory gratification, it guarantees nothing else.

Jakes's and Brett's control throughout this scene is remarkable. She keeps tears and self-pity at bay by incessant talk, by ritual toasts – 'Bung-o!' – and, above all, by focusing on the positive side of what she has done in renouncing Romero. He focuses on the minutiae of the scene around him – the name of the hotel, the train, the heat outside in Madrid (though he cannot feel it in the cold bar), his food, his drink, the details of the square outside the hotel. Understatement and a kind of facetiousness gets them both through. And the code. Observing it, Jake concentrates on the validity and the fascination of the world as it is. The height of the bar stools, the nickelled cocktail shaker, the curtained window, the excellence of the sucking pig, his pride in his meticulous recall of the way in which he located the restaurant. All these things help him distance himself from his agony. When he finds Brett asking him, apropos of nothing – she could probably have kicked herself once the words were out – a vague, conversational, half-drunk question which suddenly seems pointed – 'What do you like to do?' – he is able to turn her off with 'Oh, . . . I like to do a lot of things. Don't you want a dessert?' All they can do is touch glasses. It is, of course, an unfulfilled relationship. But their human need of each other, their openness with each other, their friendship for each other are unmistakeable. Both are in a sense desexed. She dresses like a man, has a short haircut and talks of herself as a chap, while he cannot be fully a man; yet both 'cripples' make something of their lives, something of their relationship. Within their limits they are mutually dependent and dependable. It is a relationship not without value.

The conduct of Jake and Brett in this scene is the correlative of Ernest Hemingway's prose style, of which he said:

> If a writer of prose knows enough about what he is writing he may omit things that he knows and the reader, if the writer is writing truly enough, will have a feeling of those things as strongly as though the writer had stated them. The dignity of an iceberg is due to only one-eighth of it being above water.[5]

Jake and Brett are, in their speech, such dignified icebergs. Their language embodies, as Malcolm Bradbury has noted,

> a controlled limitation of feeling, an ironic materiality in which a small number of details live starkly in clear juxtaposition. The aim of the language is double: To force attention to the economy of the gesture, the cleanness of the line, the active grace of the doing, and to convey with integrity the thing observed, to get toward some ultimate and authentic experience.[6]

But the very fact of suppression, the very presence of the submerged iceberg, of depths rarely shown, make us conscious of what lies behind and beneath.

Hemingway knows very well that his characters are more complex than their construction of the universe allows them to appear. He also believes that even if complexities are aired, they cannot be satisfied – better to stick with the simplicities which can be. And so there are repeated formula words and phrases, as if, in a diminished existence, the currency of speech has been whittled down to a minimum; only certain words are in circulation, just as only certain emotions and pleasures are possible in Hemingway's world. Emotion cannot be allowed to take over, even though it threatens. So, 'I put my arm around her and she rested against me comfortably' is followed by 'It was very hot and bright, and the houses looked sharply white.' Hemingway people pick up each other's words and phrases as in a game – but it is a serious game, the game of survival. Sophisticated small talk – 'Barmen and jockeys are the only people who are polite any more' – keeps pain at a distance; so does the artificially understated or somewhat exaggerated speech. Brett's and Jake's strategy for survival works, but only just – they are as clipped and tense as they are smooth and relaxed – and perhaps only temporarily.

Hemingway learned from Gertrude Stein how to strip language down to its essentials, how to use rhythm and repetition. A master-craftsman, he showed how well her theory could work in practice. Letting the objects live and speak as he did, he was also part of the movement to create a new kind of beauty (or re-create the old one), a spare, concrete beauty comparable with that which the imagist poets put forward. He is a fine practitioner of early twentieth-century literary theory. He is also importantly a writer who painted the expatriate scene, who evoked the postwar mood, who showed the charm of Europe and the rape of Europe. And in Jake Barnes he created a character who memorably symbolizes his author's influential vision of man in the postwar world. Jake survives but he is effectively incapacitated in an uncertain, disordered and cruel universe which will not change for the better.

The Sun Also Rises represents an extravagant but genuine reaction to the First World War and expresses the passionate conviction that a worse world ensued in spite of the lives sacrificed. Hemingway shows, movingly, how the living lost still managed to achieve positive as well as negative states of being. The novel ends sadly, however, with the image of Jake's impotence and Brett's notion of what the lost generation had instead of God: the 'ideal' of not being a bitch.

Notes

1 Ernest Hemingway, *The Sun Also Rises*, New York, 1963 (first published 1926). All quotations from *The Sun Also Rises* are taken from this edition and, unless noted otherwise in textual parentheses, from Book 3, Chapter 19, pages 243–7.

2 Leslie A. Fiedler, *Waiting for the End*, Harmondsworth, 1967, 14.

3 Ezra Pound, 'Hugh Selwyn Mauberley', *Collected Shorter Poems of Ezra Pound*, London, 1968, 101.

4 Ernest Hemingway, *A Moveable Feast*, Harmondsworth, 1966, 27–8.

5 Quoted in Brom Weber, 'Ernest Hemingway's genteel bullfight', in Malcolm Bradbury and David Palmer (eds), *The American Novel and the Nineteen Twenties*, London, 1971, 25.

6 Malcolm Bradbury, 'Style of life, style of art and the American novelist', in Bradbury and Palmer, ibid., 25.

Further reading

Baker, Carlos, *Hemingway: The Writer as Artist*, 3rd edn, Princeton, 1963.

Baker, Carlos, *Ernest Hemingway*, New York, 1969. The major biography.

Bradbury, Malcolm and Palmer, David (eds), *The American Novel and the Nineteen Twenties*, London, 1971. Especially Chapters 1 and 7.

Fiedler, Leslie A., *Waiting for the End*, New York, 1964. Chapters 1 and 2.

Hemingway, Ernest, *A Moveable Feast*, New York, 1965. An expatriate's autobiography.

McCormick, John, *American Literature, 1919–32*, London, 1971.

Young, Philip, *Ernest Hemingway: A Reconsideration*, 2nd edn, University Park, Penn., 1966.

13
Eugene O'Neill (1888–1953)

The sitting room of MRS. DION ANTHONY's half of a two-family house in the homes section of the town – one of those one-design districts that daze the eye with multiplied ugliness. The four pieces of furniture shown are in keeping – an armchair at left, a table with a chair in back of it at center, a sofa at right. The same court-room effect of the arrangement of benches in Act One is held to here. The background is a backdrop on which the rear wall is painted with the intolerable lifeless realistic detail of the stereotyped paintings which usually adorn the sitting rooms of such houses. It is late afternoon of a gray day in winter.

DION is sitting behind the table, staring before him. The mask hangs on his breast below his neck, giving the effect of two faces. His real face has aged greatly, grown more strained and tortured, but at the same time, in some queer way, more selfless and ascetic, more fixed in its resolute withdrawal from life. The mask, too, has changed. It is older, more defiant and mocking, its sneer more forced and bitter, its Pan quality becoming Mephistophelean. It has already begun to show the ravages of dissipation.

DION. (suddenly reaches out and takes up a copy of the New Testament which is on the table and, putting a finger in at random, opens and reads aloud the text at which it points) 'Come unto me all ye who are heavy laden and I will give you rest.' (He stares before him in a sort of trance, his face lighted up from within but painfully confused – in an uncertain whisper) I will come – but where are you, Savior? (The noise of the outer door shutting is heard. DION starts and claps the mocking mask on his face again. He tosses the Testament aside contemptously) Blah! Fixation on old Mama Christianity! You infant blubbering in the dark, you! (He laughs, with a bitter self-contempt. Footsteps approach. He picks up a newspaper and hides behind it hurriedly. MARGARET enters. She is dressed in stylish, expensive clothes and a fur coat, which look as if they had been remodeled and seen service. She has grown mature and maternal, in spite of her youth. Her pretty face is still fresh and healthy but there is the beginning of a permanently worried, apprehensive expression about the nose and mouth – an uncomprehending hurt in her eyes. DION pretends to be engrossed in his paper. She bends down and kisses him).

MARGARET. (with a forced gaiety) Good morning – at four in the afternoon! You were snoring when I left!

DION. (puts his arms around her with a negligent, accustomed gesture – mockingly) The Ideal Husband!

MARGARET. (already preoccupied with another thought – comes and sits in chair on left) I was afraid the children would disturb you, so I took them over to Mrs. Young's to play. (A pause. He picks up the paper again. She asks anxiously) I suppose they'll be all right over there, don't you? (He doesn't answer. She is more hurt than offended) I wish you'd try to take more interest in the children, Dion.

DION. (mockingly) Become a father – before breakfast? I'm in too delicate a condition. (She turns away, hurt. Penitently he pats her hand – vaguely) All right. I'll try.

MARGARET. (squeezing his hand – with possessive tenderness) Play with them. You're a bigger kid than they are – underneath.

DION. (self-mockingly – flipping the Bible) Underneath – I'm becoming downright infantile! 'Suffer these little ones!'

MARGARET. (keeping to her certainty) You're my oldest.

DION. (with mocking appreciation) She puts the Kingdom of Heaven in its place!

MARGARET. (withdrawing her hand) I was serious.

DION. So was I – about something or other. (He laughs) This domestic diplomacy! We communicate in code – when neither has the other's key!

MARGARET. (frowns confusedly – then forcing a playful tone) I want to have a serious talk with you, young man! In spite of your promises, you've kept up the hard drinking and gambling you started the last year abroad.

DION. From the time I realized it wasn't in me to be an artist – except in living – and not even in that! (He laughs bitterly.)

MARGARET. (with conviction) But you *can* paint, Dion – beautifully!

DION. (with deep pain) No! (He suddenly takes her hand and kisses it gratefully) I love Margaret! Her blindness surpasseth all understanding! (Then bitterly) – or is it pity?

MARGARET. We've only got about one hundred dollars left in the bank. . . . (shamefaced) . . . something's got to be done.

DION. (harshly) Will Mrs. Anthony helpfully suggest what?

MARGARET. I met Billy Brown on the street. He said you'd have made a good architect, if you'd stuck to it.

DION. . . . William A. Brown, architect! . . . One of God's mud pies!

MARGARET. He particularly told me to ask you to drop in.

DION. (springs to his feet – assertively) No! Pride! I have been alive!

MARGARET. Why don't you have a talk with him?

DION. Pride in my failure!

MARGARET. You were always such close friends.

DION. (more and more desperately) The pride which came after man's fall – by which he laughs as a creator at his self-defeats!

MARGARET. Not for my sake – but for your own – and, above all, for the children's!

DION. (with terrible despair) Pride! Pride without which the Gods are worms!

MARGARET. (after a pause, meekly and humbly) You don't want to? It would hurt you? All right, dear. Never mind. We'll manage somehow – you mustn't worry – you must start your beautiful painting again – and I can get that position in the library – it would be such fun for me working there! . . . (She reaches out and takes his hand – tenderly) I love you, dear. I understand.

DION. (slumps down into his chair, crushed, his face averted from hers, as hers is from him, although their hands are still clasped – in a trembling, expiring voice) Pride is dying! (As if he were suffocating, he pulls the mask from his resigned, pale, suffering face. He prays like a Saint in the desert, exorcizing a demon) Pride is dead! Blessed are the meek! Blessed are the poor in spirit!

MARGARET. (without looking at him – in a comforting motherly tone) My poor boy!

DION. (resentfully – clapping on his mask again and springing to his feet – derisively) Blessed are the meek for they shall inherit graves! Blessed are the poor in spirit for they are blind! (Then with tortured bitterness) All right! Then I ask my wife to go and ask Billy Brown – that's more deadly than if I went myself! (With wild mockery) Ask him if he can't find an opening for a talented young man who is only honest when he isn't sober – implore him, beg him in the name of old love, old friendship – to be a generous hero and save the woman and her children! (He laughs with a sort of diabolical, ironical glee now, and starts to go out).

MARGARET. (meekly) Are you going up street, Dion?

DION. Yes.

MARGARET. Will you stop at the butchers' and have them send two pounds of pork chops?

DION. Yes.

MARGARET. And stop at Mrs. Young's and ask the children to hurry right home?

DION. Yes.

MARGARET. Will you be back for dinner, Dion?

DION. No. (He goes, the outer door slams. MARGARET sighs with a tired incomprehension and goes to the window and stares out.)

MARGARET. (worriedly) I hope they'll watch out, crossing the street.

CURTAIN

The Great God Brown (1926)[1]

* * *

In 1916 the Provincetown Players performed Eugene O'Neill's *Bound East for Cardiff* in a warehouse at the end of a pier in Provincetown, Cape Cod, and thus serious American theatre was fittingly inaugurated in an area which had seen some of the first American settlers. Dramatists who came after O'Neill – Arthur Miller, Tennessee Williams and Edward Albee – drew on his dramatic arsenal and bore the stamp of his preoccupation with tortuous family relationships, with the plight of the artist in society, with the problem of making the outside world a home, with the difficulty of distinguishing reality from illusion. As Walt Whitman changed the nature of American poetry, Eugene O'Neill changed the face of American drama, indeed he created it, for before him there were only melodramas and minstrel shows.

The list of O'Neill's pioneering contributions to American theatre is long, but high on that list is his ability to state, within the drama, classical American themes. He structured his plays, as nineteenth-century American fiction had done, in terms of opposites – night and day, good and evil, land and sea, art and commerce, city and country. As J. H. Raleigh[2] asserted, O'Neill recalls Henry Adams's preoccupation with the dynamo, Hawthorne's New England stories and

Melville's use of sea and sailors. He covered an enormous range of American history, from Ponce de Leon's search for the fountain of youth to the twentieth century's bars, songs, sports and manners. And, like much of American literature, O'Neill's plays posed cosmic questions and often found them unanswerable.

O'Neill wrote not only out of a tradition of American culture and a sense of American history but out of profound personal and contemporary experience. His years as a sailor led to a number of fine plays, and his dissolute, nearly self-destructive life near the New York waterfront gave him the material for his penetrating studies of down-and-outs and alcoholics in such fine later plays as *The Iceman Cometh* (1946) and *Hughie* (1959). His father was a first-rate actor and matinee idol who became hopelessly entangled with the vehicle of his success, the melodrama *The Count of Monte Cristo*. Eugene's backstage exposure to the stage together with the theatricality of his home life – a father who never stopped acting, a mother addicted to drugs, a self-dramatizing alcoholic brother – gave him an acute sense of the range of 'theatre', from realism to fantasy, from bathos to tragedy. This range is well reflected not only in the autobiographical *Long Day's Journey into Night* (1956) but in his work as a whole, which pushes the medium, in all its forms, to its limits. His plays run the technical gamut from expressionism to tragedy, and run it boldly. At the end of *The Hairy Ape* (1922), for example, the despairing stoker Yank, rejected by all classes and all political organizations and driven to seek a primitive brotherhood with the ape, goes to the zoo and unlocks the cage door: '"Come on Brother. Shake de secret trip of our order." With a spring he wraps his huge arms around Yank in a murderous hug. There is a crackling snap of crushed ribs.' In the dramatic monologue of *The Emperor Jones* (1920) O'Neill has remarkable success in imaging the psychological state of the American Negro dictator of a West Indian island. In *Mourning Becomes Electra* (1931), an American tragedy, a hybrid of Aeschylus and Hugo von Hofmannsthal, O'Neill ambitiously transposes the House of Atreus into the New England family Mannon during the American Civil War. In his idiosyncratic treatment of racial intermarriage in *All God's Chillun Got Wings* (1924), we have the first American play in which a black man and a white woman embraced on the stage.

O'Neill was extremely responsive, in his early days, to social and political movements, and had a hatred of class distinction and social inequality. He abandoned his radical political commitment in the mid-

1920s, but remained faithful to a general radicalism in the sense that he continued to side with the underdog. Parties and dogmas left him increasingly unmoved, and he often articulated a philosophy of studied indifference: 'Life's all right if you let it alone' (p. 280). God he sometimes denied, sometimes affirmed, appearing at times to prefer the theory of evolution. Billy Brown was 'one of God's mud pies' – a phrase which begs the question but which also belittles the God who may exist. In *The Great God Brown* Dion Anthony speaks of 'Charley Darwin's circus', and of man as an animal escaped from that circus (p. 268). But in the same play Billy Brown also asserts that 'The grace of God is glue!', a statement which implies an incompetent if not a careless God (p. 318). On occasion no one exhibits more vociferously than O'Neill the nihilism so prevalent in the 1920s, but he denied that he was a cynic or a pessimist. Optimism he damned as a false, unrealistic and therefore hopeless philosophy. To him a hopeful life was one lived bravely in the pessimistic knowledge that what is worthwhile is almost certainly unattainable. What mattered was that man perceive the awfulness and the absurdity of existing, and transcend this through an act of defiance. In his plays, O'Neill said, what he had set out to do was 'to dig at the roots of this sickness of today as I feel it – the death of the old God and the failure of science and materialism to give any satisfactory new one for the surviving primitive religious instinct, to find a meaning for life in and to comfort its fears of death with.'[3]

Unlike Wallace Stevens, Eugene O'Neill did not hold out a great deal of hope for man as the shaper of his world and his destiny. O'Neill believed that man was so constituted that he must struggle with the universe and with himself and lose that struggle. He saw two conflicting forces at work in the sensitive human being, the Dion Anthony of *The Great God Brown*. Those forces were

> Dionysus and St. Anthony – the creative pagan acceptance of life, fighting eternal war with the masochistic, life-denying spirit of Christianity as represented by St. Anthony – the whole struggle resulting in this modern day in mutual exhaustion – creative joy in life for life's sake frustrated, rendered abortive, distorted by morality from Pan into Satan, into a Mephistopheles mocking himself in order to feel alive.[4]

Dion Anthony is composed of both Dionysian and Anthonian elements from the first. 'Dion' seeks creative joy in life for life's sake: art; but because he is 'Anthony' as well as 'Dion' he is doomed to failure. A vulnerability which is the product of heightened sensibility makes a Dionysian existence impossible, and leads to a life of conflict, deception and misery. In addition, society damns the Dionysian, if with some hypocrisy. As O'Neill sees it, the problems are inherent and insoluble. He offers no existentialist answer; he posits the existence of a malevolent, clever god, whose deceptive projection of a benevolent image deceives even Dion Anthony into worship and quest. In the face of such a god, O'Neill argues, Dion Anthony would be better employed in seeking the pagan existence, which unifies what is beautiful and what is sensuous. But the conflict between the two sides of Dion Anthony's personality renders that search fruitless. As 'Dion' becomes less like Pan and more like Mephistopheles – defiant, mocking, forced, bitter – so 'Anthony', his Christian side, becomes 'more selfless and ascetic, more fixed in its resolute withdrawal from life'. Joy, creativity, life are negated; schizophrenia prevails.

O'Neill holds up as an ideal the abandonment to intoxication and ecstasy which Dionysus represented and the creative capacities which such abandon released. He writes boldly and preaches boldness, mixing rhetoric and colloquialisms, seeking the pointed phrase – 'this domestic diplomacy', for instance, which refers to Dion Anthony's conversations with his wife. Like Stevens, O'Neill alters biblical phrases for heretical purposes: 'It's the Will of Mammon', 'Blessed are the poor in spirit for they are blind'. The beatitudes quickly give way to pork chops, in a manner reminiscent of H. L. Mencken. The polarization of language reflects not only the differences between Dion Anthony and his wife – which are the differences between the artist and society – but the conflicts within Dion Anthony himself. He oscillates between abusing his wife and caring for her, moving from frivolity to seriousness, from believing that pride resulted from man's fall and must be exorcized to aspiring to that pride 'without which the Gods are worms', without which he cannot become the creator he aspires to be.

But if the language O'Neill uses in this play is realistic, the plot and the techniques employed are not. O'Neill, who scorned photographic realism, was an inventive dramatist, nowhere more than in his use of masks in *The Great God Brown*. The mask had some obvious and simple uses – it made actors use their bodies more, it let the words play as important a part in the play as the faces of the stars, it helped with crowds, mobs or wherever a sense of impersonal or collective psychology was called for. In *The Great God Brown* the mask served four other purposes: (a) to emphasize that people do wear masks before other people who (b) mistake them for their masks, (c) to suggest that the masks change their makers and (d) that the masks themselves change, thus making the process of masking increasingly unpredictable.

For O'Neill the mask was also a potent metaphor for the isolation and the complexity of the artist. 'One's outer life passes in a solitude haunted by the masks of others; one's inner life passes in a solitude hounded by the masks of oneself,' he wrote.[5] Dion Anthony is the artist figure, born without a skin and needing a defence. He puts on a mask which he intends will meet the requirements and opinions of the environment. But the mask does not do what he intends. It does not enable the real man successfully to play a role. First it stifles him and then it perverts both the real man and itself. The dichotomy between the inner needs of the individual and the external demands made on him is thus intensified. The mask of Dion Anthony transforms his real face, 'spiritual, poetic, passionately supersensitive, helplessly unprotected in his childlike, religious faith in life', sometimes into the expression of an ascetic, a martyr and sometimes 'into the expression of a mocking, reckless, defiant, gaudy, scoffing and sensual young Pan' (p. 260). Once the mask has been put on, once the destructive process of alternating personalities is underway, Dion Anthony loses control, and neither the pagan ('Dion') nor the Christian ('Anthony') avoids the exaggeration and corruption of his original qualities. The joyful, self-centred pagan becomes as withdrawn from society as the hermit. Dion Anthony realizes the conflict and its result, laments it, but is powerless to alter the process. He is acted upon. A mundane job in Brown's architect's office and a strange friendship with a golden-hearted whore alter both the mask and the natural face of Dion Anthony still further; the Pan-like persona now has taken on 'a diabolical Mephistophelean cruelty and irony', while the face itself and the will to live have wasted away (p. 285).

Psychologists have demonstrated that it is not man's way to confront his fellow with his true face, and O'Neill embodied this insight in his play. His was an attempt, stimulated by Freud, to 'express those profound hidden conflicts of the mind which the problems of psychology continue to disclose to us'.[6] What interested most Americans was Freud's contention that the unconscious, the repository of our fundamental life drive, is almost wholly preoccupied with sex. What interested O'Neill was Freud's elaboration of the conflicting urges of a controlled consciousness and an almost uncontrollable unconsciousness. Freud emphasized the conflict between natural man and social convention, and Dion Anthony's ego could be seen as a battleground for the unbridled libido ('Dion') and the regulating super-ego ('Anthony').

In the 1920s O'Neill's interest in psychology demonstrated itself in his use of masks. *Desire Under the Elms* (1924) is an exploration of subconscious and conscious sexual motivation; its characters have 'mask-like' faces and the play would lend itself to masks as the key characters assume a variety of poses to sustain a complicated triangular relationship. In *All God's Chillun Got Wings* black Jim and his white wife Ella can only sustain a tenuous happiness when they assume the roles of children, he white, she black. 'Pretend you're Painty Face and I'm Jim Crow,' says Ella.[7] In *The Hairy Ape* masks showed how people misconceive each other – even the gorilla in his cage is masked to show that the stoker Yank is perverting reality by seeing anything like brotherhood, anything except apehood, present in the cage. Yank's ape mask shows how incongruous is his assertion that he is as low as the animals. In *Strange Interlude* (1928) whole bodies become masks as characters speak their inner thoughts in frozen statue positions on stage, and only move when they are their 'social selves'.

The Great God Brown lends itself particularly well to the use of masks, for it is a play about the divided self; about individuals torn between the natural impulse and the artificial act. The conflict leads to conflicting outer actions and amounts to a complex form of schizophrenia. O'Neill's play attempts to convey the layers of falsehood and obsession of which we are composed and with which we confront the world. The natural self is almost farcically concealed by these artificially constructed layers. The 'Dion' of Dion Anthony, the Dionysian artist figure, is never imaged in a state of unqualified happiness, unstinted abandon or unmitigated artistry. Even at the beginning of the play, when he is at his most natural, he is afraid to dance and asks himself bitterly, 'Why am I afraid to live, I who love life and the beauty of flesh and the living colors of earth and sky and sea. . . . why was I born without a skin, Oh God, that I must wear armor in order to touch or be touched' (pp. 264–5). The answer lies in the responses demanded by other people, responses which make naturalness impossible. In isolation he could perhaps be free, but man is not naturally isolated, O'Neill argues – certainly not 'Dion', whose instinctive, joyous, sensual art needs to be communicated, to be shared. The sensitive artist is, by definition, tortured, but society makes the torture worse. 'Dion' has already found a way of coping or of attempting to cope with the insoluble artist's dilemma. He will try to be an artist in private and adopt an insensitive persona in public. So he claps a mask over his face 'and his voice becomes bitter and sardonic', and he addresses 'God' no longer with a suffering bewilderment but challenges him, 'Old Graybeard, why the devil was I ever born at all?' (p. 265). The mask which 'Dion' assumes affects the 'Anthony' in him – a good example of the incalculable power of the mask.

Dion Anthony is a psychological case study. As a child he was alienated from his father. He recalls that 'When he lay dead, his face looked so familiar that I wondered where I had met that man before. Only at the second of my conception. After that we grew hostile with concealed shame' (p. 282). His father is not a sufficiently demonstrative or loving man, and he and Dion Anthony vie for the attentions of Dion Anthony's mother. Dion Anthony has a classic mother fixation. To him his mother must be all women – mother, sister, wife. He remembers her as a girl whose hands caressed and who deserted him by dying. Partly as a result of this fixation, he marries a woman who is overly maternal. 'Three mothers in one person,' he calls her (p. 282), and in Act One, Scene One, she calls him 'my poor boy', 'young man', and 'kid'. 'He'll be my Dion – my own Dion – my little boy – my baby!' she says when they become engaged (p. 264). Additionally, Dion Anthony blames his cynicism on an incident in childhood in which his best friend Billy, whom he later christens the 'Great God Brown',

> sneaked up behind when I was drawing a picture in the sand he couldn't draw and hit me on the head with a stick and kicked out my picture and laughed when I cried. It wasn't what he'd done that made me cry, but him! I had loved and trusted him and suddenly the good God was disproved. (p. 295)

Act One, Scene One of *The Great God Brown* shows the damaging effect of the psychologically scarred Dion Anthony on other people and on himself. He has had to learn to be false to himself, to compromise, to live with 'multiplied ugliness'. Having fallen short of his highest expectations of himself as an artist, having produced a family who view him with 'tired incomprehension', who think he can paint 'beautifully' (he knows he cannot), having 'created' children 'before one discovered one couldn't' (one could only bring them into the world – one could not make them things of beauty and joy), he does not fit into family or society. He can only play roles; and while playing roles and wearing masks make life momentarily tolerable, they slowly make it untenable too. The changes of mask and mood are violent, unsettling – he is, as the stage directions indicate, mocking, penitent, self-mocking, pained, bitter, irritable, sober, bitter, angry, jeering, harsh, desperate, bruised, suffering, resentful. Both his real face – the face of the would-be artist – and the face he shows the world – cynical, jaunty, sneeringly defensive – are changing. The man becomes even more withdrawn from his own practice of art and from the 'stereotyped paintings' and 'lifeless realistic detail' of his surroundings. The mask perverts the realities of the good husband, the good father, the talented young man. Now he gets up late, will not fetch the children home and does not come back for dinner. He has spent his inheritance on drink; he has burned the good, if not great, paintings he did in France. His talent to create has become a talent to wound and to destroy.

It is clear from this scene that incompatibility between husband and wife is another factor in forcing Dion Anthony to wear a mask. As he says, 'We communicate in code – when neither has the other's key!' In a striking scene at the outset of the play, Margaret, the woman Dion Anthony loves, is unable to recognize him without his social mask. She is frightened and literally chilled by the artist, by the real, sensitive and sincere man. When he puts on his mask, boldly embraces her, feigns a romantic actor's passion and speaks to her in a parody of love-making – 'Your eyes are blue pools leaning backward beneath the lips of spring' – she swam in 'an ecstasy' (p. 267). Without a mask it is difficult for Dion the artist to stoop this low, but Margaret likes Rudolph Valentino and so he plays the role of the Hollywood lover and she loves it. Poignantly, though, Margaret too has a mask which she wears to pretend to the world that all is well in the Anthony household. But with Dion Anthony (and with 'Dion' and 'Anthony') she does not need to wear it. He cannot be himself with her; she can be herself with him. The play is made even more sombre by their increasing inability to communicate unless he wears a distorting mask.

In spite of everything, there is great love between them, says O'Neill. But how can this relationship be dignified as love? For in a curious and fantastic turn of events at the end of the play, Billy Brown, who had rubbed out Dion Anthony's pictures but had not won Margaret's hand, assumes the mask and the identity of the dead Dion Anthony. The mask convention is given a new twist. Margaret is not only deceived but welcomes the rebirth of the lustier, more virile Dion Anthony. You are more like you used to be, she tells the Billy whom she now takes – or insists on taking – for Dion Anthony.

What, in allegorical terms, does O'Neill intend here? Is it a savage indictment of the superficiality of the middle-class woman, for whom any man in a certain mould or of sexual potency is an acceptable husband? Or is it a parable of the dangerous power of the artist? 'Dion', even when dead, can prevail. Or do commerce and false art get their comeuppance? For Billy Brown is the unimaginative artist who needs 'Dion's' talents to transform his pedestrian designs into something with flair, and although he inherits 'Dion's' talents when he assumes Dion Anthony's mask, increasingly Dion Anthony uses Brown. At first, under 'Dion's' spell, Brown designs fine buildings, but gradually he finds himself creating strange buildings with obscene ornamentations. Brown, helpless, loses his custom and loses to Dion Anthony in every other sense too. He cannot be sure that Margaret loves him, Billy, when she sees him as Dion Anthony; and through the action of the mask his cheerful, if envious, personality is overtaken by the diabolic, self- and other-torturing aspects of Dion Anthony. Billy Brown now becomes Mephistopheles, sneering and dissipated, defiant and mocking, and ultimately unable to bear life. Having only seen the Dionysian side of Dion Anthony, having only expected to become 'Dion', he finds he has become Anthony too, with all the life-denying asceticism that entails. His dying speech shows him in a state of Christian delusion.

> I have found Him! I hear Him speak! 'Blessed are they that weep, for they shall laugh!' Only he that has wept can laugh! The laughter of Heaven sows earth with a rain of tears, and out of Earth's transfigured birth-pain the laughter of Man returns to bless and play again in innumerable dancing gales of flame upon the knees of God! (p. 322)

O'Neill himself could not subscribe to such theological justification of suffering. He intends this speech as satire, for to him this life-denying Christianity is what always makes men fix their eyes on the next world instead of enjoying this one.

But if Dion Anthony 'triumphs' over Brown, why is the play called *The Great God Brown?* Brown has been the incarnation of material success, but he has needed 'Dion's' skills to enhance his architectural business even before he takes the mask. Perhaps there is a sneer in the title; Brown is fooled into believing in a good God, is frustrated in his relationship with Margaret and is made to fail as an architect. He is nothing but the creation of Dion Anthony. But if William Brown is destroyed, the Great God Brown as archetypal businessman, mediocre artist and insensitive human being survives in his thousands. He is as average as John Q. Public. The title, then, both deflates Brown and what he stands for and faces the fact of the dominance of his kind.

An epilogue to the play reinforces the impression that convention and the conventional ultimately prevail in O'Neill's world. Margaret survives her two husbands, and it is her lack of intelligence and artistic sensitivity, her lack of complexity and subtlety which equip her to survive. She is single-minded and simple to a fault; indeed, as the play progresses, she regresses. When she married Dion she thought of him as a child; now he is back in her womb. The play ends with her kissing the masked image of Dion Anthony, and with her words, 'My boy, I feel you stirring in your sleep, forever under my heart' (p. 325). This ending is at least as strong and in positioning seems even stronger than its antithesis, the end of Act Four, when Cybel, the earth-mother prostitute, equally mother and lover, utterly honest and utterly comforting, the only person in the play able to prefer Dion Anthony without his mask, affirms 'always, always love' (p. 322), by which O'Neill seems to mean the ability to be honest and to cherish honesty, to be responsible for ourselves and not to seek scapegoats. But the play has another moral: Margaret is loved sexually by the two men; her ability to be satisfied by a sexual relationship helps ensure her unscathed survival. O'Neill departs from Freud and suggests that such sexuality is a form of insensitivity. It is also power of a terrifying kind.

Although O'Neill affirms the inherent superiority of the artist and his vision and mockingly refers to the 'Almighty Brown, thou Kindly Light' (p. 283), he also sees the artist as a man doomed by unbearable insights into himself and others and unrealistic expectations of artistic greatness and fulfilment. The artist's dissatisfaction is a threat to society as it is, and is made more threatening by the masks that he assumes, which inexorably pervert what is already threatening. But if Dion Anthony is damned by too much introspection, by too great a self-knowledge, by too much concealment, society, as exemplified by Margaret, sets up such barriers to knowledge of others that she functions as an obstacle to change. Yet the play is ultimately ambiguous in its affirmation. The hypersensitive, profoundingly questioning, complicated Dion Anthony is the most divided self of all; he is deliberately devious and frighteningly schizophrenic. The self-defeating characteristics of Dion Anthony suggest that O'Neill finds it difficult to believe that a free self is possible; indeed Act One, Scene One suggests that the artist is primarily the victim of his art and his intellect, which set him apart and which necessitate the mask. In the play O'Neill senses and gives bold expression to the increasing divergence of art and society in America; and in a decade which suggested the possibility of infinite freedom – in clothes, dance and morals – he sounds an astringent note of dissent. The artist is stifled by the mediocre materialism of the 1920s; he is denied freedom by the clash of his Dionysian and Anthonian characteristics. He is confused and changed by a mask he at first wears at will but which comes to force itself on him.

In his quest for a joyful and perfect fusion of the senses and of the self with others, the complicated, creative 'Dion' is clearly of finer stuff than the other characters. He has a subtlety that Margaret cannot see, let alone match; even his fatal flaw – pride, with its connotations of striving for excellence – ranks higher than Brown's envy and Margaret's wilful blindness. Intrinsically, if not effectively, the destructive and unhappy artist is superior to home-makers like Margaret and home-builders like Billy Brown. They cannot come near him. If they begin to comprehend him, they are unhappy. And if he attempts to be a member of their society, he cannot be true to himself. As an artist and a Dionysian he has to put himself first. Logic dictates that he should be celibate and friendless. It is not surprising, therefore, that O'Neill described *The Great God Brown*, with its bold experimental form and its sobering message, as not only 'one of the most interesting and moving plays I have written' but a play which 'for me, at least . . . does succeed in conveying a sense of the tragic mysterious drama of life revealed through the lives in the play'.[8]

Notes

1 Eugene O'Neill, *The Great God Brown*, in *The Plays of Eugene O'Neill*, New York, 1954 (first published 1926). All quotations from *The Great God Brown* are taken from this edition and, unless noted otherwise in textual parentheses, from Act One, Scene One, pages 269–73.
2 John H. Raleigh, *Eugene O'Neill: The Man and His Works*, Toronto, 1969, 243.
3 Eugene O'Neill, 'On man and God', in Oscar Cargill, N. B. Fagin and W. J. Fisher (eds), *Eugene O'Neill and His Plays*, London, 1964, 115.
4 Quoted in Barrett Clark, *Eugene O'Neill: The Man and His Plays*, New York, 1947, 104.
5 Eugene O'Neill, 'Memoranda on masks', in Cargill, Fagin and Fisher, op. cit., 117.
6 ibid., 116.

7 Eugene O'Neill, *Strange Interlude*, in *Nine Plays*, New York, 1932, 133.
8 Quoted in Eugene M. Waith, 'Eugene O'Neill: an exercise in unmasking', in John Gassner (ed.), *Eugene O'Neill: A Collection of Critical Essays*, Englewood Cliffs, NJ, 1964, 34.

Further reading

Bogard, Travis, *Contour in Time*, New York, 1972. Especially Chapter 7.

Cargill, Oscar, Fagin, N. B. and Fisher, W. J. (eds), *Eugene O'Neill and His Plays*, London, 1964. Contains extracts from O'Neill's writings on the theatre.

Clark, Barrett, *Eugene O'Neill: The Man and His Plays*, New York, 1947.

Gassner, John (ed.), *Eugene O'Neill: A Collection of Critical Essays*, Englewood Cliffs, NJ, 1964.

Raleigh, John H., *Eugene O'Neill: The Man and His Works*, Toronto, 1969.

14
William Faulkner (1897–1962)

The three-quarters began. The first note sounded, measured and tranquil, serenely peremptory, emptying the unhurried silence for the next one and that's it if people could only change one another forever that way merge like a flame swirling up for an instant then blown cleanly out along the cool eternal dark instead of lying there trying not to think of the swing until all cedars came to have that vivid dead smell of perfume that Benjy hated so. Just by imagining the clump it seemed to me that I could hear whispers secret surges smell the beating of hot blood under wild unsecret flesh watching against red eyelids the swine untethered in pairs rushing coupled into the sea and he we must just stay awake and see evil done for a little while its not always i and it doesnt have to be even that long for a man of courage and he do you consider that courage and i yes sir dont you and he every man is the arbiter of his own virtues whether or not you consider it courageous is of more importance than the act itself than any act otherwise you could not be in earnest and i you dont believe i am serious and he i think you are too serious to give me any cause for alarm you wouldnt have felt driven to the expedient of telling me you have committed incest otherwise and i i wasnt lying i wasnt lying and he you wanted to sublimate a piece of natural human folly into a horror and then exorcise it with truth and i it was to isolate her out of the loud world so that it would have to free us of necessity and then the sound of it would be as though it had never been and he did you try to make her do it and i i was afraid to i was afraid she might and then it wouldnt have done any good but if i could tell you we did it would have been so and then the others wouldnt be so and then the world would roar away and he and now this other you are not lying now either but you are still blind to what is in yourself to that part of general truth the sequence of natural events and their causes which shadows every mans brow even benjys you are not thinking of finitude you are contemplating an apotheosis in which a temporary state of mind will become symmetrical above the flesh and aware both of itself and of the flesh it will not quite discard you will not even be dead and i temporary and he you cannot bear to think that someday it will no longer hurt you like this now were getting at it you seem to regard it merely as an experience that will whiten your hair overnight so to speak without altering your appearance at all you wont do it under these conditions it will be a gamble and the strange thing is that man who is conceived by accident and whose every breath is a fresh cast with dice already loaded against him will not face that final main which he knows before hand he has assuredly to face without essaying expedients ranging all the way from violence to petty chicanery that would not deceive a child until some day in very disgust he risks everything on a single blind turn of a card no man ever does that under the first fury of despair or remorse or bereavement he does it only when he has realised that even the despair or remorse or bereavement is not particularly important to the dark diceman and i temporary and he it is hard believing to think that a love or a sorrow is a bond purchased without design and which matures willynilly and is recalled without warning to be replaced by whatever issue the gods happen to be floating at the time no you will not do that until you come to believe that even she was not quite worth despair perhaps and i i will never do that nobody knows what i know and he i think youd better go on to cambridge right away you might go up into maine for a month you can afford it if you are careful it might be a good thing watching pennies has healed more scars than jesus and i suppose i realize what you believe i will realize up there next week or next month and he then you will remember that for you to go to harvard has been your mothers dream since you were born and no compson has ever disappointed a lady and i temporary it will be better for me for all of us and he every man is the arbiter of his own virtues but let no man prescribe for another mans wellbeing and i temporary and he was the saddest word of all there is nothing else in the world its not despair until time its not even time until it was

The last note sounded. At last it stopped vibrating and the darkness was still again. I entered the sittingroom and turned on the light. I put my vest on. The gasoline was faint now, barely noticeable, and in the mirror the stain didn't show. Not like my eye did, anyway. I put on my coat. Shreve's letter crackled through the cloth and I took it out and examined the address, and put it in my side pocket. Then I carried the watch into Shreve's room and put it in his drawer and went to my room and got a fresh handkerchief and went to the door and put my hand on the light switch. Then I remembered I hadnt brushed my teeth, so I had to open the bag again. I found my toothbrush and got some of Shreve's paste and went out and brushed my teeth. I squeezed the brush as dry as I could and put it back in the bag and shut it, and went to the door again. Before I snapped the light out I looked around to see if there was anything else, then I saw that I had forgotten my hat. I'd have to go by the postoffice and I'd be sure to meet some of them, and they'd think I was a Harvard Square student making like he was a senior. I had forgotten to brush it too, but Shreve had a brush, so I didn't have to open the bag any more.

The Sound and the Fury (1929)[1]

* * *

William Faulkner's *The Sound of the Fury* was published almost three-quarters of a century after the end of the American Civil War, but that war and its aftermath continued to be the major preoccupations of life in the South. 'The Mind of the South', in the words of the title of W. J. Cash's masterful book, resisted change. *The Sound and the Fury* is a study of the tragic repercussions for twentieth-century southerners of that resisting mind.

Despite constitutional amendments which abolished slavery and granted full rights of equal citizenship to all persons born or naturalized in the United States, state law, federal inertia, Supreme Court decisions and racism quickly reduced the black to a second-class citizen, a Jim Crow, separate and not equal. It is sometimes forgotten in the rightful and indignant concern over this denial of human rights that the war had extraordinarily far-reaching and adverse effects on the whites who seemed so eager to reassume their old supremacy. Defeat by the North meant defeat not only for the South's pretensions to govern itself and for its right to be slave-holding, but also defeat of its plantation economy and of the social, cultural and philosophical structures which went with it: paternalism (and cruelty), leisure (and indolence), elegance (and crudity).

Faulkner was from Mississippi, and as Louis Rubin has so rightly pointed out:

> Nowhere else in the South has the tension between tradition and change, between moral precept and animal instinct, between wealth

> and poverty, between order and disorder, between black and white, between aristocracy and redneck, been so sharply drawn, and so dramatically revelatory. For the worst abuses of the sharecropper system, for the most lordly of plantation dynasties, for the most vicious aspects of the race question, for the highest illiteracy rate, for the most beautiful examples of antebellum town architecture, for the most tranquil kind of pastoral existence, for the worst abuses of popular democracy and demagoguery in action, for the most dogged, tenacious stand of the old feudal *mores* in the face of twentieth-century industrial civilization, there is no place like Mississippi.[2]

In the post-Civil War period Mississippi reacted violently to martial law enforced by Negro soldiers, and took the lead in carrying out lynch-law and in disenfranchising blacks. Though from the newest of southern states, Mississippian whites did their best to sustain the traditions of antebellum life – the fact of white supremacy and the fiction of an ideal society, its men gallant, its women flawless. *The Sound and the Fury* is a response to that southern myth which was part fact, part fiction. There *was* something in the South approaching a manorial social pattern and a cavalier civilization housed in white and stately mansions. Many *did* subscribe to ideals of honour and chivalry. But this was also a world of inflammatory rhetoric, unhealthy romanticism and rampant hedonism, a culture which placed great emphasis on personal heroism and which ran the danger of producing the reckless individual and the poseur. There *was* fineness in the legendary South but there was emptiness and artificiality too. The flaws and dangers inherent in southern theory and southern practice provide context and content for the scene where young Quentin Compson, the 'i', and his father Jason, the 'he', discuss, in the anachronistic terms of southern honour, the question of Quentin's contemplated suicide.

Malcolm Cowley wrote of Faulkner's many novels and stories set in Yoknapawtawpha County, that 'mythical kingdom' in northern Mississippi and the setting of much of *The Sound and the Fury*, that they 'are like blocks of marble from the same quarry; they show the veins and faults of the mother rock'.[3] That mother rock is the deep South; the blocks of *The Sound and the Fury* were quarried during the years 1898 to 1928 and bear the imprint of that disturbed and disturbing place. Faulkner's America informs the novel too. The First World War had brought money into the region; urbanization and industrialization were beginning to change the face of the largely rural South. Small communities found themselves expanding; religious orthodoxy found itself challenged. The South had to ask itself whether it wanted to join the crassly materialistic American mainstream, whether it wanted to be as busy, as go-getting, as pragmatic as the North. Faulkner was not alone in posing and facing such questions. In 1930, a year after the publication of *The Sound and the Fury*, a group of poets, historians and sociologists published, in Nashville, Tennessee, a manifesto called *I'll Take My Stand*, subtitled 'an attempt to define the Southern or agrarian way of life against the Northern, industrial and prevailing way'. The 'Agrarians', who included a number of poets and novelists, among them John Crowe Ransom, Allen Tate and Robert Penn Warren, asserted not only that much in the North was bad – who wanted to believe, with President Calvin Coolidge, that 'the business of America is business', that salesmanship was the highest calling? – but that much in the southern way of life was good, or potentially so: family life, a sense of place, respect for individual difference, for eccentricity, even. Faulkner was altogether less optimistic than the Agrarians. What they saw as valuable he saw as debilitating. His South, imaged in Yoknapawtawpha, is less a region of strengths and more a region of epic and melodramatic error. The bloody and violent history of the Compson family illustrates this all too well. Quentin Compson is at once the product of this decadent society and the tragic victim of its errors: rhetoric, romanticism, hedonism. He demonstrates the immorality and the emptiness of southern myth and southern reality.

The Compsons are a family trying hard to preserve the standards of the old South in the face of the realities of the new and against the background of their own degeneration. Little by little the extravagant Mr Compson sells off their plantation until it shrinks to a house, a mile of land, a few servants and a cabin, but he still plays the patrician, the planter, the community leader. The Compsons are poor, they are lazy, but they insist on their gentility. Their home decays because housework is for servants and they can only afford one cook-maid. Jason Compson, the father, alcoholic and nostalgic, likes to write Latin satires and wishes 'that the lawyer's office might again be the anteroom to the governor's mansion and the old splendor'.[4] Caroline Compson, the pretentious mother, is so stiff and indifferent, so preoccupied with her hypochondria, that the children turn for comfort to the black servant Dilsey. Quentin Compson is the product of a family where there is little love between the parents, between parents and children, even among the children, who grow up not really knowing what love is. The parents act divisively on the children. Quentin remembers any number of instances in which his mother challenged his father: *'How can I control any of them when you have always taught them to have no respect for me and my wishes'*; and in which his father chided his mother: *'I will not have my daughter spied on by you'* (p. 90).

In spite of such apparent and frequent breaches of their teaching, Mr and Mrs Compson insist that unity and loyalty and ordered relationships are what count. Because Quentin is a southerner he has been brought up to have unquestioning faith in the family, to accept as gospel instruction from his father and to respect his mother regardless of the fact that she is selfish, cruel, greedy and whining. He is asked to believe untenable precepts, to live a hypocritical life. The extremes of myth and reality, so characteristic of the tensions of Mississippi, press upon him unbearably. And as in Mississippi, as in the South, so in Faulkner's novel, the solutions are violent. Quentin commits suicide.

Three of the four sections in the novel emanate from the Compson children: the first from Benjy, the youngest, now thirty-three years old but with a child's mentality; the second from Quentin, the eldest of the children; the third from Jason. Caddy (Candace), the second child and only girl, is not given a section of her own, though Faulkner called the novel 'the tragedy of two lost women, Caddy and her daughter'.[5] Her daughter, Miss Quentin, figures prominently in Jason's section and in the last section, which is narrated by the author, though emphasizing the viewpoint and the character of Dilsey, now an old woman. It is easy to see why Faulkner chose to end with Dilsey; she exemplifies that endurance, that ability to survive with integrity which he so valued. Only Dilsey is capable of unselfish love, and Faulkner associates her with Christ in a section that takes place on Easter Sunday. It is less easy to say why Faulkner did not use Caddy or Miss Quentin as the focus or the voice of a section. Perhaps it is because they weave in and out of the narrative in symbolic patterns, or perhaps because they break away from the South – Faulkner's major preoccupation.

At the beginning of the book we see Caddy dirtying her drawers in the muddy stream and climbing up a pear tree to peer in at her dying grandmother while her brothers stare up from the ground below; at the end we see Quentin climbing down the tree and leaving behind in her room a pile of cheap, bright pink underwear. Both mother and daughter are adventurous, especially in matters of sex. They are survivors, people who can get on with the practice of life without bothering too much about the theory. It is the Compson brothers who are most hurt, most changed by the life around them. But Caddy and Miss Quentin survive tragically: they most of all seek and need love, and they most of all feel its absence in the Compson household. It is Caddy who demonstrates how love is perverted and dissipated by the Compsons and the society they represent. In the context of unbalanced and selfish family relationships, she is forced to play the maternal role Mrs Compson cannot fill. One unnatural role leads to another, and she comes as well to symbolize lover to Benjy and Quentin. The demands made on her for love are excessive. She cannot meet them. In her search for undemanding love and for the love between man and woman that has been so signally lacking between her parents, she turns to promiscuity. Her search for love becomes so perverted that she abandons her illegitimate daughter Quentin to an unloving grandmother (the mother whom Caddy herself had found so impossible) and a maliciously hostile uncle (Jason Compson III, the new southerner who resents the pretensions and the errors of the old South). Too much responsibility has bred irresponsibility. Caddy has wished on her daughter an even more loveless upbringing than her own. Not surprisingly, at the first opportunity Miss Quentin runs away, with a man from a circus. His world is less freakish than hers.

It is Quentin Compson, the most intelligent and sensitive of the Compson children, who can formulate and comprehend the subtleties and complexities of life in the South. It is Quentin who offers insights into the tragedy of the Compsons, into the South in transition and into his own profoundly alienated consciousness, but at a price. The South makes impossible demands on its children, and on Quentin as much as on Caddy. He is asked to bear an intolerable burden of culture, philosophy and introspection; he turns to self-destruction. The colourful exaggerations of life in the South breed nothing but a tragic insecurity.

The extract that begins this chapter comes at the end of Quentin's section of the novel, a section which takes the form of a complex interior monologue. The monologue mixes a chronologically precise account of the last day of his life with that day's chronologically jumbled recollections of terrible and pleasurable moments in his life. Here he is remembering as clearly as when it took place (hence the present tense) what was probably his last conversation with his father on the question of suicide; then he returns to a meticulous, minute-by-minute account of his last day.

The use of the past tense makes Quentin's death seem inevitable – so much was it bound to happen that it had happened. The past tense also suggests, macabrely, that Quentin, already dead, is speaking from the future, like someone who remembers his own death. But there is another way of looking at the deliberate quality of the actions and words of Quentin on his last day. He is trying to create the illusion of death in life, to ignore the signs of life around him, to smash his watch, to ignore his shadow, to be deaf to clock chimes, factory sirens and college bells. This is not simply an attempt to avoid the appointed hour of death, nor simply an image of the chaos – or the hell – which may follow life, and which his life has already become. If Quentin can create the illusion of death in life he is, paradoxically, ordering, by an act of will and imagination, the chaos he seeks to control. But he cannot sustain this ambitious metaphysics. Often on this last day he is drawn back into life. He takes the trolley into the country outside Cambridge; he wanders about the village; he buys currant buns in the village shop; he tried to help a little Italian girl who speaks no English. Though his section is more remarkable for the chaos which takes over as his sense of the past acts on his perception of the present (he confuses a classmate who is talking lightly about women with one of Caddy's lovers, and attacks the classmate as he had the lover), at the end he does achieve some kind of control, some kind of ordered perspective. This is marked by his coming back into time and organizing his thoughts in response to the chiming clock.

> The three-quarters began. The first note sounded, measured and tranquil, serenely peremptory, emptying the unhurried silence for the next one and that's it [Quentin thought] if people could only change one another forever that way [,] merge like a flame swirling up for an instant then blown cleanly out along the cool eternal dark.

He thinks of death in physical terms now, not in metaphysical ones. He wants a swift end, and images it as a kind of consummation, the heat of sex which burns and then is doused.

The sexual reference is a poignant one because Quentin Compson was a virgin when he died, and one of the elements which drove him towards the state of mind which made him commit suicide was his preoccupation with the vaunted purity and obvious corruption of southern women, and with his own sister and her loss of virginity. Quentin finds it impossible to make sense of the southern theory of the relationship between men and women. His father tells him that *'women . . . don't acquire knowledge of people we are for that they have an affinity for evil for supplying whatever the evil lacks in itself for drawing it about them instinctively as you do bed-clothing in slumber*' (p. 90). Women are 'liquid putrefaction', 'delicate equilibrium of periodical filth between two moons balanced' (p. 118). Yet in spite of such comments and in spite of the flawed reality of Mrs Compson and Caddy's promiscuity, he *apparently* expects his son to respect all women, blindly to keep them on their pedestals. As he says to his son in this extract, 'you will remember that for you to go to harvard has been your mothers dream since you were born and no compson has ever disappointed a lady'. Quentin longs to meet this maternal 'lady', pure and loving, wise and kind. 'If I could say Mother. Mother,' he cries (p. 89).

He might have said, 'If I could say sister, sister', as his feelings for Caddy, the only love object in his life, verge on the incestuous. He sees her loss of virginity as literal and symbolic proof of the hollowness of southern myth, and yet he himself is bound up in that myth in a perverse posture of gallantry – he wants to join her in her fall by raping her. It seems, however, not to be an incestuous feeling *per se* that he has for her; rather he attempts to enact his belief that the only way he can now 'possess' Caddy is by committing as great a wrong as hers. 'If we could have just done something so dreadful that they would have fled hell except us,' he tells his father (p. 76). He tries conventional means – fighting with Caddy's lovers – but does not prevail. He tries to kill her and himself – but fails. Nor can he get rid of his obsession with her. Throughout his death day, which he tries desperately to order and plan and control, images of Caddy overcome him. He remembers their childhood, their adolescence, the times they talked and touched, the horror of receiving her wedding invitation (a pregnant Caddy finds an unsuspecting bridegroom who later throws her out). He sees her in her wedding dress, he hears what are for him the funereal strains of the wedding hymn, 'The voice that breathed o'er Eden'. His death day testifies to his obsession with her. Caddy testifies to the closeness – and the strangeness – of their relationship by naming her daughter Quentin.

Life without Caddy was a desolate prospect, but whether that alone would have driven Quentin to commit suicide is doubtful. It is Mr Compson, the cruel purveyor and destroyer of myth, who deliberately attempts to mould an immature boy into his own kind of cynic and who drives him into the intellectual and emotional position from which it becomes inevitable that he will commit suicide. Mr Compson defines man to Quentin as 'a problem in impure properties carried tediously to an unvarying nil' (p. 114). He tells him that 'mind function' is 'Excrement' (p. 74), that time is man's pointless attempt to order a meaningless universe. Yet he expects Quentin to be in every sense manly, to be a thinking person and to organize himself at Harvard. The fact that this last conversation about suicide between father and son is uppermost in Quentin's mind as he moves to complete his own preparations for suicide suggests that the Compson parody of the father/son relationship is perhaps even more significant in bringing about Quentin's death than the disparity between his real mother and the ideal southern lady; more significant than his father's ability to get him to confess that not only did he not commit incest with Caddy but 'i was afraid to i was afraid she might . . . if I could tell you we did it would have been so . . . and then the world would roar away'.

It would seem that what Quentin wants is to possess – in all senses except the physical – the only thing he comes close to loving. The relationship he suggests is as abnormal as an incestuous one. He cannot use his knife to kill her, he cannot use his penis to make love to her, he cannot bear anyone else to have her. All this forms part of Faulkner's analysis of the South, which figuratively renders its men impotent and literally perverts their potential. Southern women, real and ideal – the unloved, unloving, artificial mother, the overloved, uninhibited sister, the paragon of southern myth – all combine to make women focal, frightening, longed for and unattainable to Quentin Compson, for whom sexual urges are always associated with suffocating images of thick grey honeysuckle.

In the course of this crucial conversation Quentin's father pours scorn on a number of things which are dear to Quentin and on two things in particular that Quentin sees as quintessentially southern. One is Quentin's courage. He offers his father his projected suicide as the act of a man of courage. His father queries this and then adds, 'whether or not you consider it courageous is more important' (than whether he does commit suicide). He is leaving his son with no absolutes, no ideals. Quentin does not have courage, he implies, and courage does not exist anyway. It is an exercise in egotism, a useful, comforting, subjective device to label something courageous. Mr Compson also scorns Quentin's idealism. He tells Quentin that his anguish when what he had believed to be southern fact turned out to be southern fiction, his feeling towards Caddy, his radical alienation from the universe are none of them so extraordinary that they will not pass. A 'temporary state of mind', he says, 'and i temporary and he you cannot bear to think that some day it will no longer hurt you like this now were getting at it'. Perhaps Mr Compson is right. Here Quentin really appears to feel challenged. Certainly he now reiterates temporary, temporary as a kind of choric comment to his father's words. There is 'nothing else in the world', responds his father. If his father is right in this, then life for Quentin is untenable. The only passion and pleasure in his life will pass – there is no other in prospect, no habit of hoping. Death is preferable. Mr Compson also tells Quentin that only the most profound emotion can precipitate suicide, while he questions the existence of such emotion in general and Quentin's in particular. Thus Quentin can only 'prove' himself by suicide. His father makes this his son's only way of demonstrating the permanence of his anguish about the South and the depth of his feeling for Caddy.

It is significant that in this extract, the climax to Quentin's section, Faulkner uses unadulterated stream-of-consciousness only for the conversation between Quentin and his father. His father's taunts and his perversion of the parental role – 'whether or not you consider it courageous is more important than the act itself,' says Mr Compson when Quentin tells him of his contemplated suicide – are still unbearable. They still amaze and overwhelm Quentin. The use of the lower case – 'i' – conveys his sense of a dehumanizing process. But other people, other attitudes, other relationships which preoccupied him earlier in the section, and which were then also treated through a stream-of-consciousness technique, now begin to be expressed in ordered language. Quentin has confronted them, recognized them for what they are, and has them in perspective. However painfully, he can now face the memory of Caddy in the swing with her beaux, the cheap perfume which indicates her interest in making herself attractive to men, the love-making in the bushes, the unsecret flesh. He can recognize that to him sex is the coupling of swine.

The last paragraph uses conventional syntax less reassuringly. Following as it does Quentin's recollection of his father's remark, 'its not even time until it was' (another challenge from Mr Compson to Quentin: can he achieve the only 'time' his father admits – the finite – that moment when something ceases?), such syntax means that in tidy and logical sequence Quentin is making the final preparations for suicide. The objects of order – the coat, the watch, the handkerchief, the tooth brush, the toothpaste, the hat and the bag – are put in their ordered places, and Quentin Compson sets out to drown himself in the Charles River, weighted down by the flatirons he had bought that morning. Faulkner ends the novel with an image of order – the idiot Benjy's tyrannical serenity, which most people will do anything to maintain – as unacceptable as chaos itself. Quentin's section ends on just such a note.

It is an effective irony that Faulkner has Quentin die in the North. On the one hand, the North has exacerbated his dilemma. The piece of pasture which was one of the few things which gave his idiot brother Benjy pleasure has been sold for Quentin to go to Harvard, and thus he feels guilty. There are no funds left for a college education for his brother Jason, and this doubles his guilt. Going to Harvard has a purely symbolic function, Quentin has been told – your mother's dream which a gentleman fulfils and in fulfilling must be satisfied. But Quentin cannot recognize the validity of such symbolic actions anymore. He does not see the point of Harvard, and this triples his guilt. However, he finds life in the North of considerable interest, and he is refreshed by his new perspective on the South. It is on the train when he is going North that he begins to see blacks in perspective, to appreciate

> that quality about them of shabby and timeless patience, of static serenity; that blending of childish and ready incompetence and paradoxical reliability that tends and protects them it loves out of all reason and robs them steadily and evades responsibility and obligations by means too barefaced to be called subterfuge even and is taken in theft or evasion with only that frank and spontaneous admiration for the victor which a gentleman feels for anyone who beats him in a fair contest, and withal a fond and unflagging tolerance for whitefolks' vagaries like that of a grandparent for unpredictable and troublesome children. (pp. 82–3)

The blacks seem to him to have an instinctive wisdom denied the cerebrating whites, and an almost primitive access to emotions denied the Compsons:

> they come into white people's lives like that in sudden sharp black trickles that isolate white facts for an instant in unarguable truth like under a microscope; the rest of the time just voices that laugh when you see nothing to laugh at, tears when no reason for tears. (p. 154)

The anachronistically pretentious southern whites he meets in the North demonstrate to him as never before that the South and the Compsons must change. Blacks in the North show initiative and enterprise, they exhibit entrepreneurial skills, they thrive in a new environment. The southerner must go away and must come back determined to resist the Protestant ethic, determined to sustain the present not with inflexible southern myth but with a flexible humanism.

Quentin Compson waits almost a year before he commits suicide. His crucial confrontation with his father takes place probably in June 1909; he enters Harvard in August, he returns home for Caddy's wedding in April 1910, and he commits suicide on 10 June 1910. Perhaps the delay does not need explaining; it does not necessarily indicate a lessening of resolve. Faulkner himself wrote in 1945 that Quentin needed to stay at least a year at Harvard in order to assuage his guilt that the last piece of Compson land had been sold for an education he did not intend to complete. Another explanation presents itself in the companion novel to *The Sound and the Fury*, *Absalom, Absalom* (1936), in which, six months before his suicide, Quentin and his Harvard roommate Shrevlin McCannon piece together – with a few facts, Quentin's informed southern imagination and Shreve's unprejudiced Canadian perspective – the archetypal southern history of the Sutpens and the Coldfields, neighbours of the Compsons. During these conversations with Shreve, whom he greatly likes and respects, Quentin hears articulated for the first time a candid view of southern culture and society. What kind of a life is it down there, asks Shreve.

> I just want to understand it if I can. . . . Because it's something my people haven't got. . . . We dont live among defeated grandfathers and freed slaves (or have I got it backward and was it your folks that are free and the niggers that lost?) and bullets in the dining-room table and such, to be always reminding us to never forget. What is it? something you live and breathe in like air? a kind of vacuum filled with wraithlike and indomitable anger and pride and glory at and in happenings that occurred and ceased fifty years ago? a kind of entailed birthright father and son and father and son of never forgiving General Sherman, so that forevermore as long as your children's children produce children you wont be anything but a descendent of a long line of colonels killed in Pickett's charge at Manassas?[6]

'You cant understand it,' Quentin replies. 'You would have to be born there.' He is not even sure that he understands it himself; but with the helpful distance of Harvard and the refreshing outlook of Shreve, he is learning not to reject the South that produced his father, that produced Quentin Compson too. At the end of *Absalom, Absalom*, Shreve asks him why he hates the South. '"I don't hate it," Quentin said, quickly, at once, immediately; "I don't hate it," he said. *I don't hate it*, he thought, panting in the cold [northern] air, the iron New England dark; *I don't. I don't! I don't hate it! I don't hate it!*"'[7] But the memory of what led to his confrontation with his father, the reality of his home – now without Caddy – and his determination to prove his anguish prevail. Temporarily it makes no difference whether it is 'Mississippi or Massachusetts . . . Massachusetts or Mississippi' (p. 157). The South had irretrievably disturbed the balance of his mind.

Notes

1 William Faulkner, *The Sound and the Fury*, Harmondsworth, 1970 (originally published 1929). All quotations from *The Sound and the Fury* are taken from this edition and, unless noted otherwise in textual parentheses, from pages 159–62.
2 Louis D. Rubin, Jr, *Writers of the Modern South: The Faraway Country*, Seattle and London, 1966, 68.
3 Malcolm Cowley, Introduction to *The Portable Faulkner*, New York, 1967, xi, xv.
4 William Faulkner, 'Appendix: The Compsons', in *Portable Faulkner*, ibid., 709.
5 Quoted in Jean Stein, 'William Faulkner: an interview', in Frederick J. Hoffman and Olga Vickery (eds), *William Faulkner: Three Decades of Criticism*, New York, 1963, 73.
6 William Faulkner, *Absalom, Absalom*, Harmondsworth, 1971, 297.
7 ibid., 311.

Further reading

Cash, Wilbur J., *The Mind of the South*, New York, 1941.
Cowan, Michael H. (ed.), *Twentieth Century Interpretations of 'The Sound and the Fury'*, Englewood Cliffs, NJ, 1968.
Millgate, Michael, *The Achievement of William Faulkner*, London, 1966.
Rubin, Louis D., Jr, *Writers of the Modern South: The Faraway Country*, Seattle and London, 1966.
Scott, Anne Firor, *The Southern Lady*, Chicago, 1970.

Bibliography

Aldridge, John W., *After the Lost Generation*, New York, 1951.
Allen, Frederick Lewis, *Only Yesterday*, New York and London, 1931.
Beach, Joseph W., *American Fiction 1920–40*, New York, 1941.
Bewley, Marius, *The Complex Fate*, New York, 1954.
Bewley, Marius, *The Eccentric Design: Form in the Classic American Novel*, New York, 1959.
Bogan, Louise, *Achievement in American Poetry*, Chicago, 1951.
Bone, Robert A., *The Negro Novel in America*, New Haven, 1958.
Bridgman, Richard, *The Colloquial Style in America*, New York and Oxford, 1966.
Brooks, Van Wyck, *America's Coming-of-Age*, New York, 1915.
Butcher, Margaret J., *The Negro in American Culture*, New York, 1956.
Cargill, Oscar, *Intellectual America: Ideas on the March*, New York, 1941.
Coffman, Stanley K., *Imagism: A Chapter in the History of Modern Poetry*, New York, 1961.
Cooperman, Stanley, *World War I and the American Novel*, Baltimore and London, 1967.
Cowley, Malcolm, *Exile's Return: A Literary Odyssey of the 1920s*, New York, 1934, and rev. edn, 1951.
Cowley, Malcolm (ed.), *After the Genteel Tradition*, New York, 1937.
Dembo, Lawrence S., *Conceptions of Reality in Modern American Poetry*, Berkeley, 1966.
Downer, Alan S. (ed.), *American Drama and its Critics: A Collection of Critical Essays*, Chicago and London, 1965.
Fiedler, Leslie A., *Love and Death in the American Novel*, 2nd edn, New York, 1969.
Frohock, Wilbur M., *The Novel of Violence in America*, Dallas, 1957.
Geismar, Maxwell, *The Last of the Provincials, 1915–25*, Boston, 1949.
Geismar, Maxwell, *Rebels and Ancestors, 1890–1915*, Boston, 1953.
Geismar, Maxwell, *Writers in Crisis, 1925–40*, Boston, 1942.
Ginger, Ray, *The Age of Excess: The U.S. from 1877 to 1914*, New York and London, 1965.

Glaab, Charles N. and Brown, Theodore, *A History of Urban America*, New York and London, 1967.

Gregory, Horace and Zaturenska, Manya, *A History of American Poetry, 1900–40*, New York, 1946.

Gross, Seymour L. and Hardy, John E., *Images of the Negro in American Literature*, Chicago and London, 1966.

Hays, Samuel P., *The Response to Industrialism, 1885–1914*, Chicago and London, 1957.

Hoffman, Frederick J., *The Twenties*, New York, 1962.

Kazin, Alfred, *On Native Grounds*, New York, 1942.

Kenner, Hugh, *The Pound Era*, New York, 1971.

Krutch, Joseph W., *The American Drama Since 1918*, New York, 1957.

Leighton, Isabel (ed.), *The Aspirin Age, 1919–41*, New York, 1949.

Leuchtenberg, William E., *The Perils of Prosperity, 1914–32*, Chicago, 1958.

May, Henry, *The End of American Innocence, 1912–17*, New York, 1959.

Pound, Ezra, *Make it New*, New Haven, 1935.

Quinn, Arthur H., *A History of the American Drama from the Civil War to the Present Day*, New York, 1951.

Rubin, Louis D., Jr, and Jacobs, Robert D. (eds), *Southern Renascence: The Literature of the Modern South*, Baltimore, 1961.

Sinclair, Andrew, *Prohibition: Era of Excess*, London, 1962.

Stearns, Harold, *Civilization in the United States*, New York, 1922.

Tanner, Tony, *The Reign of Wonder*, Cambridge, 1965.

Walcutt, Charles C., *American Literary Naturalism: A Divided Stream*, Minneapolis, 1956.

White, Morton and White, Lucia, *The Intellectual Against the City*, Cambridge, Mass., 1962.

Index